Willis Pope Hazard, Thomas Robinson Hazard

Recollections of Olden Times

ISBN/EAN: 9783337379117

Printed in Europe, USA, Canada, Australia, Japan

Cover: Foto ©ninafisch / pixelio.de

More available books at **www.hansebooks.com**

Recollections of Olden Times:

Rowland Robinson of Narragansett and His Unfortunate Daughter.

With Genealogies of the Robinson, Hazard, and Sweet Families of Rhode Island.

BY

THOMAS R. HAZARD,

"Shepherd Tom,"

IN HIS EIGHTY-FIRST AND EIGHTY-SECOND YEARS.

ALSO GENEALOGICAL SKETCH OF THE HAZARDS OF THE MIDDLE STATES.

By WILLIS P. HAZARD,

OF WESTCHESTER, PA.

NEWPORT, R. I.:
PUBLISHED BY JOHN P. SANBORN.
1879.

Entered according to Act of Congress, in the year 1879, by
JOHN P. SANBORN,
in the office of the Librarian of Congress, at Washington, D. C.

Willis Pope Hazard, Thomas Robinson Hazard

Recollections of Olden Times

ERRATA

Page 10, fourth line from bottom of page, for "great-grandfather" read *father*.

Page 76, fourth line, "Rowland Robinson" should read *Rowland Hazard*.

Page 76, thirteenth line, "vessel" should read *pier*.

Page 148, " Mary, Rowland, Sarah, Ruth, numbered 9, 10, 11, 12, all children of John, the son of Rowland Robinson and consequently grandchildren of the last named."

Page 150, "Joscan" should be *Toscan*.

Page 152, fifth line from bottom, "eighth son" should be *eighth child*.

Page 153, fourth line from bottom, "Minturn" is the son of Theodore and Mary Wright.

Page 161, after fourth paragraph from the bottom, there should be added to the list of children of Benjamin Robinson: 6. Hannah who married the late Elisha Watson, of Wakefield, R. I. 7. Benjamin. 8. Philip Wanton, who died when a youth.

Page 191, twenty-fourth line, "ten" should read *two*.

Arms of the English Hassards or Hazards. Family Crest, the escallop shell proper, denoting pilgrimage to the Holy Shrine of St. Jago de Compostella, and the Palm, pilgrimage (Crusade) to Jerusalem.

Preface.

The following narrative and genealogies first appeared, simultaneously, in the "Newport Mercury" and "Narragansett Times," in the latter part of the year 1877 and early part of 1878. Their perusal having excited some interest among the public, it is thought advisable by some, including the undersigned, that the papers should be embodied in book form.

THOMAS R. HAZARD.

Vaucluse, R. I., May 1, 1879.

Table of Contents.

CHAPTER I.

Rowland Robinson.—Marquis Lafayette.—Extract from Mrs. Mary Hunter's Diary.—Governor Brenton.—Large Landed Estate in Narragansett.—Robert Hazard the great farmer.—Gov. John Potter.—Judge William Potter.—Jemima Wilkinson.—Hon. Elisha R. Potter.—Abolition of Slavery in Rhode Island.—Wealth of South Kingstown and high price of land in "olden times." - - - - - - - - - - - 9

CHAPTER II.

Old Time Costume.—Count Rochambeau.—Thomas Robinson of Newport and his daughter Mary.—William Gardiner.—Dr. Sylvester Gardiner.—Slaves from Guinea landed at Franklin (now South) Ferry.—Murder of Jackson by William Carter.—Tower Hill. - 19

CHAPTER III.

Dr. Job Sweet.—Rowland Robinson's Children.—The Unfortunate Hannah.—Sarah Robinson of Newport.—Mrs. Mary Hunter's Diary. - - - - - - - - - - - 30

CHAPTER IV.

Personal Beauty of Hannah Robinson.—Thomas Hornsby.—Madame Osborne.—Mr. Peter Simons.—Dr. William Bowen.—Col. Harry Babcock.—Dr. Joshua Babcock.—Dr. Franklin.—John Case.—Queen of England and "Crazy Harry." - - - - - 34

CHAPTER V.

Richard Smith.—Daniel E. Updike.—Lodowick Updike.—The great Indian Swamp Fight.—Canonchet, the Indian Chief.—King Tom.—Queen Esther.—King George the last King of the Narragansetts.—Hannah Robinson elopes and marries Peter Simons in Providence.—Simon and Ray Mumford.—Gov. William Robinson imports the Narragansett pacing horses from Andalusia.—Ridge Hill. - - - - - - - - - - - 41

TABLE OF CONTENTS.

CHAPTER VI.   PAGE
Mr. Simons takes his bride to Newport, and thence to Providence, to reside.—The "Unfortunate Hannah" deserted by her husband.—Her sickness and return home with her father.—Miss Belden. - 48

CHAPTER VII.
The Sweet Families of "Natural Bone-setters."—John Hazard.—Alexander Gardiner, and Ephraim Hazard.—MacSparran Hill.—St. Paul's Church.—Pettaquamscutt Lake.—Gilbert Stuart.—George Rome.—Lawyers Bowne and Joe Aplin.—John Randolph of Roanoke. - - - - - - - - - - - - 59

CHAPTER VIII.
Gen. Nathaniel Greene.—Colonel Whalley the regicide.—The Willets of New York and Narragansett.—"Stout Jeffrey" Hazard.—Dr MacSparran.—Pettaquamscutt River.—George Hazard, father of Thomas G.—The War Brig Orpheus.—Narragansett Pier.—Pacing Horses. - - - - - - - - - - 67

CHAPTER IX.
Pattaquamscutt Rock.—Great Snow-storms.—Christopher Champlin.—James Gould.—Otter Sheep.—Jeremiah Niles.—Captain Kidd.—"Nailor Tom" Hazard's "Blue-book." - - - 77

CHAPTER X.
"Old Benny Rodman's Horsewhip."—Augustus Hazard of Enfield.—Continuance of the subject of Great Snow-storms. - - - 85

CHAPTER XI.
Great Snow-storms continued.—Great distress in Newport in 1780.—Samuel Elam.—Vaucluse.—Historic Trees.—David Buffum.—Dr. Abernethy. - - - - - - - - - - - 87

CHAPTER XII.
September Gale of 1815.—William Knowles drowned.—Tower Hill first settled.—Rowse J. Helme, C. J., Rowland Brown, Commodore Oliver Hazard Perry.—Thomas Hazard's testimony against slavery.—Moses Brown, John Woodman, Jeremiah Austin. - 96

CHAPTER XIII.
Thomas Hazard, first settler.—Robert his son.—Thomas Hazard's Will.—Importation of the famous Arabian Stallion Snip.—Job Watson.—Mrs. Mary Hunter's Diary.—George Gibbs.—Governor Nichols.—Judge Stephen Hassard.—William Hunter. - - 103

CHAPTER XIV.
William T. Robinson.—Count Vernon.—Headquarters of Count Rochambeau.—Colonel Wanton.—Capt. Wallace.—Mrs. Mary Hunter's Diary.—Abigail and Anne Greene.—John Allen. - - 112

TABLE OF CONTENTS.

CHAPTER XV.
PAGE

Updike's History of the Narragansett Church.—Old Time Customs.—Nicholas Gardiner.—"Dorothy Hollow."—"The Crying Bog."—Gooseberry Island.—The French Hermit.—"The Palatine Ship." 119

CHAPTER XVI.

The Unfortunate Hannah on MacSparran Hill.—Singular state of the atmosphere.—Mrs. Simons' nice sense of hearing.—Her conductors take her from the hill and proceed homeward. - - 127

CHAPTER XVII.

Pettaquamscutt Bridge.—Mrs. Simons arrives home.—Dr. Robert Hazard.—Death and burial of the "Unfortunate Hannah."—Lines contributed by Miss Eliza Gibson Hazard. - - - 136

CHAPTER XVIII.

Genealogical Tables of the Robinson Family of Narragansett. - 146

CHAPTER XIX.

Genealogical Tables of the English and Irish Hazards, or Hassards. 165

CHAPTER XX.

Genealogical Table of the Rhode Island Hazards. - - - - 181

CHAPTER XXI.

Historical Sketch and Genealogical Table of the Hazard Family of the Middle States. - - - - - - - - 226

CHAPTER XXII.

Genealogical Table of the Sweet Family, the Natural Bone-setters of Narragansett. - - - - - - - - - 265

Recollections of Olden Times.

Rowland Robinson of Narragansett and his Unfortunate Daughter.

CHAPTER I.

About one mile west of Narragansett Bay, and a half mile north of the old colonial highway that leads to and from the South Ferry, formerly called "Franklin Ferry," there now stands a gambrel-roofed house, occupied at present by Mr. Rowland F. Gardiner, and built by Rowland Robinson before the middle of the last century. Originally, the house including the negro quarters was one hundred and five feet in length, the stone foundations of the whole being now visible; but the present structure measures but fifty-four feet front. The west front room on the ground floor is twenty feet square. This room is paneled and elaborately finished in the best architectural style of that day. The timber was cut on the estate, and is very large. In a recent visit to the premises I took especial note of the middle cross-beam that supports the chamber floor over the west front room. It is twenty feet long and twelve inches square, and is without support underneath its full length; yet I could not perceive that, in the century and more that have passed since it was placed there, it had sagged or bent in the least degree. All the rooms in the house are finished after the same costly pattern, and most of the fire-places ornamented with the old-fashioned Chinese tiles. The dining-room is twenty-two by twenty feet in dimensions. On the panel over the fire-place in a back room on the ground floor is a large, ancient painting in which the artist has, in a more graphic than finished style, sketched in oil a stag or deer hunt that occurred on the premises while the house was being built. The huntsmen are depicted fully accoutered in their sporting costumes, with high flap boots, and sitting, or rather standing very erect in their stirrups.

The chamber over the west room was occupied for some time during the Revolutionary war by the Marquis Lafayette, and has ever since been designated by the successive occupants of the premises, "The Lafayette Chamber." In making some recent repairs two one-ounce bullets were found embedded in the plank in front of this room. Whether there is any historical significance attached to this incident, I have not learned.

A large apartment over the dining-room is called to this day the "Unfortunate Hannah's Chamber," from its having been occupied by a beautiful daughter of Mr. Robinson by that name, whose tragic story is briefly told in Updike's "History of the Narragansett Church." The cupboard is still shown in which her lover used to retreat when the steps of her irascible father were heard on the stairs.

Rowland Robinson was born October 8, 1719, and was the eldest son of Gov. William Robinson, who owned and improved an estate, in the beginning of the eighteenth century, lying in Point Judith and extending west of the River Saucatucket, the Indian for "dead man's brook," of several thousand acres, most of which had descended to him by inheritance from his great-grandfather, Rowland Robinson, who came to Narragansett from England, and purchased a large tract of land directly from the Indians, on which he built not far from where the old Gov. William Robinson house, with the exception of the negro quarters, is now standing, a little north of the pond in Point Judith called "Kit's Pond."

Updike, in his History of the Narragansett Church, p. 179, says: "In Narragansett, resided the great landed aristocracy of the colony. Their plantations were large, some of them very extensive. Major Mason of Connecticut, in a letter to the commissioners of that colony, dated August 3, 1670, persuading them to relinquish all further claim of jurisdiction over the Narragansett country, says: 'Those places that are any way considerable, are already taken up by several men, in farm and large tracts of land, some having five, six and ten square miles—yes and I suppose some have much more, which some of you or yours may see or feel hereafter.'"

If the following account, taken from Mrs. Mary Hunter's diary, written some fifty years or more ago, is correct, it would seem that the first Robinson who came to Rhode Island, though of an ancient and highly respected English family, was nevertheless in some respects a self-made man.

"Rowland Robinson the first ran away from his parents and escaped on board a ship from England to the colonies, and bound himself to a carpenter. By good behavior he soon got advanced in business, and bought from the Indians large tracts of land on which he built, partly with his own hands, the homestead in Point Judith. He married a rich farmer's daughter, had many children, and from his eldest son, William, the Robinson family are descended."

Wm. T. Robinson, son of Thomas and father of Mrs. Mary Hunter, used to relate an amusing anecdote of one of the early Robinsons who, it appears, had joined the Quaker Meeting. Governor Brenton had placed him on a farm belonging to him, situated on the south end of the island, adjacent to Brenton's Point, and stocked it largely with sheep. In a violent snow-storm, such as used to prevail more frequently than of late in New England—though I have known several in my day, perhaps equally destructive—, these sheep having been left in an exposed position, were driven by the inclement tempest of wind and sleet off the rocks into the sea, where they perished. When Robinson communicated the loss of the sheep to Brenton, the Governor being a man of hasty temper, as most of the early settlers of Newport and King's—now Washington—counties in Rhode Island seem to have been, he flew into a towering rage with his tenant, and reproached him in unmeasured terms for the loss of the sheep through, as he charged, gross neglect. To all the abuse heaped upon him Robinson answered not a word, which submissiveness seemed only to increase Brenton's ire, who at last, in his frenzy, declared that Robinson should pay for the lost sheep, and bid him choose a man to arbitrate their value, while he chose another, which Brenton did on his part *instanter*. It was now Robinson's turn to choose his man. "Friend Brenton," said he, "I know of no one whom I should prefer to trust my interest with than thou! I think I will choose thee for my man." This was too much for the governor, who, after bursting into a fit of laughter, told his unmanageable tenant to go back to the farm and he would venture to trust one more flock of sheep to his care.

The extent of Governor Robinson's farming operations may be guessed at from what my paternal grandmother, who was his daughter and a sister of Rowland by his first wife, used to say, that after her father had given several large tracts of land to his sons, including the Governor Sprague, Little Neck and Narragansett Pier estates, he used to congratulate himself upon having his *parlor* and *kitchen* family reduced in the winter season to seventy persons all told.

Nor was Governor Robinson the only large land-holder in those days. Robert Hazard, my father's grandfather, improved, including large cattle ranges lying adjacent to Worden's Pond, several thousand acres, two thousand of which lay in the rich southern portion of Boston Neck and on the

Tower Hill slope adjoining Governor Robinson's estate on the north. My father said that his grandfather used to ship to the West Indies about one hundred horses annually, all of which were raised on the farm he improved, and that he employed twelve women, each with a young assistant, to manage his dairy, and sent occasionally two schooners from the South Ferry to the West Indies, laden entirely with produce and live stock from his own farms. For a more detailed account of Robert Hazard's farming operations, see Updike's History, pages 179-181.

Updike also states that Colonel Staunton owned one tract of land in Narragansett, four and a half miles long and two miles wide. Colonel Updike owned three thousand acres, lying adjacent to Wickford. Mr. Sewall owned all the land in Point Judith lying south of Governor Robinson's estate, now constituting six largs farms, whilst the Champlins, Potters, Noyeses, Babcocks, Gardiners, Perrys, Browns, Nileses, Brentons, and many others, owned and occupied large landed properties.

The Champlin estate lay for the most part in Charlestown, and I can remember when the old family mansion-house was in pretty good repair, and have traced the lines of the race-course, lying on the plain south of the house toward the sea, where the old-time gentry used to prove the speed of the horses that were reared on their own estates.

Farther still to the east lay the Colonel Staunton estate, the manor-house of which, situated on the old post-road, I think may yet be standing..

Still farther to the east used to stand, since my recollection, what was called the "Old Hull House," being one of the first six houses that were built by the early settlers of Narragansett between Franklin Ferry on the east and Pawcatuck river, which made the western boundary of the country of the once powerful Indian tribe of Narragansetts. It was in the parlor of this house that the first murder in Narragansett was perpetrated, under the following circumstances. A daughter of the host had been married during the day, and whilst in the evening the friends were celebrating her wedding, a rejected lover approached in the dark a window where the newly married couple stood conversing, and, placing the muzzle of his gun within a few feet of his victim, sent a bullet through her heart.

Still farther to the east, on the south side of the old post-road, stood the old mansion of Judge Samuel Perry, who, since my memory, was held to be the largest land-holder in Southern Rhode Island. It was from this family that Commodore Oliver Hazard Perry descended, he having been named after his grandfather, Oliver Hazard, the fourth in degree from the first settler, Thomas Hazard.

Yet still farther to the east, used to stand beside the "Potter Pond," on the old post-road, the Governor John Potter house, which was removed some score or two years ago by the late James and John—Jimmy and John—Sherman, who lived and died in the old mansion-house, which still stands near the west bank of Saucatucket river, one mile or more north of Peacedale. The Governor John Potter house was built and finished throughout in a really palatial style, as I can well remember. The stone steps leading to the front door were circular in form, and very lofty. The ceilings of the lower rooms were nearly or quite twice the ordinary height. On the panel over the fire-place in a chamber I used to observe a full-length portrait of Governor Potter's daughter, which was said to have been painted by an Italian artist whom he had employed to embellish the walls of his house.

Tradition used to say, that, taking advantage of the father's somewhat prolonged absence on a certain occasion, the perfidious Italian painted himself kneeling at the feet of the charming Miss Potter. This, however, gave such offence to the irate old gentleman, that immediately upon his discovery of what had been done in his absence he drove the poor artist from his house, and afterwards employed another to expunge the kneeling figure. The lovers, however, were not thus to be separated, and shortly after Miss Potter eloped from the parental roof and was united in wedlock with the fascinating stranger.

The late Daniel E. Updike, of East Greenwich, who was a perfect gazetteer in old time recollections and anecdotes, used to tell a great deal of "Old Booca Chicca" John Potter, who, I have since been told, lived on Little Rest Hill. Were it not for this fact, I should think the nickname might be a corruption of the Italian word *Boccaccia*, signifying "ugly mouth," bestowed upon the old gentleman by his vindicitive son-in-law. At any rate, the coincidence is rather singular.

About one mile north of the village of "Little Rest," now Kingston, used to stand, since my recollection, the fine old mansion of Judge William Potter, who owned a large landed estate adjoining. In about the year 1780, Judge Potter became a devoted follower of the celebrated Jemima Wilkinson, and, to accommodate herself and adherents, "he built a large addition to his already spacious mansion, containing fourteen rooms and bedrooms, with suitable fireplaces." It was probably from this cause that the house used to be popularly called "The Old Abbey," partly on account of its spaciousness, and partly from the character of its occupants.

Updike, in his history of the Narragansett Church, page 235, says, "that in consequence of his devotion to this artful woman, Judge Potter was compelled to mortgage his estate; and finding it impossible to redeem it in its deteriorated condition, he finally, in 1807, sold the remainder of his interest in it and settled in Genesee.

"The late Hon. Elisha R. Potter purchased the homestead, but the elegant garden, with parterres, borders, shrubbery, summer-house, fruit orchard, his ancient mansion, with the high and costly fences, outhouses and cookery establishment, and the more recent erections for the accommodation and gratification of the priestess of his devotions, were in ruins, and, within a few years, the whole buildings have been removed." To this account, I may add in parenthesis, that a somewhat similar fate as attended the Potter estates has fallen on score upon score of others that were occupied by the gentry of the olden time.

A stranger now visiting Narragansett and observing the unthrifty and worn-out appearance of most of the farm-houses and lands, the latter to a great extent disfigured with dilapidated walls and loose boulders and cobble-stones, and fast being overrun with briers and bushes, could hardly believe that scarcely a century ago this beautiful, though now desolate-looking, farming country, teemed with a superabundance of dairy and other agricultural products, and was studded throughout with princely mansions, a few skeleton specimens of which only are now left standing.

As Updike in his History narrates, the original owners and occupants of the soil of Narragansett were for the most part high-toned, highly cultured English country-gentlemen, who, with their accomplished and carefully educated families, constituted a social fraternity which was certainly not surpassed in polite culture, refinement and hospitality in the British American colonies. This fascinating social structure was, however, based upon and sustained by the unrequited toil of the African race, and has been visited with the blight that always, sooner or later, follows in the foot-prints of human slavery.

In an address delivered by him before the Rhode Island Historical Society, February 19, 1851, the Hon. Elisha R. Potter said, " All along the belt of land adjoining the west side of Narragansett Bay, the country, generally productive, was owned in large plantations by wealthy proprietors, who resided on and cultivated their land. They had the cultivation which would naturally result from a life of leisure, from intercourse with each other and with the best informed men of the colony, and from the possession of private libraries for that day large and extensive."

Says Updike, p. 184, "The gentlemen of ancient Narraganett were well informed, and possessed of intellectual taste. The remains of these libraries and paintings would be sufficient testimonials if other sources of information were defective. Doctor Babcock, Colonel Staunton, Judge Helme, Captain Jones, Colonel Potter, Colonel Willet, Colonel Robert Brown, the Hazards, Captain Silas Brown, the Brenons, owned valuable libraries. Doctor McSparran, Doctor Fayerweather, Colonel Updike, and Matthew Robinson possessed rich collections for that day in classical and English iterature."

In alluding to the subject of slavery, Judge Potter, in his address, said, "From the nature of the climate, the expense of supporting slaves was greater than in more southern lattudes, and public opinion would not sanction overwork or ll-treatment. The children of their owners were brought up n leisure, with little acquaintance with any profession or business, and when, in the course of time, slavery was abolshed and they were brought into contact with men educated o labor and self-dependence, the habits, they had acquired rom slavery proved the ruin of most of them, and their property was encumbered and passed into other hands.

"The equal division of property upon the death of the parent contributed to the breaking up of these large plantations, and probably contributed also to the abolition of slavery itself. Until 1770, the eldest son inherited, by law. the whole estate of a person dying without a will; and after hat time until 1792, he was entitled to a double portion. But public opinion and the common sense of right were stronger than the law; and except in a very few cases property was equally divided by will. And so strong was his feeling that in many cases where the eldest son, for want of a will, became entitled to the whole, he voluntarily gave up his legal rights, and admitted the other children to share in the estate.

"The abolition of slavery [in Rhode Island] was gradual. In 1774, the importation of slaves was prohibited, and every slave brought into the colony was declared free. Large numbers of them joined our Revolutionary army, and were declared free on enlisting. They were among the best of the American troops, and rendered efficient service in the war, and finally in 1784, all children of slaves, born after that year were declared free."

It is an historical fact that the first regularly organized body of American colored troops that ever engaged in battle, was during the Revolutionary war under General Sullivan in Portsmouth, Rhode Island, where they bravely withstood the charge of British troops and more than once repulsed them. (See Hon. S. G. Arnold's Centennial Address, 1878.)

Even at a time to which my memory extends, when dairy products, the staples of Narragansett, were less than half the price they now are, farming lands in South Kingstown sold for twice the sum that can now be obtained for them. The Gov. George Brown farm, containing nearly four hundred acres, which formerly constituted one of the most eligible tracts of the Hazards' Boston Neck estates, has been recently sold, as I am told, after long advertisement, for less than ten thousand dollars; and yet I have heard my father say that his ancestors paid in early colonial times as high as sixty dollars per acre for land in the same vicinity.

I well remember when the late Elisha Watson, Esq., more than fifty years ago, purchased the farm lying north of Governor Brown, containing about three hundred and thirty acres, for which he paid in coin *seventeen thousand dollars.*

Arnold says, in his History of Rhode Island, that so late as 1780, "South Kingstown was by far the wealthiest town in the State, paying double the taxes assigned to Newport, and one-third more than Providence."

CHAPTER II.

Rowland Robinson, though perhaps a little too much after the brusk order of Fielding's "Squire Western," was a fair specimen, in temper and manners, and a perfect beau ideal, in costume, presence· and person, of the old-time country gentlemen who constituted the semi-feudal aristocracy of Narragansett. In person he was portly, tall and erect. His features were Roman, slightly tempered with the Grecian type. His clear blonde complexion, inclining to red, and undulating brown hair, worn in a cue behind, attested his Saxon descent. When in full dress Mr. Robinson generally wore a dark silk velvet or brown broadcloth coat, light yellow plush waistcoat with deep pockets and wide flaps resting partly on the hips, short violet colored velvet breeches buckled at the knee, nicely polished white-top boots, or silver buckled shoes, fine cambric shirt profusely ruffled and plaited at the bosom and wrists, with white silk neck-tie to match; the whole surmounted and set off by a looped-up, triangular hat on his head and a stout gold-headed cane in his hand.

I have heard it said by persons acquainted with Revolutionary *data*, that such was the admiration inspired by the fine appearance and courtly bearing of Rowland Robinson, though then far beyond the prime of manhood, who occasionally came to his brother Thomas Robinson's house in Newport, where Count Rochambeau, commander of the French land-forces, resided for some time as a guest, that many of the count's officers sought introductory letters to Mr. Robinson, that they might obtain access to and share in the hospitalities of his home in Narragansett. To what extent Mr. Robinson's beautiful and accomplished daughter, then deceased, might have contributed as a further element of attraction had they seen her when in the zenith of her glory, to the proverbially gallant and *light-o-love* Frenchmen, can only be surmised. I do, however, know that a fair cousin of Hannah's, Mary by name, was sent to Narragansett and placed by her parents in the care of her uncle and aunt (my grandparents), that the lovely maiden might be removed from the society of the numerous young French officers, one of whom, under the cloak of calling at her father's house to see his general, Count Rochambeau, had nearly succeeded through his blandishments in pursuading the little Quaker beauty to exchange her drab bonnet for a Parisian hat and become his bride, before the alarming plot was discovered and its further *denouement* arrested by keeping the lovers separated until his "most Christian Majesty's" land-forces took their final departure from Newport.

Thomas Robinson, of Newport, the father of Mary, the Quaker beauty, and his brother-in-law, Thomas Hazard, of Narragansett (my grandfather), were two of the earliest, as well as the most active and efficient, advocates for the abolition, not only of the slave trade but of slavery in any form in the British colonies. In Thomas Robinson, the wronged and oppressed, whether white or black, were ever sure to find a friend, and I have heard my father and others narrate deeds of daring performed by the Quaker philanthropist in defense of outraged humanity, truly heroic.

On one occasion, learning that a negro had been abducted for the purpose of being sold into slavery, and was then on board a vessel in Newport Harbor just about to sail for the West Indies, Mr. Robinson, accompanied by only one man, proceeded in a row-boat to the vessel, which he boarded, and demanded of its ruffian captain that the man should be given up to him. This, after torrents of foul oaths and threatenings, the pirate was finally compelled to do, although Mr.

Robinson had no legal warrant with which to enforce his determined demand.

Nor did his sympathetic nature manifest itself in one direction only. I have heard "old Thomas Goddard"—that prince among his peers and gentleman by natural right—say that he had known Thomas Robinson to come to his house early in the morning, when the weather had suddenly become stormy and cold, and hand to him thirty dollars or more at one time, with directions to spend it all in furnishing wood to such poor families as he might find in need; and this, too, although his own income was quite limited.

Though irritable and passionate beyond measure or reason when crossed or opposed, Rowland Robinson's nature seemed wholly devoid of malice and as compassionate and full of tenderness when not angered as any woman's. When quite young I used to hear many anecdotes told illustrative of these traits in his character, some of which I will narrate.

In the year 1741, Mr. Robinson married Anstis Gardiner, daughter of Colonel John Gardiner who lived in a house yet standing on the old family estate a few furlongs south of the South Ferry, in Boston Neck. Dr. Sylvester Gardiner, of Boston, the ancestor of the Gardiners of Maine, was a son of William (grandfather to Anstis), and was born in the house before mentioned. Sylvester's constitution being frail, his father sent him to Boston to be educated as a physician, and finally to England and France, where he remained for eight years under the medical instruction of the most distinguished practitioners of the healing art. (See Updike's History of the Narragansett Church.)

Previous to establishing his household Mr. Robinson engaged with others of his friends in sending a vessel from Franklin Ferry to the Guinea coast, for slaves, out of his portion of which he proposed to select most of his domestic servants and farming hands and dispose of the remainder by sale, as was the custom in those days. Up to the time of the return of the vessel—such was the force of education and habit—the cruelty and injustice involved in the slave-trade seemed never to have entered Mr. Robinson's mind, but now when he saw the forlorn, woe-begone looking men and women disembarking, some of them too feeble to stand alone, the enormity of his offense against humanity presented itself so vividly to his susceptible mind, that he wept like a child, nor would he consent that a single slave that fell to his share—twenty-eight in all—should be sold, but took them all to his own house where, though held in servitude, they were kindly cared for.

I have heard it said by old people that these Africans arrived at Mr. Robinson's at a season of the year when rye was fit for harvest; that he had a large field of this grain on the east side of his farm which was bounded on Narragansett Bay; and that not being provided with a sufficient quantity of sickles to supply all the men, a part were set to work furnished with case-knives for want of better implements with which to gather the grain into sheaves.

Among the African slaves imported by Mr. Robinson was a woman who after her arrival was called by the name of Abigail. Abigail became in time so pleased with her Narragansett home, that she solicited and obtained the consent of her master to return to Guinea for the purpose of bringing to Narragansett her only son. Mr. Atmore Robinson, of Wakefield, had at one time in his possession the account-books of old Rowland Robinson, containing the expenses for outfit and passage of Abigail on board a slave-ship to Africa and return with her son. In this schedule the articles deemed by Mr. Robinson essential to their comfort while on board ship are minutely inventoried. The entries in the book include table-linen, bedding, cooking utensils, dishes, spoons, knives and forks, etc., etc. Abigail successfully accomplished her mission, and returned in safety with her son, who was thereupon domesticated into Mr. Robinson's family.

Rowland Robinson held many responsible positions under both the colonial and state governments; and among others that of sheriff of Kings county.

Sometime during the winter of 1741, two travelers stopped late in the afternoon at the house of a widow Nash, who lived in one of the six old houses before alluded to, which I think is yet standing near a small rivulet on the east side of the old post-road, about one mile from Dockray's corner. Mrs. Nash had the kindness to dress their hair, and playfully remarked to the smaller of the two whilst so engaged, that if he was murdered she could identify his person by a round black lock of hair that marked his head.

About sunset the two men proceeded on their journey with the avowed intention of reaching Franklin Ferry that night and passing over to Newport in the morning.

It subsequently came to light that one of the men, whose name was Jackson, had started from Virginia with a horse load of deer-skins which he intended to convey to Boston, and that he was joined on the way by a Captain William Carter, an old privateersman of Newport, Rhode Island, who had been shipwrecked somewhere on the coast south of the Chesapeake, and was making his way home on foot. After leaving Mrs. Nash's, and when passing over the southern portion of Tower Hill in the evening, it also appeared that Carter knocked Jackson from his horse by hitting him on the back of the head with a stone. Jackson, however, recovered himself and ran to an old uninhabited house near by—which was the only semblance of a habitation within a mile and more of the spot—where he was pursued and beaten to death by Carter, who then proceeded on his way with Jackson's horse and pack, having previously dragged his victim nearly a mile down the hill to a salt water estuary called Pettaquamscutt Cove, and shoved the corpse under the ice, from whence it was fished up some days after by a man whilst jabbing for eels with a spear and identified by Mrs. Nash as the stranger with the *black spot* on his head, to whom she had unconsciously spoken so ominously.

The place where Jackson was first knocked down by Carter is still marked by a stone at the base of the road wall directly west of the exact spot, with the figures "1741" engraven on it. This stone is not far from the junction of the road and the north line of the lot on which the late Nicholas Austin some years ago erected a house on the very same site where the ruins of the old "Carter and Jackson chimney" since my remembrance stood.

This monument, in commemoration of the murder, is situated a few rods south of the print of the horseshoe made in a stone, as tradition said, by the Devil, who left his home among the Massachusetts Puritans in Cotton Mather times, in pursuit of an old Indian squaw, who, after honestly forfeiting to him her soul, meanly attempted to escape out of her sable creditor's own proper jurisdiction into Rhode Island, just before the penalty became due.

The Devil's first step can now be traced by the print of a giant foot—called to this day "the devil's foot"—in a rock situated in the old post-road, some half way between East Greenwich and Wickford, from whence he struck next on Chimney Hill, having previously, in order to disguise his route, caused his cloven foot to be shod with an old horseshoe. From this point the Devil landed at the next stride on Block Island, where he captured his victim, and seizing her by the hair of the head, delivered her into the hands of his Puritan children in Boston to be shipped to the Barbadoes and exchanged for rum and sugar on his account.

Rowland Robinson, who was sheriff of Kings (now Washington) county, at the time of the murder, arrested Carter on the "Point," in Newport, where he found him at his sister's, holding her child on his knee, and without aid brought the criminal, who was a remarkably powerful and desperately resolute man, over both the ferries and lodged him in jail at Tower Hill, which was the county seat, whence he was taken, tried, convicted and condemned, and shortly after hanged in gibbet at the eastern foot of Tower Hill, on what is now called the "training lot," lying between the highway leading to the South Ferry and Pettaquamscutt river.

When I was a boy I used to sit in the kitchen chimney-corner and listen, with my hair on end, to "Uncle Sci" and other old negroes as they told how *scared* they used to be when they rode by of a dark night and heard the chains creaking in the wind, and ever and anon one of Carter's bones fall *cajunk* to the ground.

Whilst on the way from the ferry to the jail, a distance of four miles, Carter, who was walking, showed signs of weariness; upon observing which Sheriff Robinson, who rode a powerful black horse, after loosing the bonds of his prisoner, made him mount and ride on the crupper behind him.

My father was named for his maternal uncle, Rowland Robinson, who, after the death of his wife and children, bequeathed to him a large part of his landed property, which, under time-honored semi-feudal usage, rendered it morally incumbent on him to make comfortable provision for the support of the superannuated negroes and other dependents who had become domiciled on his deceased uncle's estate. One of these, an old negro, by the name of Cuddymonk, used to occupy a few acres of land and a small house of my father's, that stood on the pleasant promontory that projects from the west side of the Wakefield mill pond, a little north of the dam.

It used to be told that Cuddy once raised the earliest potatoes that were ever dug from the ground in South Kingstown. The old man had just finished planting one day when a friend chanced to call unexpectedly, and Cuddy was obliged to dig up his newly-planted potatoes to furnish his guest with a dinner.

Cuddymonk was quite a philosopher in his way, and his ideas on the abstruse questions of finance and political economy might well be favorably compared with some of the theories that have been broached of late, on the floor of Congress, by members who stand high in the estimation of a majority of their constituents.

Cuddy used to fatten yearly two pigs on corn that he

bought, the pork from one of which he cured for his own use, whilst he sold the other. In making up his accounts and finding that the money received for his pig scarcely paid the cost of the corn it had consumed, Cuddy used to remark that "times would never be good in dis country, till corn was pistareen (20 cents) a bushel, and pork pistareen a pound."

Another old retainer (of Welsh descent) who had lived from boyhood with Mr. Robinson and claimed to have been his head farmer, by the name of Benjamin Nichols, also occupied a tenement of my father's for many years. I knew the old man well, and used, some sixty years ago, to like very much to talk with him about "old times." Let the subject commenced with be what it might, it was pretty sure to run into some anecdote or relation on his part connected with "old Rowland Robinson," whose memory he fairly idolized. Many of the stories he used to tell, like the following, strikingly illustrated the peculiarities of Mr. Robinson's hasty and undisciplined, but yet kindly, nature.

Mr. Robinson had furnished an old Guinea negro that he imported, named Steppany, who was a notorious thief, with a little home some miles away. Steppany fell sick one time, and sent his boy to his old master. The boy happened to come about noonday, when Mr. Robinson and his work people were going home from the field. Noticing the boy in the company behind him, the old gentleman asked Nichols who he was, and was told it was Steppany's boy, who had come to tell him that his father was sick. Upon this Mr. Robinson turned to the boy and said, excitedly, "Boy! what makes your father such a thief?" and, as he walked along, continued to berate Steppany most vehemently. After a little time, looking over his shoulder and not seeing the boy, Mr. Robinson hastily inquired where he was, and was told by Nichols that he had frightened him so that he had taken to his heels and run away! "Run quick and catch him, Benjamin!" cried Mr. Robinson. Nichols accordingly started, but the boy seeing himself pursued only ran the faster and got clear away.

The same afternoon a horse was laden with necessaries and sent by Mr. Robinson's body servant, Prince, to the relief of the "thief," by his old master.

This boy was afterwards killed by a stroke of lightning. Mr. Robinson lost no time, after being apprised of the fact, in going to see Steppany. On his arrival at the old negro's house he found him sitting beside the body of his child and looking very glum. On Mr. Robinson offering some words of condolence, Steppany gruffly said, "Yes, massa! s'pose God ormighty tink he do some big ting when he kill dat little boy," adding defiantly, "nex' time let him try his thunder on ole nigger!"

Another thief, by the name of Jerry, lived in a small tenement of Mr. Robinson's, for whom he had worked as a farm-hand a great many years. Mr. Robinson kept a large flock of sheep, from which Jerry used occasionally to take one by night for his family's use. Against these proceedings of his old farm servant Mr. Robinson had made no decided protest until in one of his sheep-stealing expeditions Jerry accidentally got hold of a fine English ram which Mr. Robinson had recently imported and, without the knowledge of the depredator, turned in with his flock. One morning Nichols discovered that this ram was missing. On informing Mr. Robinson of the fact, the old gentleman flew into a frenzied rage and without hesitation declared that the rascally thief Jerry must have stolen it, and ordering his horse he rode at once to the delinquent's house. Jerry was cutting wood at the door, but espying Mr. Robinson hastily approaching in the distance he slipped into the house and hid beneath a bed. When the thundering rap of Mr. Robinson's heavy cane was heard on the door it was tardily opened by Jerry's wife, who, in answer to his angry demands to see the "rascally thief," told him that her husband had gone fishing "to get something for his children's dinner." This the exasperated old gentleman knew to be false, as he had got a glimpse of Jerry just as he was entering the door on his approach, and moreover readily divined by the odor that reached him through a broken window, that a portion of his English ram was at that moment in process of being cooked. Amidst Mr. Robinson's loud and angry threatenings that he would cane the "rascally thief" to death, Jerry was finally forced to show himself at the door, when, raising his cane aloft. as he sat on his horse, the irate old gentleman roared at the top of his voice, " Come here, you rascally thief, while I break every bone in your body for stealing my English ram!" The trembling culprit knew it would naught avail to deny the main fact, and sought to palliate his offense by alleging that owing to the darkness of the night he did not discover, until he came to dress the mutton, that he had made a mistake in catching the ram under the supposition that it was " a big wether sheep." To the hypocritical old sinner's entreaties for mercy Jerry's wife joined her tearful appeals, aided by some half-dozen, ragged, whimpering children, that she brought forward to the rescue, who, if her asseverations could be relied upon, had been for the week past suffering from sheer starvation. Altogether, the aggregate forces were too much for Mr. Robinson's placable and compassionate, though untrained and fickle, nature to resist, and after striving in vain to maintain his angry deportment he was at length forced to capitulate and turn away hastily—lest the gathering moisture in his eyes should be observed—with the semi-angrily expressed caution and threat that if Jerry did not want every bone in his old body broken, he had better be careful in future how he mistook his " English ram for a wether sheep."

Old Benjamin Nichols used to relate that on another occasion, whilst Mr. Robinson was assisting Jerry in driving some young cattle through an open bar-way between two of the adjoining famous six "Smith meadows," that are bounded northerly on the South Ferry road and easterly on the Ferry estate, the old gentleman became very much excited because of the persistence of the cattle in refusing to leave the lot they were in—as experienced farmers are aware is often their most provoking wont under similar circumstances. Again and again, the cattle were driven up to the bar-way, and just as they seemed in the act of passing quietly through would suddenly start back and race away across the field. On the last of these occasions Mr. Robinson, who was on horseback, in an excessively angry freak, threw his cane, missed the steer at which the blow was aimed, and broke Jerry's leg short off below the knee. Upon this Mr. Robinson's angry passion was at once succeeded by one of a different mood. Jerry was tenderly conveyed home, a messenger having been previously dispatched in haste to Point Judith to obtain the immediate services of old Job Sweet, who, with his son Jonathan and his grandsons Job and William of Sugar Loaf Hill in South Kingstown, were never known to fail in replacing and healing a fractured or dislocated bone out of the thousands or tens of thousands they had operated upon, save in one remarkable instance, wherein the patient's spine, being broken, was forced inward in a position where it was impossible to be reached or pressed against by the hand.

Old Benny used to say that scarcely a day passed from the time Jerry was hurt until his substantial recovery, on which Mr. Robinson did not ride over to inquire after his health, whilst during the whole period of confinement he amply provided for the wants of Jerry's family. After Jerry got entirely well, and again went to work on the farm, he used to say that he wished Mr. Robinson would break his other leg, that his family might live as they did whilst the one he broke was getting well!

CHAPTER III.

Rowland Robinson made a large dairy, and his fancy was to have none but what were called "blanket cows," that is, cows that are entirely white all around the body between the shoulders and hips. His ambition, old Nichols said, was to have in his yard exactly one hundred "blanket cows," neither more nor less, and he took great pains to keep this number good by raising or purchasing animals so marked, but never fully succeeded. He could manage to keep ninety-nine pretty readily, but whenever the hundred was made up one or more were sure to sicken and die, or be lost through some accident.

Rowland Robinson was the father of three children only, viz.: two daughters named Hannah and Mary, both of whom were very beautiful, but especially the first named, and William, his only son. William, who in gentleness and amiability of disposition was the very opposite of his father, married Ann (called Nancy), the daughter of George Scott, of Newport, and lived and died in the fine old mansion that still stands at the north-east corner of Broadway and Mann avenue in that city.

From all I have heard, William Robinson must have been a man most singularly beloved by his fellow-townsmen. He died in October, 1804, and the late Stephen Ayrault Robinson told me that in his boyhood he used to hear that the whole town of Newport mourned his loss, and that strong men, not his especial personal acquaintance, were seen to shed tears on the mere mention of his name days after his funeral.

The death of his second daughter, Mary, in early womanhood, by consumption, and the tragic fate of his eldest daughter soon after, called ever after the "unfortunate Hannah," greatly weakened Mr. Robinson's mind, whilst the subsequent loss of his wife and that of his only and dearly beloved son in addition, proved altogether too much for his sensitive and undisciplined nature to bear up against, and his mind soon relapsed into a state of second childhood.

Many were the anecdotes that used to be told of eccentric sayings and doings of the old gentleman after his faculties had become thus impaired. Among scores of others the following: One day while in the ferry-boat, on his way to Newport; a fellow passenger made some remark derogatory to the Society of Friends, for which Mr. Robinson reproved him in not very gentle terms. "Are you a Quaker, sir?" said the stranger. "No," was the quick reply, "but I know and love the Quakers so well that I would fight knee-deep in blood in their defense."

The wife of his brother Thomas Robinson, of Newport, whose house is now standing on the "Point," having recently been put in full repair by his great-grandson, Benjamin R. Smith, of Philadelphia, who has considerately made the repairs in harmony with the ancient architectural design, was a remarkably fine woman and a great favorite of her brother-in-law, Rowland Robinson, who, in case of serious difficulty or trouble, used in his latter days always to resort to her for counsel and comfort, though it necessitated several miles' travel by land and the passing of two long ferries together measuring seven miles.

One day he came to Mrs. Robinson in a towering rage against one of the Robinson family in Narragansett, with whom he had quarreled. After stating his grievance to his sister, "Sal," said he (as he always called her), "the Robinsons are all rogues." "Why, no," said she, "that cannot be so, brother Rowland, for in that case thou, being a Robinson, must be a rogue thyself." "I believe I am, Sal! I believe I am!" was the old gentleman's quick reply.

On another occasion Mr. Robinson crossed the ferries to Newport to enter a complaint against my father, with whom he had become offended. "Sal," said he, "Rowland Hazard and I have quarreled, and I don't intend to leave him a cent." "And what have you quarreled about, brother?" mildly asked Mrs. Robinson. After trying a few moments to gather in his thoughts the old man testily replied, "I can't remember now, Sal! I can't remember now! but I dare say it was something about money matters!"

Sarah Robinson, the wife of Thomas Robinson, was a daughter of Thomas Richardson, who lived in the gambrel-roofed house now standing on the west side of Thames street in Newport, next but one north of Marlborough street, and occupied by Micah W. Spencer. Mr. Richardson was a man of the strictest probity and honor, and was for many years treasurer of the colony of Rhode Island. The original of the following love-letter addressed by Mr. Richardson to Miss Ann Newberry, who afterwards became his wife, has been preserved in the family of his great-grandson, Rowland T. Robinson, of Ferrisburgh, Vermont. It is printed precisely in the language of the original:

"——, YE 17TH OF 6 MO., 1703.

DEAR ANN:

I have long thought for an oportunity to present thee with a few lines whereby (if thou wilt but Pleasure me So much as to read them) thou may in part perceive the Distemper which Continually Greives mee that is (first) the unhappiness that I ly Under by reason of the Great Distance between us so that thereby I am debared from that felicity of Injoying the Company of Thy Person whom I Dearly Love but that is not all for I hope in a Short time to see Thee,

(Secondly) that which Greives mee most is the want of Some Assurance of being excepted in to thy honnourable favour (for as I told Thee) if it stand with God's will that I Injoy Thee for my Dearest friend I should esteeme it a great Blessing even beyond all other this world can afford beside therefore Dear Ann I beseech Thee if thou hast but ye least spark of respect for my happiness honnour mee with a line of Incorredgment Whereoff I take leve and subscribe myself Thy Constant Lover Until Death."

But though childlike in intellect, Rowland Robinson retained his activity of body—owing, probably, in a measure, to his passing so much of his life on horseback—up to almost the day of his death, which occurred in the year 1807, in the 88th year of his age.

The late Mrs. Mary Hunter, wife of Hon. William Hunter, formerly United States Minister to Brazil, in moralizing in a diary she kept some half a century ago upon the situation of her great-uncle after the decease of his wife and children, makes this entry : " Rowland Robinson was thus left alone in his grandeur, a man of violent passions, which was characteristic of the Robinsons, but of a noble, benevolent nature."

His remains lie buried in the family vault, beside those of his wife and children. The vault is about twenty feet long by fifteen broad, and is situated on an elevated mound that commands a beautiful land and sea view, some three furlongs west of the old family mansion in Boston Neck. Formerly North Kingstown and South Kingstown constituted one town—Kingstown, in Kings county, which was a part of the old " King's Province "—, and in running a division line between the two towns, when it was subdivided, it is said the line across Boston Neck was veered a little to the north to meet Mr. Robinson's expressed wishes that his house and family place of burial might be included in the town of South Kingstown, within the limits of which he was born and where most of his family, relatives and friends resided.

CHAPTER IV.

From all I used to hear related in my young days concerning the "unfortunate Hannah Robinson," her personal charms and accomplishments must have been of a character almost exceeding belief. She was described as being rather above the medium height, her figure just a trifle inclined to *embonpoint*, of a clear complexion delicately tinted with the rose, dark hazel eyes, Grecian features of the finest mould throughout, surmounted with a faultless head of auburn hair that fell in luxuriant ringlets about her swanlike neck and shoulders, all of which was made the more bewitchingly attractive by a surpassingly lovely expression of countenance and an incomparable grace in speech, manner, and carriage. As had been the custom of the Narragansett gentry in times past, the parents of Miss Robinson spared neither pains nor expense in the education of their children, and, when advanced in her teens, their daughter was placed in the care of an aunt at Newport, that she might receive instruction in the more polite branches under the care of the celebrated Madame Osborne, a most accomplished lady, whose fame as an instructor of young ladies was not confined to Newport, where she resided, nor to America.

It was said that Madame Osborne was a Swedenborgian in belief, and very devotional in her nature. Most of her patrons were ruined in property, or greatly impoverished by the events of the Revolutionary war, and she was left in quite destitute circumstances in her old age, but yet her faith never wavered from an entire assurance, that she would be provided with everything necessary for her comfort during her sojourn on earth.

Old Thomas Hornsby, of Newport, whose life was devoted to nursing and attending on the sick, for which his gentle breeding and sympathetic nature pre-eminently qualified him, used to tell me a curious anecdote in this connection. Mrs. Osborne lived in chambers for which she paid five dollars a quarter rent. As the time for a quarterly payment drew near, it was the practice of some of her friends to ascertain the prospect she had of getting the needful cash, so as to assist her, if necessary. On one such occasion it seemed to them very doubtful whether this would be forthcoming; the old lady, however, manifested no uneasiness, but simply said, when queried with, that she would certainly have the amount in season. The day of payment, notwithstanding, arrived with not a cent in prospect to meet the quarter's rent. Still Madame Osborne manifested no alarm, and maintained that the money would come in due season. This did not satisfy, and her friend begged her to inform him whence she expected the money to come. Thus urged, the old lady exhibited some impatience, and rather sharply replied that she did not know whence it was to come—it might be "from France, for all she knew;" but that she would certainly get it in season to meet the payment!

Scarcely had Madame Osborne pronounced the last word, when a rap was heard at the door, which was opened to a genteel stranger, who, after satisfying himself of the identity of the lady present, proceeded to say that he was from Paris, and that shortly before he left the city, in an interview with a friend of his, who was formerly an aide on Rochambeau's staff in Newport, he requested that if, in his contemplated visit to America, he chanced to visit Newport, he would much oblige him by seeking out his old friend, Madame Osborne, of that town, and handing her with his kind regards this sovereign (just $5), as a small token of his remembrance of the pleasant hours he had passed in her society.

It was while taking lessons under Madame Osborne's roof that Miss Robinson first saw M. Pierre Simond, or Mr. Peter Simons, a young and highly accomplished teacher in music and other branches of *belles-lettres*, the scion of a Huguenot family of some note, who were obliged to flee their country during the persecution of the French Protestants, in the reign of Louis XIV. Almost from the hour they met, a sentiment of affection sprung up in the hearts of the young tutor and his lovely, unsophisticated pupil, which had ripened into a strong mutual attachment before Miss Robinson's return to her parents' home in Narragansett. The lovers were aware that it would not do for one in Mr. Simons' position in life to venture into Mr. Robinson's house as a suitor of his daughter, and that it might be equally unsafe to conduct a correspondence by post. In this dilemma fortune seemed to favor the young people. Miss Robinson's maternal uncle, Col. William Gardiner, who lived less than two miles from her father's house, found it most convenient to educate his children partly at home. With this purpose in view, in looking about for an accomplished private tutor, through the recommendation of Madame Osborne and others of his Newport friends he engaged Mr. Simons to go with him to Narragansett and occupy that position in his family. Thus situated, it may be readily divined that the lovers enjoyed many opportunities of seeing each other, especially as Colonel Gardiner, who was of a kind and easy disposition, on becoming aware of the strong attachment that existed between his lovely niece and her former tutor, sought rather to promote opportunities for interviews between the lovers than otherwise.

It was not until her mother's suspicions were aroused on account of the unusual frequency of her daughter's visits to her uncle Gardiner's that Miss Robinson confided to her the secret of her love. After trying for months in vain to persuade her child to discard her affianced lover, and finding that nothing could induce her to prove false to her plighted faith, Mrs. Robinson forbore further opposition. Thus encouraged by the mother's tacit consent, if not approval, of his suit, it was mutually arranged by the lovers that Mr. Simons should occasionally walk over from Col. Gardiner's of an evening, and, on the appearance of a signal light in Miss Robinson's chamber window, approach the house and secrete himself in a large lilac bush that grew beneath it, whence billets might be easily passed; or they could converse in whisper without being detected. In fact. so emboldened did the lovers become by the unbroken success that attended this stratagem that they finally arranged for occasional meetings in Miss Robinson's own chamber, her mother lending her presence and countenance to the dangerous adventure, rendered all the more critical because of it being the undeviating practice of Mr. Robinson to bid his daughter good night before he retired, even if it required his going to her own chamber or elsewhere. Hence it was necessary to have a convenient place, like the cupboard before alluded to, into which Miss Robinson's lover might retreat on untoward occasions.

Though not yet grown to mature womanhood, Miss Robinson, as might be readily surmised, had many admirers.— Among these was a Dr. William Bowen, of Providence, who was ardently attached to the fair damsel, and earnestly sought her, with her father's full approval, in marriage. Miss Robinson, however, graciously declined his addresses, and that he might not indulge in delusive hopes, imparted to him in confidence, the fact that her affections were irrevocably engaged to another.

The heart of that rudely chivalric and perfect "dare-devil" Col. Harry Babcock, of Narragansett, but known the world over as " crazy Harry Babcock," was perhaps never subdued by female charms but once. He was the eldest son of Dr. Joshua Babcock, of what is now Westerly, in Narragansett, a gentleman of refinement and wealth, at whose house

Benjamin Franklin used always to stop—as he also did with his friend, John Case, Esq., who lived on Tower Hill—in his yearly journeyings on horseback to and from Philadelphia and Boston.

Updike, in his History, relates a characteristic anecdote of Dr. Franklin, while he was stopping at Dr. Babcock's. Mrs. Babcock asked him if he " would have his bed warm‑ed." " No, madam, thank'ee," he replied; " but if you will have a little cold water sprinkled on the sheets I have no objection."

It was on one of these annual journeyings that Dr. Franklin happened to arrive at a tavern near New London on a cold evening, where he found every place around the blazing wood fire closely occupied. No one offering to relinquish his seat, the doctor called upon the landlord to give his horse a peck of raw oysters, which order was repeated in a more decided tone upon the host hesitating to comply with his request. The oysters were accordingly carried out by the landlord, followed by the individuals who had monopolized the seats around the fire, they all being curious to see a horse eat oysters. The landlord soon returned and told the doctor, who, by this time, was comfortably ensconced in the arm-chair in the warmest corner, that his horse refused to eat the oysters. " Poor, foolish beast!" said the doctor ; " he don't know what is good ; bring them to me, and see if I will refuse them!"

Alluding to "Crazy Harry," Updike says : " Doctor Babcock's eldest son, Col. Harry Babcock, was a brilliant and extraordinary man, formed by nature and education to be the flower of his family and an ornament to the country which gave him birth. His biography, written by one who had the requisite documents, talent and leisure, would form a curious, interesting and instructive work."

During England's wars with France, in colonial times, Colonel Harry Babcock performed many marvelous feats of valor, both by land and sea, and in all his engagements and fights he never once, it is said, succumbed to a foe.

Before the Revolutionary war he went to London, and on the night of his arrival attended a play at Covent Garden Theatre. There being no seat vacant, the Colonel stood in a passage-way. A policeman, seeing his tall, gaunt figure standing erect, with a big slouched hat on his head, touched his shoulder with his baton and told him to be uncovered. Col. Babcock thereupon took off his hat, and, reaching up to a chandelier near by, hung it over one of the lights. A murmur of disapprobation ran through the hall, and the police were about to eject the rude intruder, when some one present, called out, "Colonel Harry Babcock!" Upon this announcement the performers in the play ceased acting their parts to join in the uproarious applause that greeted the presence of the far-famed hero, "Crazy Harry Babcock."

A short time after this, Col. Harry Babcock received an invitation to the palace, and was introduced to the royal family. When the Queen, in accordance with usage, offered him her hand to kiss, the gallant colonel sprang from his knees to his feet, briskly exclaiming, "May it please your majesty, in my country it is the custom to salute, not the hand, but the lips of a beautiful woman!" and suiting the action to his words, he seized the Queen by the shoulders and impressed on her lips a loud and hearty smack!

Rowland Robinson chancing once to meet Col. Babcock on Little Rest Hill (now Kingston), during a session of the court in February, asked the eccentric colonel to go home with him and stay the night. "Ah, ha!" said Crazy Harry; "so you want me to see Hannah, that I've heard so much of, do you? Well, I will go, but don't expect me to fall in love with her, as so many fools have done."

As was the general custom in those days, they both rode on horseback, and when they came near to McSparran Hill, one of the longest and probably the steepest hill road in Rhode Island—the ground being covered with ice at the time—, Mr. Robinson cautioned his friend against the danger of descending on a smooth-shod horse, as his appeared to be, and advised him to dismount and lead his beast down the descent. Instead of heeding the well-meant caution, when they reached the brow of the hill, and Mr. Robinson was in the act of dismounting, "Crazy Harry" suddenly exclaimed, "Now, Mr. Robinson, I will show you how the devil rides!" and putting spurs to his horse, he went slipping and sliding down the steep declivity, fortunately without accident, on the full run. When they shortly after arrived at the house, the colonel was in high and outspoken glee at the prospect, as he said, of seeing "the prettiest woman in Rhode Island," these words being spoken in a loud, jocular tone, just as they entered the door of the sitting-room, where Miss Robinson was at the time engaged in sewing. With a slight flush on her cheeks, and a look of surprise, she arose with her customary dignity and grace to receive her father, and welcome his boisterous guest, whose eyes no sooner fell upon the beautiful vision than the rough-spoken hero seemed to have been suddenly overcome by some charmed spell. As Miss Robinson, on being introduced by her father, extended toward him her hand, the "crazy colonel" reverentially took it gently in his, and gazing in her face with a subdued look of wonder and admiration, he dropped on his knee before her, and, with a voice tremulous with emotion, softly and slowly said: "Permit, dear madam, the lips that have kissed unrebuked those of the proudest Queen of earth, to press, for a moment, the hand of an angel from heaven."

Scarcely less flattering, though in a different vein, was a compliment that was once paid to Miss Robinson's charms by an old Quaker preacher, who chanced to meet her at her uncle Thomas Robinson's, while she was yet attending school. After gazing steadfastly in her face for some minutes, the old man drew his chair to her side and remarked, "Friend, thou are wonderfully beautiful!"

CHAPTER V.

Though Dr. Bowen kept inviolate the secret of her engagement imparted to him in confidence by Miss Robinson, her naturally frank and unsuspicious father, nevertheless, began to imagine that there must be some cause unknown to him to account for his daughter's rejection of the addresses of so many suitors, and especially of Dr. Bowen, who seemed every way qualified to confer upon her happiness in domestic life.

It was not long before his suspicions were confirmed. Chancing late one evening to step suddenly out of the front door of his house which had been left ajar, Mr. Robinson caught a glimpse of his daughter's arm reaching down from the window above, just as she was about to drop a billet into the extended hand of her lover. Instantly seizing a heavy buckthorn cane that stood near the door he thrust it violently into the lilac bush, from which, upon the stick coming in contact with his person, rushed forth a man who was quickly lost to sight in the darkness, but not until Mr. Robinson recognized him to be no other than the young teacher of music he remembered to have occasionally seen at the house of his brother-in-law, William Gardiner. Frantic with rage the incensed parent hastened to his daughter's chamber, and upbraided her in unmeasured terms for her unfilial conduct in disregarding his wishes respecting the choice of a husband in every way befitting her, and thus throwing herself away upon a wretched "French dancing master," as Mr. Robinson ever after designated Mr. Simons. The poor girl answered not a word, either in way of confession or denial, but remained mute as a statue under all her father's reproaches. This only exasperated the choleric and undisciplined parent the more, and it may be readily conceived there could have been but little hope of peace or happiness for Miss Robinson whilst under her father's roof in the future, or at least so long as she refused to discard the addresses of the man upon whom she had irrevocably placed her affections.

"If she walked," says Updike, p. 189, "her movements were watched; if she rode, a servant was ordered to be in constant attendance; if a visit was contemplated, he immediately suspected it was only a pretence for an arranged interview; and even after departure, if the most trifling circumstance gave color to suspicion, he would immediately pursue and compel her to return. In one instance, she left home to visit her aunt in New London; her father soon afterwards discovered from his windows a vessel leaving Newport, and taking a course towards the same place. Although the vessel and the persons on board where wholly unknown to him, his jealousies were immediately aroused. Conjecturing it was Mr. Simons intending to fulfil an arrangement previously made, he hastened to New London, arrived a few hours only after his daughter, and insisted on her instant return. No persuasion or argument could induce him to change his determination, and she was compelled to return with him."

It was fortunate that at this crisis the engagement of Mr. Simons with Colonel Gardiner was about expiring; otherwise a breach of friendship and intercourse between the two families might have been the consequence. Mr. Simons, however, found another, though more distant, home in Narragansett, and still persevered in his suit, the story of which had now become widely spread abroad.

On account of Mr. Robinson's rabid and unreasonable opposition to his daughter's wishes, and the rigid measures he adopted to prevent the lovers meeting, nearly the whole neighborhood became interested in their behalf, and almost every connection of the family was ready to assist in forwarding opportunities for their interviews. These, however, were attended with great difficulty, as her father never permitted his daughter to leave home without being attended by a confidential servant on whose vigilance and faithfulness he could rely. For this reason months sometimes passed without the affianced lovers meeting each other, although through the agency of an attached and confidential friend of Miss Robinson—a Miss Belden, from Hartford—, who was staying at the time with her Uncle William Gardiner, who married an aunt of Miss Belden, a secret correspondence was kept up between them.

The life of anxiety and worry Miss Robinson was subjected to, finally began to affect her health so seriously, that even her mother, though she did not actively abet, took no pains to frustrate, a plan she strongly suspected was perfecting, whereby, with the aid of friends, Miss Robinson had consented to embrace the first favorable opportunity to elope from her father's house and unite herself in wedlock with her lover. Nor was it long before such an occasion presented itself.

It was the custom in those days for wealthy families in Narragansett to entertain on an extensive scale, nor were the invitations confined to the locality alone, but were sent by post to friends in Newport, Providence, Boston, and other distant parts. A ball of this kind was announced some days beforehand, to be given by Mrs. Lodowick Updike, who was a sister of Mrs. Rowland Robinson. It would in that hospitable time have been considered a breach of etiquette, were not some of Mr. Robinson's family to attend on the occasion, and it was finally arranged, with many misgivings on his part, that his two daughters, Hannah and Mary, should go to the ball and stay the night with their aunt. Prince, Mr. Robinson's body servant, as a matter of course was to wait upon and keep watch and guard over the beautiful sisters, especially the elder.

Mr. Updike owned and occupied a large landed estate in North Kingstown, and lived in the fine old mansion still standing a little north of Wickford, on the east side of the old post-road, on the site where, Updike's History says, was erected by Richard Smith, the first settler in Narragansett, the first English house or "fort" built in that district of the country. This fortified house must have been standing in 1675, as I have heard the late Daniel E. Updike, of East Greenwich, relate that after the great Indian swamp fight, which occurred in South Kingstown in 1675, a Connecticut regiment encamped for the night on his great-grandfather's estate, and that on the next morning the officers of the regiment, who lodged at his house, took a fine-looking young Indian warrior, whom they had captured after the battle, into the orchard, and, out of "pure cussedness" and for sport, placed his head on a tree stump and chopped it off with a wood axe.

For this dastardly attack on the Indians for which the people of Narragansett were in no way responsible, as they had kept faith and lived in the immediate neighborhood in peace and harmony with them up to the very night of the battle, the governments of Massachusetts and Connecticut are alone answerable at the bar of eternal justice.

I have heard old people say that on the very day preceding the massacre, the Indians had exchanged neighborly kindnesses with a family by the name of Knowles—one of the most ancient and respectable of Narragansett families—, who resided within a short distance of their encampment on the elevated knoll in the swamp.

In referring to the outrageous extermination of the most powerful, warlike and numerous of the New England tribes of aborigines, Updike, in his History, says:

" Canonchet, the son of the brave but unfortunate Miantonomi, was the last sachem of the race. He commanded the

Indians in the great swamp fight of 1675. This battle exterminated the Narragansetts as a nation. He was captured near the Blackstone river, after the war, and executed for the crime of defending his country and refusing to surrender the territories of his ancestors by a treaty of peace. It was glory enough for such a nation to have expired with such a chief. The coolness, fortitude and heroism of his fall stands without a parallel in ancient or modern times. He was offered life upon the condition that he would treat for the submission of his subjects; but his untamed spirit indignantly rejected the ignominious proposition. When the sentence was announced to him that he must die, he said, 'I LIKE IT WELL, THAT I SHALL DIE BEFORE MY HEART GROWS SOFT, OR THAT I HAVE SAID ANYTHING UNWORTHY OF MYSELF.'

"The splendid dignity of his fall extorted from one of the prejudiced historians of the times the sentiment that, acting as if by a Pythagorean metempsychosis, some old Roman ghost had possessed the body of the western pagan like an Attilius Regulus! Thus ended the last chief of the Narragansetts, and with Canonchet the nation was extinguished forever."

Ninnegret, says Updike, was the sachem of the Nyantics— since called the Charlestown tribe—, and only related collaterally "to the family of Canonicus, who was the grand sachem of the Narragansetts when the whites first settled Plymouth." Ninnegret was succeeded by a son of the same name, and he in turn by his son George. "George left three children, Thomas, George, and Esther. Thomas, commonly called 'King Tom,' was born in 1732, and succeeded as sachem in July, 1746." (See Potter's History of Narragansett.)

The arm-chair in which King Tom was crowned, and which represented his throne, is now in the possession of Rowland G. Hazard, of Peacedale, in a good state of preservation.

King Tom was succeeded by Esther. William Kenyon, late of Charlestown, writes (see Updike's History): "I saw Queen Esther crowned over seventy years ago [about

1776]. She was elevated on a large rock, so that the people might see her. The council surrounded her. There were present about twenty Indian soldiers with guns. They marched her to the rock. The Indian nearest the royal blood, in presence of her counselors, put the crown on her head. It was made with cloth covered with blue and white *peage.* When the crown was put on the soldiers fired a royal salute and huzzaed in the Indian tongue. The ceremony was imposing, and everything was conducted with great order. Then the soldiers waited on her to the house, and fired salutes. There were five hundred natives present, beside others. Queen Esther left one son named George; he was crowned after the death of his mother. I was enlisting soldiers and went to him and asked him to enlist as a soldier in the Revolutionary war; the squaws objected, and told me he was their king." King George was killed by the limb of a tree, while felling timber, in the twenty-second year of his age. "No king," says Updike, " was ever crowned after him, and not an Indian of the whole blood now [1847] remains in the tribe."

Queen Esther, I think, must have inherited a good deal of the spirit of the illustrious Narragansett chiefs, to whom, Updike states, her family was only collaterally related. I used to hear the late Molly Hazard, a granddaughter of Gov. William Robinson, say, that Queen Esther was a frequent visitor at her father's (Sylvester Robinson's) and her grandfather's, and that she was very much attached to the family of Robinson, but could not be induced to converse in English, declaring through her interpreter, to the last, that she would never "speak the language of the destroyers of her people."

An anecdote used to be told me of an instance wherein Queen Esther attended upon the last moments of a little girl to whom she was devotedly attached, but whose earnest appeals that she might speak one word to her in English before she died, was resisted to the last, although tears rolled down the poor Indian's cheek under the severe conflict her contending feelings of affection and pride were forced to undergo.

It was the cruel treatment of the Indians by the colonists of Connecticut and Massachusetts, and the banishment of Roger Williams and the Baptists, together with the whipping and hanging of the Quakers by the latter, that doubtless gave rise to the old-time three-plied religious creed, which, when I was young, used to be inculcated into the ductile minds of infant children in nearly every well ordered family in Narragansett, viz.: 1st. "That ye love one another," and "your neighbor as yourselves;" 2d. That ye hate the Puritans of Massachusetts with a perfect hatred ; 3d. That ye hold the Presbyterians of Connecticut in like contempt.

Under such unfavorable circumstances it may readily be surmised that when Parson Kendall, irreverently called " the six-fingered parson" from a supernumerary finger on his left hand, was sent as a missionary from Connecticut, that his preaching met with little success. It was even said that on an occasion wherein old Sim Hazard happened to be present, when the parson was holding forth with unusual heat, the irreverent listener got up and left the meeting-house, declaring that he'd be d—d if he would sit by and hear anybody so shamefully abused as the Connecticut six-fingered parson was abusing the devil, if he was black !

In fact, I cannot call to mind of ever hearing of more than three of the regular " blue" sort of the denomination living in all eastern Narragansett, in my younger days.

One of these was old Parson Torrey, who lived and died before my memory in a house that stood about one mile from the village, on the south side of the road running west from Tower Hill, on what is now called the " Tory lot."

I the more particularly remember old Parson Torrey, from a uniform way my father used to tell me, when I was a small boy, the old Presbyterian had of reproving his son, a very naughty boy, to whom he would say, with great emphasis, when he behaved amiss, "Why! I am ashamed of you, John! I am ashamed of you!"

Were it not for this circumstance I should probably have forgotten hearing of Parson Torrey, as I probably might have forgotten ever seeing his successor, Parson Kendall, were it not for his extra little finger, which attracted my boyish attention more than his whole body, limbs and all beside.

The two others were brothers, both rising eighty, named Simon and Ray Mumford, who owned and occupied a brick house in Point Judith, that was demolished some years ago to give place to a new structure erected for Mrs. William Sprague.

I doubt even if the orthodoxy of these could be relied upon; for old Ray used to say that a Bible and a Life of Oliver Cromwell were the only books in their house, and that after more than forty years' examination of the two neither he nor his brother Simon had been able to determine which was the best book!

I knew both of these old gentlemen pretty well. Old Simon used to sit a good portion of the warm season of the year on a rock on the top of a conical hill that rises some two or three furlongs south of the present Tower Hill Hotel, on the Mumford land, his occupation being to watch his son Nathaniel's cattle and sheep, who was proverbially careless of his fences.

CHAPTER VI.

To return from this long digression: Mr. Simons was, of course, apprised by Miss Belden of the contemplated visit of Miss Robinson to her aunt's in North Kingstown, and it was arranged that he should meet her on the way and the lovers make their escape to Providence. When the morning of the day of Miss Robinson's departure—perhaps forever—from the home of her childhood, rendered sacred and dear by a thousand tender recollections, arrived, the struggle in the poor girl's breast between filial duty and sisterly affection on the one side and that all-conquering sentiment which is implanted by nature in every female heart, that compels a woman to disregard, as it were, even against her own will, every consideration that stands between her and the man she loves, on the other, was pitiable to contemplate. Still Miss Robinson maintained, in a good degree, an outward appearance of composure until the moment came to take leave of the household. After especially bidding Phillis, the cook, and Hannah, her own waiting-maid, an affectionate farewell, and charging them both to take good care of her little spaniel Marcus, and Felis, her favorite cat, she threw her arms around her mother's neck and sobbed as if her heart was breaking. Still the high-spirited girl, the victim of what in the end proved a misplaced affection, persevered in her resolution to remain faithful to her vows. Mounting from the stone horse-block her splendid Spanish jennet or "Narragansett pacer"—from whose sire and dam, imported by her grandfather Robinson from Andalusia, sprang a race of horses unrivaled for the saddle in America—,Miss Robinson and her companions rode away.

It was fortunate for the success of the ill-starred adventure that Miss Robinson had taken leave of her father an hour before her departure, he having been unexpectedly called away on urgent business; otherwise the heart-rending emotion that overcame her just before leaving might have given rise to suspicion in his breast that would have led to a positive forbiddance of her departure from home.

When the ladies attended by Prince reached an "elbow" turn in the highway on Ridge Hill, a thickly wooded spot, they encountered Mr. Simons with a closed carriage, into which the affianced bride, after dismounting and bidding her sister an affectionate adieu, and charging Prince to see well to Selim, her pony, assisted by her lover, hastily stepped, and was driven rapidly away on the road towards Providence, in spite of the frantic appeals and remonstrances of Prince. Mr. Simons had thoughtfully secured the attendance of his sister for the occasion, who had provided an addition to Miss Robinson's necessarily scanty wardrobe, and in a few hours the lovers, with the aid of the pastoral services of a regularly ordained minister of the Episcopal church, were indissolubly united in the bonds of wedlock.

Miss Mary Robinson and her sable attendant proceeded no farther on their journey, but returned to her father's house, where, as may be readily inferred, there was but little quiet or sleep that night. Suffice to say, that Mr. Robinson, after fully comprehending the fact that his daughter had really eloped from the parental roof, and was then undoubtedly wedded to the wretched "French dancing master," he so thoroughly despised, was for a time completely beside himself with rage. He offered a large reward to any one who would make known to him the person or persons who aided in her escape, but wholly without success.

But now approaches the most sorrowful part of the story

of "unfortunate Hannah Robinson." After her marriage, Mr. Simons took his bride to reside for a time with his father, Peter Simons, who lived in the fine old, two-story, hip-roofed house, still standing on the north side of Bridge street, near Thames street, in Newport. This house is at present owned and occupied by Mr. Zenas L. Hammond. The elaborately finished front door, and the accompanying portico, which was formerly mounted with a carved pine-apple, after the manner of the old State House, together with the heavy carriage gate-way, have been recently remodeled. The premises in other respects remain the same as when first established, and are still in good repair. The nicely finished paneling, extending all around the lower front rooms from the floor to the ceiling, is apparently as perfect as when first placed there, some century and a half ago. Here Miss Robinson, now Mrs. Simons, remained for some months, when her husband obtained a professional situation in Providence, and removed his wife to that city, where they took a house in which she resided for some one or two years, up to the time she went home to die.

Mr. Simons, though of a pleasing person and seductive manners and address, proved to be an unthrifty, unprincipled man, who, finding that his wife was likely to be wholly discarded and disinherited by her father, began not long after his marriage to treat her with neglect, and to indulge in his naturally dissipated propensities, until he became totally reckless and almost entirely deserted her. After striving with all her might for a time to arrest the downward course of her husband, whom she continued to love to the last moment of her life notwithstanding his cruel treatment, the poor lady's health broke down completely and she was obliged to keep her bed.

As yet, with the exception that her mother had contrived to send to her hapless daughter, soon after her flight from home, her wardrobe and her little dog, Marcus, who seemed inconsolable for the loss of his mistress, she had not received any recognition or assistance whatever from her relatives. In the meantime Mrs. Simon's sister Mary had died with the consumption, whilst her mother's health under her complicated anxieties and suffering had given way, so that she was unable to go to her daughter, to say nothing of the opposition she might have met with from her still exasperated husband, had she made the attempt. Upon learning the forlorn condition of her suffering child, Mrs. Robinson did, however, manage, through the instrumentality of her stripling son William, and occasionally through the assistance of others, to convey to her the needed wherewithal to supply her most pressing material wants, and keep advised of the progress of her sickness. It was in vain, however, that she pleaded with her incensed husband to mitigate his rigor toward his unfortuate daughter and to permit her to be brought to his house.

It soon became pretty evident to Mrs. Robinson that, notwithstanding the acrimonious demeanor her husband habitually manifested externally towards his absent, undutiful child, there was still a soft place left in his proud and sorely wounded heart for her memory to nestle in. She had observed that when he returned home after a day's or more absence, in case Hannah's cat was not in sight, he would wander abstractedly from room to room until he encountered the *real* object of his search, when, without seemingly noticing the animal, he would sit quietly down. More than once, too, Mrs. Robinson had, unconsciously to her husband, observed him conveying stealthily a tid-bit from his own plate under the table to Felis, and on one occasion on coming unexpectedly into the sitting-room, she found the sorrowing father, his eyes suffused with tears, pressing the dumb favorite of his truant child to his bosom. Prince also remarked that since his mistress left home, Mr. Robinson went twice as often to the stable to see Hannibal, his own favorite saddle horse, as he ever did before, and that he always patted Selim on the neck the very last thing he did when he was about to go away.

As all the accounts received from Providence went to show that the health of Mrs. Simons was rapidly declining, Mr. Robinson began to manifest symptoms of serious alarm, and one day, after consenting to the entreaties of his wife that Mrs. Simons' maid, Hannah, should go and stay with her young mistress, he told her of his own accord that Hannah might come home if she would consent to reveal to him the names of those who had aided in her elopement; but on no other condition, let the consequences be what they might.

On being informed of this proposition of her father, Mrs. Simons wrote to him an affectionate letter, in which she lamented in moving terms having been a cause of so much trouble to him and feelingly expressed her gratitude for his kind offer to permit her again to return to the loved home of her childhood. She added in lines that showed that the feeble hand by which they were indited trembled with increased emotion, that bitter as was the alternative, the sentiments of honor her dear parent had instilled into her mind from childhood would not permit her, even with life at stake, to betray the confidence that had been reposed in her by those who had so seriously offended him on her account. On receiving his daughter's letter, Mr. Robinson read it eagerly, and with apparent satisfaction, until he reached the last paragraph, when tossing the missive contemptuously to his wife, he angrily exclaimed, "Then let the foolish thing die where she is!"

As the accounts received of Mrs. Simons' health, however, grew more and more alarming, it became evident that a terrible struggle for mastery was going on in the wretched father's breast, between an overweening, untamable pride, wounded to the quick and supported by an indomitable will, on the one side, and parental affection, as true and unconquerable as ever found place in the most tender and susceptible human breast, on the other. The conflict at length became unendurable, and one day, pushing from him his plate of untasted food, he arose from the dinner table and ordered his horse to the door. He at once mounted, and, telling his wife not to expect him back for a day or two, rode rapidly away. That night he lodged with his friend and kinsman, Lodowick Updike, who resided at the old family seat, some eight miles on the way toward Providence. The next forenoon Mr. Robinson reached his daughter's house, and, riding up to the steps without dismounting, rapped on the door with the head of his cane. The door was opened by his daughter's maid, Hannah, who was born in his house a short time after the birth of her young mistress and called after her name. Overjoyed to see her master, the servant girl stopped not to talk with him, but hastened to her mistress' chamber with the glad tidings. Mrs. Simons was too ill to leave her bed, but sent her entreaties to her father that he should come to her. "Ask your mistress," said Mr. Robinson, "whether she is ready to comply with her father's wishes, and say to her that if she is, he will come to her; but on no other condition!" Though again to refuse compliance was like taking life from the poor invalid, Mrs. Simons could not find it in her noble nature to betray her friends, and was obliged to again deny her father's request. On his daughter's answer being communicated to him, Mr. Robinson hastily turned away, and without saying an intelligible word, rode back without stopping for refreshment for man or beast to his friend Updike's, where he again passed the night, and so away to his solitary home in the morning.

But the warring elements which had been only momentarily allayed by his journey continued to rage with increased violence in the father's breast, until they became so overpowering that the unhappy man could neither eat nor sleep, and, urged on by contending passions, but a day or two elapsed after his return from the first visit when Mr. Robinson again started on the road to Providence, stopping a night with his friend Updike on his journey to and fro as before. These visits he continued to repeat, at intervals of two or three days only, for some weeks. In every instance, he would ride up to the door of the house where his sick daughter lay, and, without dismounting from his horse, simply say to the servant he had summoned by a knock of his cane on the door, "How is Hannah?" and on receiving an answer he would immediately turn the head of his horse, and ride away.

Miss Belden, of Hartford, and Mrs. Simons' uncle, William Gardiner, who had married an aunt of Miss Belden of the same name and city, were the only individuals that were implicated in the demand of Mr. Robinson, and so soon as the former became acquainted with the pitiable dilemma in which her unfortunate friend was placed, she dispatched a letter by post to Mrs. Simons, in which she not only absolved her from all obligations of secrecy, but commanded her to make the confession required by her incensed father, irrespective of any consideration on her account.

About the same time, Mrs. Simons' uncle, William Gardiner, called to see his niece in Providence, and insisted upon her making a clean breast of the whole affair to her father, regardless of any obligations of secrecy she felt bound by in relation to him. Thus set at liberty, the next time her father called Mrs. Simons sent word that if he would come to her bedside she would tell him all.

Trembling with emotion, Mr. Robinson dismounted and ascended the stairs to his sick daughter's comfortless chamber. Until then he had formed no conception of the extremity to which his poor child was reduced. As he approached the bed and took her hand, thin almost to transparency, in both of his, and looked into the scarcely recognizable face, but a few years before so surpassingly fair, but now so wan, so sorrowful, so despairing, with naught remaining of the beauteous complexion that once outrivaled the lily and the rose, save the fearful hectic tint that death's messenger sends before to announce to those the angels love best their near approach, the flood-gates that had when braced by opposition so long withstood the promptings of his better nature gave way, and the long pent-up affections of the father's heart burst forth in one uncontrollable tide of tenderness and love. No wish nor thought was then in the wretched parent's breast to wring from his poor daughter the hitherto coveted secret, and the strong man, falling on his knees by the bedside, bathed the pale, cold hand of his dying child with tears, and wept aloud.

After he had somewhat regained his composure, he handed some pieces of gold to his daughter's waiting-maid, and charged her to see that her mistress lacked for nothing that would promote her comfort, until his return. Mr. Robinson then tenderly kissed his broken-hearted child, and mounting his horse, delayed not on the road save for needed refreshments, until he arrived late in the evening at his house in Boston Neck.

In those early times, when roads were rough, and four-wheeled carriages almost unknown, litters for the sick were indispensable articles in all well-appointed households in Narragansett, and, as old Benny Nichols used to relate, immediately after Mr. Robinson arrived home, he was summoned from his bed and ordered to take four strong men and proceed with them and the litter, in his pleasure boat, as fast as sails and oars would speed them, to Providence, and there await his arrival.

The next morning by break of day Mr. Robinson himself started on horseback, attended by Prince and a led-horse for his daughter's maid-servant. On their arrival before the door of her residence, he sent his man with the three horses to Macomber's tavern, and entering the house, apprised the invalid of the arrangements that had been made for conveying her to Narragansett, by which it was proposed to stop at her uncle Updike's the first night, and, if her strength permitted, to reach home the next day.

In the meantime, the boat bringing the litter and men to carry it had arrived at the wharf, and on the next morning by nine o'clock the whole party were slowly wending their way towards the homestead in Boston Neck. They arrived safely at Mr. Updike's with less fatigue to the poor invalid than was feared, and as it had been previously arranged, there the party rested for the night.

The sun had almost reached the meridian before it was deemed advisable to move onward again. A refreshing shower had fallen in the morning, which imparted a sparkling loveliness to the whole vegetable kingdom, that seemed to be rejoicing in the summer rays of a clear, unclouded sun. It was in the lovely month of June, when the rose, the syringa, the wild honeysuckle and sweet-scented clover, were all in bloom, and those most glorious of all earthly parterres, the apple tree orchards along the road, now in full blossom, and glittering with rain drops, conveyed to the senses of the beholder, more delightsome sensations, than any assemblage of the more gaudy but less fragrant foliage of tropical climes can bestow.

As the mournful party moved forward, ever and anon, little striped chipmunks were to be seen, skipping along the tops and sides of the rough stone walls that lined the way, whilst larger individuals of the species, the bush-tail, red and grey squirrels, were at times espied amidst the thick foliage af their favorite chestnut and walnut trees, leaping from branch to branch in playful sport. Occasionally, too, native rabbits were seen in the adjoining woods, and the homely woodchucks, or groundhogs, seemed to be all abroad, and on the nearer approach of the slowly moving cortege would scamper to the entrance of their holes in the ground, and maintaining their guard the while, stand upright on their haunches, as if to take a better view of the unwonted group that were passing by. Innumerable birds were holding their accustomed jubilee, after the shower had passed away, filling the air with music, too divine to be learned elsewhere than of the angels who dwell in the mid heavens, where the feathered songsters alone are permitted to soar.

The black-bird and mocking-bird seemed everywhere

vying with each other in their melodious powers, whilst the quavering note of the meadow lark responded to the whistle of the quail, and the bob-o-link, that sweetest songster of them all, winged himself from lily to lily in every field, attuning his voice in harmony with the swaying to and fro of each flowery perch, until its tinest vibration ceased when the sweet warbler would fly to another and another, and encore its own song from its highest to its lowest note.

When the spot was reached on Ridge Hill where Mrs. Simons had formerly met her lover, and bid a final adieu to her now deceased sister Mary, it was noticed by Prince that she covered her face with both hands and seemed to be weeping. When asked a few days after this, by a friend of the family, to tell him what Mrs. Simons did on the occasion referred to, Prince answered that "Missus Hannah didn't do nothin'! she eny just put both hands over her face and cried! That wer all!"

CHAPTER VII.

On reaching John Hazard's, who was a family connection and intimate friend of Rowland Robinson, the party were met by Mrs. Robinson, who, though not at all well, had ventured so far to meet her returning sick child. As may be readily supposed, the meeting between mother and daughter, after being so long separated under such trying circumstances, was affecting.

Stopping with their friends a short time to rest and take some refreshments, the party again moved forward. At the same time Mrs. Robinson left for home in her one-horse chaise—imported from England at great cost, as all covered carriages were in that day—and arrived before the sun went down.

Old Alexander Gardiner, Sr., lived at that time in a house, I remember well, that stood on the west side of the post-road, nearly opposite where the lower McSparran, or river, road, turns off to the east. The old man being aware of the coming of the party had dressed himself in his "go-to-meetin'" or "roast meat", *i. e.*, Sunday dinner, suit of yellow nankeen short breeches, with waistcoat to match, and a semi-military blue coat, ornamented with a long row of silver Spanish dollar buttons in front, and stood in his door to welcome their approach by politely removing from his head his imposing cocked hat, and making three several low conges, first to the poor lady in the litter, next to Mr. Robinson, and lastly to the attendants.

More than fifty years after this event I remember seeing

Aleck Gardiner, Jr.—then an old man—, standing in the same door, wearing a blue coat ornamented with dollar buttons, and upon my remarking on the tasty style of his garment the old man told me that he had inherited the coat from his deceased father, some forty years or more before, and he hoped to hand it down to his son in about as good condition as it was when he received it.

This was in the days when shoddy was unknown, and cloth was made to wear rather than to sell, and when "go-to-meeting" boots passed from generation to generation in the same way. It was a custom with many farmers, as soon as they returned from "meeting," to fill these last named expensive articles 'of wear with beans or flax-seed and hang them up on pegs until some extraordinary occasion or "meetin' day" called for their use again. The use of flax-seed was finally pretty much abandoned, because of a mischievous boy, on occasion of his father's whipping him one day, hitting the old man's suspended boots now and then a sly rap with the broom-handle for several days in succession, in consequence of which, when his father took them down on the next Sunday, he found both split at the toes, through the pressure of the slippery flax-seed.

Some half-mile to the north-west of Aleck Gardiner's there lived, since my memory, Ephraim Hazard, a white-headed, venerable-looking old man, whom I personally knew, and who, Thomas B. Hazard—called Nailor Tom, a man of inexhaustible anecdote—used to say, was the first discoverer of a machine that involved in its mechanical construction the only true principle of the then much mooted question of perpetual motion. In compliance with Ephraim's repeated solicitation, "Nailor Tom" called one day to see this wonderful invention. He was taken by Eph. into the garret, where stood an old woolen yarn spinning-wheel, some four feet in diameter. To one of the spokes of this there was tied a pair of kitchen tongs, whilst from the opposite there dangled a flat-iron. Taking hold of the rim, the old man gave the wheel a smart turn with his hand that sent it flying around with great speed until the flat-iron dropped to the floor. "There, cousin Tom," exclaimed the ingenious mechanic, "if that flat-iron had been a little weightier than them kitchen tongs, and them kitchen tongs had been a little weightier than that flat-iron, and that old tow string hadn't broke, that wheel would have gone round and round, just like the world, for ever and ever."

On the opposite side of the road, a little to the south of Aleck Gardiner's, there now stands a house in tolerable repair, in which old Polybius—pronounced *Polibus*—Austin lived since my remembrance, in connection with whom I have heard Joshua Custis tell the following anecdote. Mr. Custis, who was a deputy-sheriff or constable, having in his possession an execution for a debt of some two dollars and costs against Polybius that was near expiring, called at his house to collect the money. Polybius, not being prepared to respond to the demand, was told by the constable that he must in that case go with him to Little Rest and be lodged in jail. Polybius had three tall, bony, spinister daughters in the house, ranging anywhere from the age of forty to fifty years, to whom the old man turned in his extremity, and tearfully exclaimed, "Gals, are you going to let Josh take your old father to jail?" Upon this frantic appeal of their poor father, Waity seized a brand of fire with a huge pair of iron tongs. Mehitable followed suit with a shovelful of glowing coals, while Thankful snatched up a birch broom that filled the water pail, into which she plunged it, so as to be ready for action. Thus equipped all three came at the poor constable at once, as if driven by "Old Nick" himself. Thus set upon by three furies, armed with both fire and water, with a most hellish meaning in their eyes as well as hands, poor Joshua was glad to make a retreat from the premises as speedily as possible. Nor did the discomfited sheriff ever dare to invade the old man's castle thereafter, preferring to pay the dram-seller the amount of the execution from his own pocket, rather than run the risk of receiving such a baptism, as he had just escaped from, in an attempt to enforce a second demand on an old sinner who was so efficiently guarded and protected by three affectionate daughters. When the party were approaching a point a little west of the summit of McSparran Hill, a delightful spot, marked by a huge boulder, where Mrs. Simons had passed so many happy hours and days in her girlhood, she requested her father to permit the bearers of the litter to leave the road, and take her a short distance across the fields to the highest point of the hill. Her wish was of course complied with, and the litter was set down on a ledge that forms the almost perpendicular rock-bound brow of the hill, a little to the eastward of the big boulder that is yet a landmark for vessels arriving on the coast.

Directly at the foot of the hill, and extending some two miles northward, lies Pettaquamscutt Lake, one of the most beautiful sheets of water imaginable, that is destined in the future to become the Killarney of New England. Among other points of interest connected with its white, graveled, wood-fringed shores, there still stands in good repair at the extreme head of the lake, a two-story house, built by Gilbert Stuart. In the north-east chamber of this house his son Gilbert was born, in April, 1756, whose fame as an artist will remain so long as the memory of the great original of his Washington is revered by the citizens of these United States.

The records of St. Paul's church, in Narragansett, contain the following entry (see Updike's History, p. 252): " April 11, 1756, being Palm Sunday, Dr. McSparran read prayers, preached, and baptised Gilbert Stuart, son of Gilbert Stuart * * * * Sureties the doctor, Mr. Benjamin Mumford and Mrs. Hannah Mumford."

For the following, see "The Early History of Narragansett," by Elisha R. Potter, Jr., member of Rhode Island Historical Society, 1835, page 309:

"Stuart.—Gilbert Stuart, the celebrated portrait painter, was a native of Narragansett. His father came from Scotland, and here married an Anthony. Gilbert was born near Narrow (Pettaquamscutt) river where his father lived. In 1775, he went to England, and became a pupil of Benjamin West. From London he went to Ireland by invitation from the Viceroy, the Duke of Rutland, but did not arrive there until after the Duke's decease. He spent several years in Ireland, and then returned to his native country, for the express purpose of painting General Washington. While abroad he married a lady of English family. His last years were spent in Boston. For a longer account, see Knapp's Lectures on American Literature, page 193, and Dunlap's History of the Art of Design. The latter is said by Stuart's friends 'not to be entirely correct.'"

The pond from which the small river flows that empties into the Pettaquamscutt Lake—a little below the old homestead of the Stuart's—called the Snuff Mill Pond, formerly abounded with numerous pike or rather pickerel, reaching in some instances more than twenty pounds in weight.

To the north and the west of the pond above named a large tract of woodland extends, while to the north and east lies the George Rome—pronounced *Roome*—estate of some seven hundred acres. I can remember when the mansion-house of George Rome was in tolerably good repair.

Updike, in his history of the Narragansett church, says: "The mansion-house of Mr. Rome was highly finished and furnished. The beds were concealed from view in the wainscots—the rooms might be traversed throughout and not a bed for the repose of his guests be seen. This was a matter of astonishment for the colonial observer. When the hour for retirement arrived, a servant would just give a touch to a spring in the ceiling and the visitor's bed, by means of a self-adjusting process, would protrude itself as if by the effects of magic, ready prepared for the reception of its tenant. His garden contained the rarest native and exotic varieties. He lived in splendor and entertained his friends with sumptuous hospitality."

"Mr. Rome," says Updike, "sometimes styled his residence 'my little country villa,' and again 'Bachelor's Hall.' 'My compliments,' writes Mr. Rome to a friend, 'to Col. Stewart. May I ask the favor of you both to come and eat a Christmas dinner with me at Bachelor's Hall, and celebrate the festivities of the season in Narragansett woods? A covy of partridges or bevy of quails will be entertainment for the colonel and me, while the pike and perch pond will amuse you.'

"He occasionally gave large parties, at which the ladies and gentlemen of Boston, Newport and Narragansett, would equally mingle. Punch was the fashionable beverage at that period, and the entertainments at Bachelor's Hall were extravagant."

It was at one of these entertainments that the most extraordinary answer to prayer, probably on record, occurred. It seems that Lawyer Bourne, of Providence, had indulged to such an extent in libations from the enticing punch bowl, that his senses became so stupefied, that his boon companions really feared life was extinct. It was conceded by the host and all present, that something must done, and there being no minister of the gospel at hand, in the emergency, Lawyer Joe Aplin, of Little Rest Hill—more than half-seas over himself—was appealed to by the company, as the next best qualified, to offer up a prayer for the restoration of his friend.

Though totally unused to the vocation thus suddenly cast upon him, Lawyer Joe commenced in the vein in which he was accustomed to address a Rhode Island judge of the Court of Common Pleas, "thinking to be heard for his much speaking" rather than from any mitigating circumstances he had to offer in behalf of his drunken client. After some half an hour's maudlin supplication by his friend, poor Bourne still showed no signs of returning life, and Aplin closed with an impassioned call on the "Lord Jesus, to have mercy on poor Bourne, even as he had mercy on the thieves on the cross, he being a much greater sinner than either of them!" Simultaneous with the last words uttered by Aplin, a loud snort issued from the nostrils of Bourne, followed by an uproarious burst of laughter, and he was well from that moment, and probably the most sober man in the company. The last appeal made in his behalf, Bourne said, was too irresistibly ludicrous even for a dead man to resist.

It was with Lawyer Joe Aplin that the phrase "bodily wit" originated in this wise. Aplin with two of his friends went one day fishing for trout in the Silver Spring brook, in North Kingstown. After a hard day's sport they went to Congdon's tavern in Wickford, to stay the night. On the landlord's asking "What luck?" Aplin replied, they had caught just three trout which would give them one each for their breakfast. On mine host asking further "How big?" Lawyer Joe told him that one of the fish was about as long as his finger whilst the other two were rather small! Aplin being rather tired went to bed. His companions taking advantage of this, had all three of the trout cooked for their supper.

Next morning not seeing the fish on the breakfast-table, Aplin asked the landlord to explain, and was told that they had been eaten for supper by his two fellow fishermen the night before. This brought the response from the disgusted lawyer before indicated, "D—n such bodily wit!"

Congdon's tavern was also associated with a pleasant anecdote in connection with the famous "John Randolph, of Roanoke." Edmund Randolph, Secretary of State under Washington, accompanied by his kinsman, John Randolph, of Roanoke, and John R. Smith, of Philadelphia, left the city of New York on horseback and hastened to Newport to see the French minister on official business. From the time the travelers left New York until they reached Wickford, they had been unable to get scarce a thing to eat but fried bacon and eggs. Wherever they stopped for the night and inquired what was to be had for supper, the reply of the host of the tavern was uniformly the same—"fried ham and eggs!"—greatly to the distaste of the wearied travelers and more especially to the disgust of John of Roanoke.

Wickford has ever been celebrated for both its soft and hard shelled clams, the latter being then called by the Indian name "quahog." On the arrival of the guests at Congdon's tavern, in answer to the usual question, the landlord replied "that he could give them clams for supper." At this announcement John of Roanoke was so pleased that he absolutely rubbed the palms of his hands together through gleeful emotion. This lasted, however, but a few moments, when "mine host" again opened the door to say to his guests "that he was sorry the tide was too high to allow of getting clams, but that he could give them some capital quahogs. "Good God!" exclaimed John of Roanoke, "more bacon!"

CHAPTER VIII.

Looking over and beyond the Rome estate and the village of Wickford still farther to the north, may be seen the picturesque country bordering on Narragansett Bay, called by the Indians Quidneset. Still farther in the same direction lies Potowomut Neck, whereon since my memory the blacksmith's shop stood in good repair in which Rhode Island's hero—greatest among the great all save one of his countrymen—forged, with sturdy arms, anchors to hold storm-tossed ships to their moorings, until at liberty's and his country's call he forged his sledge hammer into a sword, and went forth to constitute himself one of the two bower anchors that held with a vice-like grip the ship of state to her moorings amidst the storms that assailed the tempest-riven bark through the dark days of the Revolution.

A half-mile or less south of Snuff Mill Pond may yet be seen from the hill a gentle declivity on the eastern side of the lake, on which since my memory stood a homely cottage in which lived for many years Theophilus Whalley, the regicide, and whose location is mentioned in President Styles' history of the Judges of King Charles the First. I extract the following from "Potter's Early History of Narragansett," page 311:

"Whale or Whalley.—The following account is abridged from Styles' history of the Judges of King Charles I. Theophilus Whale lived on the Willett farm. He came there from Virginia about 1679-80, built an underground hut at the north end of the pond, and lived by fishing and by writing for the settlers. From his name he was supposed to be the judge, and when questioned answered obscurely. Colonel Francis Willett said that the gentlemen who visited them from Boston in his father's time treated Whale with great respect and furnished him with money. In Queen Anne's war, a ship of war whose captain's name was Whale anchored near there, and they visited and recognized each other as cousins. Whale always used to say that he was of collegiate education, had been brought up delicately, and had been a captain in the Indian wars in Virginia. He knew Hebrew, Greek, &c. He subsisted part of the time by weaving. Whale died about 1719-20, aged 104 years."

A few rods only south of the site of the regicide's former residence is the farm which was inherited by the Rev. James Carpenter from his father, Willett Carpenter, a descendant by the mother's side of the Willetts, and who formerly owned and occupied the estate. On this farm is quite a large piece of woodland, bordering on the eastern shore of the lake, that was planted by Francis Willett, grandson of Thomas Willett, an early mayor of the city of New York, who purchased a large tract of land in Boston Neck from the Indians, and willed it to his son Andrew, the father of Francis.

Tradition says that Francis Willett having but little woodland on the estate he inherited from his father, and thinking he had been defrauded by a neighbor of whom he was in the habit of purchasing that needful article, he in a fit of passion vowed that his heirs should not be obliged to submit to similar impositions, and, with a will and perseverance characteristic of the period, proceeded to plant a large open field with acorns and have the young trees cultivated with the hoe until they attained a size that rendered farther cultivation unnecessary.

Following the shore of the lake less than a mile from this point south, we come to the first bridge that was built in Narragansett, on which Deputy Sheriff Cranston, of North

Kingstown, was in the olden time compelled to dance under the following circumstances. The constable had in his possession an execution for some three or four dollars against one Elias Wilbour, and called at the Rowland Robinson farm—then owned and occupied by the late Peleg Gardiner—, where the old man was at work in the hay field, to collect it. The debtor, pleading inability to meet the demand, was told that he must then go to jail. To this arrangement Elias readily consented, merely stipulating that he should be allowed first to see his employer. The two proceeded to the house where Wilbour obtained from Mr. Gardiner five dollars due him for past work. The debtor, thereupon expressing his readiness to proceed to jail, was told by his custodian that it was now unnecessary to take him from his work, as he had in his possession more than enough money to discharge the execution. Elias, however, who was something of a wag in his way, could not be made to understand the officer's logic, and insisted that he could not part with any of his money, as he should want it all to pay his jail board! "But," said Cranston, "pay the execution with a part of the money only, and I won't take you to jail." The force of such reasoning, however, old Wilbour could not be made to appreciate, and they proceeded on their way towards the jail, the constable trying his utmost in the meantime to induce his prisoner to discharge the debt and return to his work, but without success. From the first, Cranston had no intention of taking Elias to jail, only meaning to frighten him into paying the debt, and when they arrived at the bridge, finding he could do nothing with the stupid or obstinate old man and his own way thereafter not lying in the direction of the jail, he told Elias he might go back to his work and let the debt remain unpaid. This proposition, however, was repeatedly declined by Wilbour, who reminded Cranston that he had told him "he would take him to jail, and to jail he meant to go, even if obliged to go alone"! After a good deal of colloquy on the subject

Wilbour finally consented to go back on the condition that he himself should be permitted to sing "Old Charmany [Chalmouny] Fair" whilst the deputy sheriff danced it out to his tune on the bridge. The latter's business being urgent, he finally dismounted, and throwing off his coat complied with Wilbour's demands to the letter, after which Cranston went on his way rejoicing that he had got rid of his ugly customer, who then went back to the hay field and resumed work.

Less than two miles to the south-easterly from this bridge stands the Governor George Brown house, which was occupied by Geoffrey Hazard, called "Stout Jeffrey," who if the half that is told be true, must have approached nearer in physical strength to the fabled Hercules than almost any other man known in modern times. I have heard old people say that Stout Jeffrey was remarkably broad across the shoulders, and so thick through the chest that when he stood with his face fronting you his head looked as if it were set unnaturally far back on his shoulders, and that when his back was towards you, it looked as though he stooped, his head seeming to project so far in the contrary direction.

Most marvelous stories used to be told and vouched for within my memory of the feats of strength performed by Stout Jeffrey, and also those of a sister who married a Wilcox. There may now be seen on the lawn in front of Rowland Hazard's house at Peacedale, in Narragansett, a blue stone weighing by the scales sixteen hundred and twenty pounds, that Mr. Hazard had drawn with oxen some years ago from Stout Jeffrey's homestead in Boston Neck, with which the following tradition is associated. Several negroes were engaged in laying a wall on the premises, when Stout Jeffrey, chancing to observe a large stone lying near by that they had neglected to build into the wall, asked why they had left it out. "Cos, massa, it be too heavy," was the reply. Thereupon Stout Jeffrey stooped down and taking the stone partly on his knees, carried it some twenty feet from the wall and dropping it on the ground said, "Let *that stone* lie there until a man is found strong enough to put it back again."

It was said that Stout Jeffrey and his sister would alternately lift in playful sport a full barrel of cider—thirty-one gallons—by the chimes and holding it up drink at its bung—a thing hard to believe in these degenerate days.

One mile or more farther south stands a large gambrel roof house that was built by George Hazard, the father of Thomas G. Hazard. Thomas G. Hazard was a successful and wealthy farmer, and is said to have been the first agriculturist in Rhode Island who used kelp, or sea-weed, as a fertilizer. He was the father of the late Dr. Enoch and Benjamin Hazard, of Newport, the last named of whom was justly styled "the Daniel Webster of Rhode Island." Mr. Hazard was the father of six sons, the two above named and George (the eldest son), Thomas, Easton, and John. John was purser of the frigate General Greene, and died at sea when a young man. All the sons were Hazards of the true "snip" breed, and did their own thinking, in morals, religion and politics. Dr. Enoch, who was surpassed in his day by no other physician in the State in the successful treatment of disease, was once solicited to unite with his medical brethren in putting down quacks! "Quacks!" he indignantly exclaimed, "all we have ever learned of medicine has been from quacks!"

Thomas G. Hazard married the daughter of Jonathan Easton, a lineal descendant of the first Nicholas Easton, one of the original proprietors of Aquidneck Island, who, with the first Thomas Hazard and Robert Jeffries, laid out the town of Newport.

Thomas G. Hazard's remains lie in the Nicholas Easton burial ground, a little south of the Bath road in Newport, on the farm now in possession of the heirs of the late Robert H. Ives. The spot is marked by a plain slab of stone, on which is the following highly appropriate inscription:

"In memory of

"THOMAS G. HAZARD;

"A lineal descendant of one of the first emigrants to New England and one of the original proprietors and settlers of Rhode Island. He inherited that strong cast of character, that firmness of purpose and resolute perseverance and unconquerable love of freedom, for which that race of men were so signally distinguished."

Immediately in front of the spot where the party rested, near the foot of the hill, some one hundred yards from the shore of the lake, there still stands the old parsonage house known as "the Glebe," with the lilac bushes blossoming in their season, which were planted by Dr. McSparran—a great uncle by marriage of the unfortunate Hannah—in about the year 1721, when he first assumed his ministerial duties as pastor of St. Paul's Episcopalian church. The former site of the church building might recently have been discerned near what is called "Pender Zeke Gardiner's corner," on the old post-road a little north-west of McSparran Hill.

Raising the eyes and looking east, Newport presents itself so distinctly to the view of the beholder that, though some ten miles distant, it appears to be less than five. With the help of a glass the hands of the clock on the State House may be so plainly seen, that it used to be the practice of old John Hazard—called Wickham John—, who lived near the summit of the hill, to regulate his time-pieces by it.

Passing the eye around the horizon northerly, almost the entire area of Narragansett Bay is brought within the scope of vision, from Providence to the ocean, with its most distant shores and lovely rock-bound islands, dotted with towns and villages, and hundreds of farm-houses and other buildings and objects of interest; the whole checkered and intersected with numerous arms of the sea and broad sheets and straits of shining water, upon which scores of vessels of all descriptions with their white sails glistening in the sun are to be seen winding to and fro.

The whole of Boston Neck, some ten miles in extent from north to south, and reaching from the high bluff called the "Bonnet," and Westqueag pond and beach of the same name and the western coast of Narragansett Bay on the east, to the Pettaquamscutt lake and river on the west, lies at the beholder's feet.

I used to hear it told that one of the early Gardiners of Boston Neck employed a Dutchman who, by means of big pumps operated by wind, drained Westqueag pond entirely dry, with the view of applying the land so obtained to agricultural purposes. Why the original design was not carried out, I have never heard.

There used to hang a large picture in the old Colonel John Gardiner house, since my remembrance, in which a wrecked ship that ran ashore in a storm on Westqueag beach was represented. The ship was from some port in Europe, and was freighted in part with live cattle, which were graphically pictured struggling toward the shore amid the lofty breakers.

Less than two miles south of the Westqueag beach the ship Wampoa, freighted with French brandy, silks and fancy goods, was run on shore during our last war with Great Britain, by the British brig-of-war Orpheus. In 1839, I came from Liverpool in the steamship Liverpool, Captain Frayer, R. N., Commander. He had been a lieutenant on board the Orpheus, and as soon as he learned that I came from Narragansett his heart seemed to warm to me as if he had found a long-lost friend. Throughout the voyage he insisted on my sitting at his right hand at the table, and bestowed upon me the most marked and even affectionate attention. The Orpheus had cruised in the Rhode Island and adjacent waters as a blockader during almost the entire war, and Captain Frayer seemed thoroughly acquainted with every inlet, rock and landmark on the Narragansett coast.

The captain told me that he commanded one of the boats that were sent from the Orpheus to fire upon the militia that lined the coast, and to destroy the Wampoa, and that he would very much like to see an old Quaker that was ploughing with a yoke of oxen near the shore, a little to the north of where the Wampoa lay stranded, who, so far as he could observe, never once deigned to look toward the armament from which the cannon and musket balls were raining in his direction, but kept on turning his furrows to and fro as regularly as though nothing unusual was occurring. I have since learned that the "old Quaker," as Captain Frayer erroneously supposed him to be, was the late John Perry, Gov. George Brown's head-farmer, the father of Robinson Perry, of Wakefield, and five other grown-up sons, all of whom are now living. This reckless man was cousin to Commodore Oliver Hazard Perry, who showed still greater coolness of temperament on an occasion where bullets and cannon balls were falling thick around him somewhere on Lake Erie, while he was passing in an open boat from his own burning ship to another, to lead her into the thickest of the fight, and to victory.

I remember that the commander of the Orpheus was very desirous of obtaining one of the far-famed "Narragansett pacers," to present to his wife in England, and that agents from Block Island scoured the Narragansett country to find a horse of that breed, but without success. Many years before most of the favorite pacers had been bought up and shipped to wealthy Cuban and Jamaica planters, who paid high prices to obtain the easiest going and most sure-footed saddle beasts in the country for their wives and daughters.

After this an agent from Virginia located himself on Tower Hill, with orders to buy every full-blooded mare he could find, without limit as to cost. Hence, the pure Narragansett pacers are now extinct, although I remember when the late James Robinson, grandson of Governor Robinson, used to own one of the mixed breed, that on an urgent occasion he rode from New London to the South Ferry, a distance of forty miles, without stopping for refreshments or rest.

To return from this digression: From this point on McSparran Hill the Pettaquamscutt river may be seen nearly its whole length, winding like a belt of burnished silver for several miles in a southerly and easterly direction until its waters are lost in the sea beside a huge pile of granite called the Cormorant Rocks, that lies opposite the north end of the magnificent beach that extends in a southerly and westerly direction more than a mile to the old Narragansett Pier, from which the new pier lies about half a mile south.

This pier was first constructed by John Robinson, a son of Gov. William Robinson, not far from the middle of the 18th century. He then owned most of the land where the far-famed summer resort is now located. I have heard my father say that when the pier was in process of building a son of John Robinson came very near being devoured by one of the monstrous sharks called "man-eaters," that frequently in those days followed in the track of slave-ships plying their horrid traffic largely from Newport and Bristol, in Rhode Island, to the Guinea coast, and preyed upon the dead and dying negroes that were thrown into the sea from their decks. It was said that these sharks, after thus gorging themselves during their way across the ocean, became ravenously fond of human flesh, to the exclusion of all other species of food. The boy was swimming outside the breakers, where his father observed the fins of a shark moving from seaward toward his son. Mr. Robinson with great presence of mind called kindly to him to see in how short a time he could swim to the shore! The little fellow at the bidding did his best, but had scarcely been caught up in his father's arms while still in the water before an enormous "man-eater," ravenous and eager in the pursuit, turned on his back and desperately darting toward his coveted prey, grounded on the sand not many feet from shore, and was dispatched by carpenters who were working on the pier, with their broad-axes.

This pier, now called the "North Pier," passed from the Robinsons into the hands of Rowland ~~Robinson~~ sometime previous to 1812. It used occasionally to be washed away by the violence of the waves. Once after being thus destroyed it was rebuilt by Mr. Hazard with cabbage palm posts brought from Charleston, South Carolina. These posts were deemed to be worm proof. Some years after this Mr. Hazard exchanged the pier with Captain Robinson Potter, of Newport, for a part of the ship Frederic Augustus. Joseph Congdon, of Point Judith, for many years a resident of Shelter Island, afterwards bought the ~~vessel~~, and resold it to George C. Brown, son of Peleg. Mr. Brown in turn deeded it to the Narragansett Pier Company. This company built the heavy stone wharf of which only a part is now standing, the violence of the sea having reduced it to a ruin.

As late as 1823 only one little sloop, of about sixteen tons burthen, was employed at the Pier, and this vessel ran almost exclusively to Newport. When it was contemplated to send her to Providence, placards were posted giving notice two or three weeks before the sloop sailed for that city.

The construction of the South Pier was commenced in 1845 by Joshua Champlin, who built it mostly with his own hands, supporting himself in the meantime by fishing with hook and line. There is now more business done at the South Pier in one week than there ever was at the North Pier, previous to its transfer to the Pier company, in many months.

CHAPTER IX.

To return: In its course the river, some two miles or less below the old bridge, passes the Pettaquamscutt rock, situated a furlong or more from its west bank, and from which the river, according to tradition, received its name, as did also the Narragansett country from an island in Point Judith Pond, called by the Indians, Nahigansett. (See Potter's History, page 4.) Before the bridge was built east of Tower Hill village, there was a ford in the Pettaquamscutt river opposite the mountain rock, over which I have passed on horseback. Between this ford and the sea the Indians called the river Monkotage, and all above the ford Mettatuxet.

I have heard old people say that in the great storm in the winter of 1780, a snow-drift commencing on a level with the east side of this rock—which must be from sixty to one hundred feet in perpendicular height—, extended on a regularly inclined plain beyond the eastern bank of the frozen river into Boston Neck. This seems almost incredible, although since my remembrance there have been several snow-storms in which, I think, snow-drifts have been formed twenty feet or more deep.

Early in the winter of 1811-12, I left West Town school in Westchester county, Pennsylvania, and came with my father to Narragansett. A short time before I left school, in answer to a question in geography, I said that snow sometimes drifted so deep on the coast of New England as to cover up sheep to the depth of several feet. For this assertion the teacher reproved me, and told me not repeat so improbable a story again, if I expected to be believed.

Our arrival in Newport was shortly after the great Christmas snow-storm of 1811, when I learned that not only had hundreds of sheep perished in the vicinity by being drifted up and freezing in the storm, but many cattle and several human beings also. Among the latter was Joseph Cundall, of Portsmouth, who became so exhausted and bewildered while but a few rods from his house in what is now called "The Glen," that he gave up striving, and sat down in a deep gorge a short distance south of the mill, where his corpse was subsequently found under a snow-bank.

Close by the town of Newport, a farmer—I think the late William Bateman—went out with his men to arrest, if possible, the progress of a hundred fat wether sheep that were drifting before the blinding tempest toward the sea-shore. But all their efforts were in vain. To shield themselves from the beating of the storm of sleet and snow, the sheep in the rear would circle round and round to get in the lee of those in front of them, until all were finally edged into the sea and lost, with the exception of a few whose throats were cut by one of the men, with his jack-knife.

I may just here remark, in parenthesis, that in those early days there were but few cattle barns, while sheep-sheds were unknown in Rhode Island. Their introduction would doubtless have been considered an innovation to be punished with ridicule by a vast majority of farmers, on the same principle that the clergy of different sects, when taking their turn in power, used to torture and burn innovators upon the practices and beliefs of their respective time-honored creeds; or as the doctors of medicine now fine and imprison, in several States of this free Union—"God save the mark!"—,any outside innovators on the mediæval modes of their death-dealing craft.

As we walked along the road on our way to Narragansett between the two ferries on Jamestown, we passed by the carcases of two dead cows, both of which were under the north wall, with nothing but their horns and heads to be seen, the snow having been removed so far while their bodies were covered some feet deep in the drift.

We also heard of an instance that occurred near the Ferry road, either in that or a previous snow-storm, wherein a colored man had noticed for some days that the cattle he was in the habit of foddering never touched a lock of hay that he had thrown on a little sharp rising in the snow. This he was at a loss to account for until one morning, in passing, he struck off the top of the crust with his hay-fork, when there was revealed to sight an old Indian woman sitting bolt upright on a stone heap, with her chin resting on both hands, and her elbows on her knees, looking, as he said, "for all the world as natral as life, only the poor old squaw was frozen stiff as an icicle."

I think if my West Town teacher had been present he might have made with perfect propriety an entry in his journal similar to one I have heard of, wherein an old Newport Quaker, who had never been off the Island, took a trip in the stage as far as Bristol Ferry, on the north end, and on his return made the following memorandum in his diary:

"The seventh day of the fifth month. I have this day taken the longest journey I ever made in my life, having traveled so far as Bristol Ferry, a distance of nearly twelve miles. The journey was fatiguing, and, as it seemed to me, not without peril to life and limb, which, however, I think I may say, I am not without compensation for, inasmuch as I was mercifully preserved from all danger, and have learned through many experiences that traveling expands the mind."

I remember seeing the frigate President—the largest ship then of the United States navy—of forty-four guns, Captain Rogers, lying in Newport harbor, which Mr. Samuel Moses informs me drew her anchor quite a distance whilst in the inner harbor during the storm. Mr. Moses says that the sloops-of-war Essex, Argus, and Nautilus also wintered in Newport harbor that year.

When we arrived at Narragansett I heard of many other disasters similar to those I have mentioned. The late Nicholas Hassard, father of the late Edward Hassard, who recently kept the extensive livery stable at the corner of Spring and Touro streets in Newport, then leased the great Champlin farm of Christopher G. Champlin, who was a lineal descendant of the first proprietor. The farm borders upon a lake of salt water in Charlestown, in which all of Mr. Hassard's sheep were driven through the violence of the storm and perished.

I do hate to pile digression upon digression, but I must be allowed to insert here, in parenthesis, one more anecdote. Whilst representing Rhode Island in Congress, Mr. Christopher Champlin got involved in a duel with a hot-tempered southern member, and received a pistol shot in his face, the mark of which he carried to the grave. When his term of service expired, and he was again put forward for re-election, an opponent of Champlin learning that old James Gould, father of the late Isaac, and grandfather of the present David Gould, was an advocate of Champlin's re-election, asked the old man how one of his cloth could support a candidate for office who had been shot in the face in a duel. "I would not vote for friend Champlin," replied the plain old Quaker, "if he had been hit in the back."

James Gould first commenced his tailoring establishment in the year 1763 on the same site where his grandson, David Gould, still continues to carry on the business. It is probably the oldest establishment of the kind in the United States, and has from the beginning always been one of the very best conducted and most reliable in all respects, whether in Newport or elsewhere. The following three charges follow consecutively on James Gould's day-book, now in possession of Mr. David J. Gould:

"July 22, 1775.
   General Nathaniel Greene,

Blue regimental coat and white broad-cloth jacket, £29 0 0
2 white jean jackets and white jean breeches,   29 0 0
54 buttons, one yard osnabergs, 32s. for wrapper, 4 6 0

£62 6 0

This was probably the first full military suit ever worn by the Revolutionary hero, costing, reckoning the pound at twenty shillings colonial currency, nearly two hundred dollars. Then follows:

"Gilbert Stuart,
"White breeches.
"Abram Redwood,
"2 jackets and pair jean breeches and pair black knee breeches."

At the time of the great storm before alluded to, my father had a small flock of sheep which was placed under the care of old Benny Nichols, so often referred to in these papers. Among these sheep were two ewes of the creeper or otter sheep, so called, it is supposed, from the peculiar shortness of their legs. One of these sheep lay drifted under a snow-bank twenty-one days. The place where it lay was discovered by old Benny, from chancing to notice a small hole in the snow not bigger than his finger, called "a breathing hole," that was made, as is usually the case, by the warm breath of the sheep underneath. When taken out the poor thing was almost naked, having eaten off its own wool as far as it was within reach. Old Debby Nichols—Benjamin's wife—fed the sheep, at first very cautiously with a little warm milk, gradually increasing the quantity until it got strong enough to digest its ordinary food. When restored to health, the old woman dressed the naked sheep in a suit of clothes made out of old ragged garments of her husband's. It was several days, however, before the flock would permit its approach in so unsightly a garb. My father gave me these two creeper sheep, and their two years' fleeces, together with one fleece from their progeny, constituted the sole capital with which I engaged in the woolen manufacturing business, in 1814, when I was in my seventeenth year.

I have since learned that the first creeper sheep originated on an island in Maine or Massachusetts, on occasion of the mother being frightened, when conceiving, by an otter. If this is so, I think the sudden shock may have imparted to the incipient embryo not only some of the external characteristics of the otter, but some of its instincts also; for I remember, that when these two otter sheep—then old—were put on the other side of a wide mill pond, in the year 1819, away from the usual haunts, they both took to the water and swam back again. A peculiarity of these creeper sheep is that their progeny are always born either with limbs of the ordinary length, like other sheep, or with the short otter legs, but never of a medium length.

From the year 1812 until about the year 1865, I was never without more or less of this breed. At one time, having a very fine creeper buck, I made the attempt to propagate a distinct breed. I, however, was soon forced to abandon the project, as I found there would nevertheless still be about an equal number of long-legged and short-legged lambs, and that while many of the latter would be as perfect and beautiful as pictures, many others would be born objects of deformity, with crooked, ungainly legs, some so short that the wool on the belly of the unsightly thing would actually drag on the ground, as it went waddling along, more like an old farm duck in its motions than a four-legged animal. Strangely enough I have not owned an otter sheep for several years past, nor until just after I finished the last paragraph, when my attention happened to be called to a lovely, little, long-tailed, black-faced ewe lamb of the genuine breed, that had recently been brought from Quidneset, in North Kingstown—the first I had seen for some years. I purchased it and now have it at Vaucluse.

The winter of 1818-19 was so mild that farmers ploughed in every month. That of 1819-20 was correspondingly severe. There were in this winter three separate snow-storms in one week. During the last there was the deepest fall of snow ever remembered by the oldest inhabitant in South Kingstown. At that time I was living with my father in a house situated on the old "Jeremy Niles estate"—called Delacarlia—within the south-eastern limits of Peacedale on the old colonial highway opposite the Point Judith road. My father purchased this property before the year 1819, of Jeremiah Niles Potter, who was a family connection or descendant of the Niles family. I think I can remember seeing old Jeremiah Niles riding out with a scarlet coat, cocked hat, and sword by his side, attended by a servant on a horse in the rear. Of this fact I am not, however, entirely certain, though I feel sure as the school-boy said that " I almost remember it." and think there is little doubt that the old gentleman was the last who adhered strictly to the olden time custom of the Narragansett gentry in these respects.

Some two or three furlongs to the west of the old Jeremy Niles house—which is yet standing in a dilapidated condition—there stood within a few years on a pleasant rising ground a little to the east of the Saucatucket river where it is lost in the Wakefield mill pond, the homestead house of Thomas B. Hazard, called "Nailor Tom."

Nailor Tom's blacksmith shop stood on a little abrupt knoll on the west side of where the road between Peacedale and Wakefield now runs, nearly opposite the remains of an old mill-dam, the first that was built in Narragansett. The house was said to have been one of the first six houses —before referred to—that were built between Franklin Ferry and the Pawcatucket river. It was here, if tradition is to be relied upon, where the crews of pirate vessels used to resort in olden times when the coast was sparsely peopled, and hold high carnival. I remember to have seen a rusty portion of the scabbard of a sword, and I think some other relics of the kind, that were ploughed up in the adjacent ground. Of course Captain Kidd buried a treasure box in the neighborhood, and with it one of his crew to keep guard over the gold, as was always the custom of that terrible freebooter. Of this there is little doubt, as I saw when a boy a big hole that was dug one night in the Wilson woods by some one who was said to be in search of money. I have also seen another pit of the same kind at Adams' Hollow, a little north of the borough of Bristol in Pennsylvania, and have heard of other excavations being made for like purposes in various localities along the sea-coast of the Eastern and Middle States.

Thomas B. Hazard was a most remarkable man. His fund of anecdote and old time historical and biographical knowledge seemed inexhaustible. During the most of a long life he kept a daily record of passing local events, which was so often brought into court as evidence that the "Blue Book," as it was popularly called, was at length "ruled out of court," on the alleged ground that its endless memoranda of dates and corresponding events, when sworn to by Nailor Tom, tended to unsettle not only the titles of real estate, but, through litigation, the peace of the community. I learn that the Blue Book is now in the Redwood Library. I think it might more properly be deposited with the Rhode Island Historical Society. Thomas B. Hazard died in 1845, aged ninety years.

CHAPTER X.

I can remember when there were but seven houses on both sides of the Saucatucket river and Rocky brook, within the limits of the three villages now containing many hundreds.

The first was the old Robert Rodman house on Rocky brook, which is still standing.

The second was the old Benjamin (Benny) Rodman house, at Peacedale, which stood on the site of J. Newbold Hazard's present fine résidence. I knew old Benny Rodman for many years well. He was as harmless a man as ever walked on God's footstool, although like the Newport Quaker before alluded to, he had seen but little of the world. In conversing with the old man one day, I chanced to refer to "the head of the Pettaquamscutt cove," a rather noted locality about a mile and a half from the house where he was born and had then lived nearly ninety years, and remarked that he was of course well acquainted with the locality. "No," replied uncle Benny, "I have not traveled much, and have never been there." There now stands on the west end of the Peacedale mill-dam a large buttonwood tree, called to this day "Old Benny Rodman's horse-whip," which is said to have grown from a twig the old man stuck into the ground when a small boy, after having used it for the purpose indicated. He died aged ninety and over. Just before passing away, in answer to a friend's inquiry as to how he felt with death in near prospect, the old man replied, "as the saying is, I feel 'as easy as an old shoe.' "

The third was the Thomas B. Hazard house, before referred to, that stood on the site of the house built and occupied by the late Thomas Armstrong.

The fourth was the old Enoch Lewis house—now demolished—that stood directly on the bank of a deep gully or gulch near the Wakefield mill pond, in the elbow of the road, now called Columbia corner.

It was on the morning of a second day of the week that Friends passed this point on their way to Tower Hill monthly meeting under a clear sun, and when they returned less than three hours later, several thousand cartloads of earth had been removed by a heavy fall of rain that took place in a thunder shower and washed out the gully.

Speaking of Enoch Lewis, Updike in his "History of the Narragansett Church," says: "Mr. J. P. Hazard, in a communication, states that 'within ten years one of my aged neighbors (Enoch Lewis), since deceased, informed me that he had been to Virginia as one of the riding boys, to return a similar visit of the Virginians to this section, in a contest on the turf; and that such visits were common with the racing sportsmen of Narragansett and Virginia, when he was a boy. Like the old English country-gentlemen from whom they were descended, they were a horse-racing, fox-hunting, feasting generation.'"

The fifth was the Rodman Carpenter house, built by Daniel Coon, a former owner of the "old mill" as the grist-mill at Wakefield used to be called. This house has been recently taken down by Robert Rodman, a descendant of the old Narragansett Rodman family, and present owner of the Wakefield mills, who is, from all I hear, probably a man of as sterling qualities as any other in the State of Rhode Island. Both in Mr. Rodman's person and that of a family connection of his, the late Augustus Hazard of Enfield, Connecticut, the old adage, "Blood will tell," has been amply verified.

Thomas S. Hazard, the father of Augustus and Clark Rodman, the father of Robert, were lineal descendants of ancient and highly respected families, although they both became so reduced in circumstances that they were obliged to support their families by daily toil. The two families lived at one time in adjoining tenements belonging to me, for which they paid twenty dollars each per annum. The late Augustus Hazard, the son of Thomas S., finally earned, through his own industry, superior business qualifications and upright dealing, the Enfield powder works, which supplied a very large portion of the ammunition that was used in our late fratricidal war. He left an immense estate to his heirs. A daughter of Augustus married Governor Bullock, of Massachusetts.

Robert Rodman worked, when a boy, in a woolen manufactory. From this condition he rose to become the owner of several cotton and woolen mills. When the like pecuniary misfortunes assailed him that often sweep away the earnings of thousands, he compromised with his creditors, and commenced business anew. Fortune smiled on his honest and intelligent efforts, and in a few years he earned enough to pay every creditor in full to the last cent, principal and interest, and now stands in the community as a continual rebuke and rock of offense to the thousands of unpunished villains who live in luxury on the plunder of corporations —not sparing even the mite of the widow nor penny of the orphan that had been entrusted to their deceitful keeping in savings banks and otherwise—,and in the sight of God,"that noblest of his works, AN HONEST MAN!"

The sixth was the old Cuddymonk house, before referred to, that stood on the west side of Wakefield mill pond near the dam, on the site occupied by a house built some half century since by Jonathan N. Hazard for his mother and sisters.

The seventh and last was the old Thomas Gould house, yet standing on the west side of the road that runs north from Wakefield on the west side of the pond, about a half mile from that village.

I feel that I owe repeated apologies to my readers for these everlasting departures and ramifications, but the fact is, that to me the Narragansett country is so affluent in associations that I cannot commence on one subject without its suggesting or leading me off into scores of incidents that offer themselves as readily to my mind as Sancho Panza's never ending proverbs, piled one upon another, did to his, to the great annoyance and disgust of his master Don Quixote.

To return to the great snow-storm of 1820. I had at that time one flock of sheep in a field about thirty rods from my father's house, and another flock of about two hundred on a meadow of eighty acres in extent on a farm now owned by my brother Joseph, lying a little to the south of Narragansett Pier, on which "Hazard Castle" stands.

The tempest was fearful throughout the night, and the next morning, so soon as the day dawned, if indeed it might be said to dawn at all, I got up, and after telling a sturdy Irishman by the name of Daniel Harris to see to my sheep near home, I, without eating a mouthful, left our front door on my hands and knees and proceeded on my way to the Point Judith farm, a distance of more than three miles. Occasionally I came to bleak spots where the snow was blown away so that I could walk short distances, and occasionally to deep hollows where the snow lay from ten to thirty or more feet in depth, on which I was obliged to lie down at full length and make my way, hand over hand, in a swimming position. I could not look an instant to the windward because of the blinding snow, but kept my course solely by what I discerned dimly to the leeward. When I got to the conical hill in the Mumford land, that lies to the south of where the Tower Hill House now stands, I found there a goose with its neck all bloody, it having no doubt been abandoned by a fox, after in vain endeavoring to lug it through the storm and over the drifts of snow. This goose I took in charge and dragged it with me to Nat. Mumford's, where I left it with him at his back door, none of the family having been out of doors as yet.

After some hours' unabated effort, I arrived at the "Great Meadow," where I found that some two-thirds of my sheep lay under a snow-bank that made out from a hay-stack yard, in the lee of which they sought shelter. I next went some eighty rods to a house, one end of which was occupied by Tom Aaron, a full-blood Indian, and his family, and the other by a half-blood named George Ammon, in order to borrow some tools with which to dig out my sheep. All the implement I could obtain was a common field hoe, the blade of which was broken short off in the middle.

I will stop just here to say that I borrowed this half hoe of George, who occupied the east end of the house. The room I entered had a big snow-bank under the window, most of the panes of which were broken and their places supplied with bundles of rags, through one of which the wind and snow were blowing without hindrance. Upon my asking George's wife why she didn't stop up the broken pane, she told me the rags with which it had been stuffed had blown out and then lay on the floor underneath the snow-bank, and moreover, she was "afeared to stop up the whole of the lights, lest the window should all blow in, in a heap!" The entire furniture of the room consisted of the broken hoe, two old milking-stools, a water-pail with a tow-string for a bail with a squash-shell-dipper frozen within it, a broken-handled skillet, and a stub broom. Nor was there a stick of wood or brush to be seen in or about the house. Three shivering, half-naked little children sat huddled together, partly covered by a torn, threadbare, scanty blanket, with their feet thrust into the cold ashes, "playing," as the drunken father, with a comical, maudlin grimace, observed between his hiccups, "make b'lieve warm themselves!" The children were trying to munch some small potatoes that had been twice frozen, once before they were boiled, on the previous day, and again after the brush fire had burned out and left them to freeze in the skillet where it stood. On my remarking to the mother that I should think the poor things would cry with the cold and hunger they were enduring, she said " she guessed the little varmints mout if they had ever larnt how !"

Again, I want the reader to bear with me while I relate an anecdote about George Ammon and Tom Aaron. Tom claimed that he was entitled to a bounty, on the alleged ground that he served his country during the Revolutionary war. Taking George with him, the two procceded to Providence, where Tom laid his claim before a commissioner for pensions. The commissioner asked Tom for proof of his having served in the war. Tom referred him to his friend George, who was about half Tom's age. George was accordingly qualified, and swore point-blank that he knew Tom "sarved in the war, sartin." The commissioner queried with George to know how so young an Indian as he appeared to be could know anything of the facts. " Why," said George, " I know Tom sarved at Red Bank fight, for he told me so hisself, and I never knowed him to lie more'n a dozen times in all my life." The parties were dismissed unsatisfied.

With the broken hoe I succeeded in rescuing all my sheep alive except four, which were found dead some weeks later, after the melting of the snow. I fed the flock with hay, and then worked my way on my hands and knees most of the way, to Solomon Carpenter's, some fifty rods south, and engaged his son Hazard to feed my sheep until the snow froze or a path was beaten so that I could attend to them myself.

A tenant of my father, named Benjamin Northup, had at this time keeping on hay he had mown at the "Great Point Judith Meadow," some thirty or more head of cattle. These had all sought refuge in the swamp lying on the west end of the farm, where I followed them, every inch of the way on my hands and knees, as the snow lay level among the bushes three or more feet deep, and succeeded in making them wallow through it half a mile or more, measured on an air line, to a stack of hay near the sea, belonging to the owner of the cattle, where I foddered them.

By this time the storm had somewhat moderated in violence, but not until a large group of my sheep had been drifted up a second time. I again rescued these and then took my departure by the sea-coast line, wading in the water at times knee-deep, as the tremendous seas advanced. The snow had been piled up in a line on the beach by the ebbing and returning waves, in some places three or four feet in height, in a perpendicular sea-wall, over which I found it at times difficult to climb in time to escape from the breakers that ever and anon threatened to overtake me. As I passed the Indian and Flat rocks the scene was too grand to be conceived of in its absence, much less described. Thunder could scarcely have been heard amid the roar of the wind and waves. In their mighty sweep the latter would draw back, leaving the ocean bed almost bare a long distance from the shore, and then return with a force that would seem to shake the foundation of those "everlasting rocks," merging them entirely in their foaming crests and casting their spray in showers many rods upward on the sward. I have seen Niagara more than once, but in grandeur and sublimity of power that stupendous fall of water bears no comparison to the upheaval of the ocean's waves and war of the elements I then beheld.

I kept the coast line until I came opposite the house of the late James Robinson, which is now built intact into the Sprague Castle as a component part—the two gable ends of the old mansion only are to be seen—where I supped and stayed the night. It was about dark when I arrived. From daylight I had not taken a morsel of food or drink, nor had I for one minute relaxed my efforts, having been in a perspiration every moment of the time. The easiest part of my journeying was when I was walking on the edge of the breakers, a large part of the way on slippery stones, and at times half knee-deep in water. I must have gone over not less than ten miles of ground, or rather snow during the day, three-quarters of that distance at least on my hands and knees.

The snow froze that night so as to bear, and I reached home with comparative ease the next morning. As I walked along on the frozen crust I was for a long while unable to account for an unusual sound that was constantly assailing my ear, resembling the wheezing of a broken-winded horse. I stopped repeatedly, but could see nothing but the pure white snow in every direction. I became really alarmed, and was about to conclude that the unwonted sounds proceeded from some supernatural source, when I luckily discovered that they came from my own lungs, having absolutely "broken my wind" through the violent and prolonged effort I had been subjected to on the day previous. From this malady I did not recover for many years, if, indeed, I have fully surmounted it yet, of which fact I have some doubt, as at times I fancy I can detect signs in my constitution of the no distant approach of premature old age.

On enquiring of our stout hired man, when I got home, how the sheep near the house had fared, I found that he could not tell me, as he had not been able, as he said, to get to them. Nor could I hear of a single person in the town who had left the house on that terrible day, beside myself; nor did a vehicle of any kind, or horse, pass the post-road for several weeks after this last of the three snow-storms that all occurred in the same week in the winter of 1819-20.

On examining my pockets I found that I had lost everything they contained when I started in the morning, consisting of a pen-knife, silver-case pencil, pocket comb, two English guineas, some silver change and other trifles. All had been deposited probably in drifts of snow, varying from five to twenty feet in depth.

Some few years after this I foddered with my own hands, on several separate lots, on what is still called the "Hundred Acres," a little south of the village of Tower Hill, about eight hundred sheep and some sixty head of young cattle. Samuel Clark, a neighbor, who then lived on my grandfather's homestead estate, came along just as I had finished feeding the sheep with hay, and we both agreed that a more lovely winter evening was never seen by either of us. The sun was shining mellow and bright when it went down, and the air was imbued with such a gulf-stream-like softness that one might seemingly bathe in it. As I proceeded homeward—some two miles, in a south-western direction—I observed ahead of me a smooth bank rising in the horizon. Before morning a snow-storm commenced which, though not so deep, exceeded in severity in some respects, the one just referred to.

As in the former instance I left the house at break of day and made my way by beating to and fro against the storm and sleet, as a vessel makes its way against a head wind until I reached the Hundred Acres. When I got there I found myself utterly powerless to do anything whatever for the relief of my cattle and sheep amidst the blinding tempest that fairly outroared the ocean waves and darkened the heavens above. My cattle had all sought refuge in the recesses of a thick swamp, whilst my sheep, that I had left on the lovely summer-like evening before feeding contentedly in the golden sunshine, had been driven and scattered in all directions to the leeward before the icy gale and drifted under the hard packed snow on the lee sides of the stone walls by fifties and hundreds. As before, I stayed on the ground until night, without a mouthful to eat or drink, and became so utterly exhausted that I found myself, by repeated experiments, unable to relax my muscles a single moment by resting on the handle of a hoe I carried in my hand, without simultaneously nodding. Being aware of the danger of my situation, I combated with all my might an almost irresistible inclination to give way to sleep, until I reached home, by which means my life was probably preserved.

Unlike the storm of 1820, the snow in this instance, instead of lying loosely on the drifted sheep, packed itself so closely and hard that a large part of those under the banks were smothered to death. For many days after the storm subsided I employed men to search with rake-stales the drifts for hundreds of rods in extent to feel for any sheep that might be beneath, by which means some hundreds were found, not less than one hundred and fifty of which had been smothered to death.

CHAPTER XI.

I have known several other snow-storms in my life similar to those I have described, in which, through their severity, many sheep and cattle perished in the southern part of Rhode Island, where the snow drifts much worse than in the interior. Several such snow-storms occurred in the winter of 1740. "The following," says Updike, "is from the Rhode Island Republican, dated the 26th of February, 1840, communicated by Henry Bull, Esq. It is stated in a paragraph recently published in several papers, that during the cold winter of 1740 a man drove a horse and sleigh on the ice from Hurlgate, near New York, to Cape Cod. That this feat was actually performed is rendered highly probable by the following memorandum, made by Gov. William Greene, of Warwick, and found among his papers by one of his descendants, Richard W. Ward, Esquire, of the city of New York:—
'Memorandum of the winter of 1740, O. S.—This winter, by all accounts, was the coldest known in New England since the memory of man. It began in the early part of November with extreme cold, and so continued with considerable snow until the first week in December. The weather was then fine and warm for three or four days (the General Assembly sitting at Newport). Soon after this the weather was again so exceedingly cold that the Narragansett Bay was soon frozen over, and people passed and repassed from Providence to Newport on the ice, and from Newport to Bristol. Occasionally, however, the ferry-boat passed to Fox Hill. The storms of snow fell one upon another until it was almost knee-deep,

and it lay until the 11th or 12th of January, when a sudden thaw laid the earth bare for a few days. This was again succeeded by violent cold weather, and in a very few days by snow-storms, till the 28th, 29th and 30th of January, when the snow fell full three feet deep, in addition to what lay on the ground before. * * * The snow in the woods, where it had fallen on a level, was supposed to be three feet deep on the 10th of March. During the great snow there was a great loss of both cattle and sheep; some were smothered, and a great number of sheep were driven into the sea by the wind. * * * In the midst of the winter it was frozen from the main to Rhode Island, and from thence southward out to sea it was reported by the inhabitants that they could see nothing but ice.' "

Again, says Updike: "Dr. McSparran, in a letter to Henry Cary, in Ireland, 1752, says: ' As from my house I can see the Atlantic Ocean, I have seen it froze as far as the human eye could reach'—undoubtedly referring to the same winter."

Again, says Updike, p. 201, "Watson, in his ' Historic Tales of Olden Times in Pennsylvania,' speaks of it thus: ' The winter of 1740–1, a great snow. The winter was very severe during the continuance of the great snow. It was in general more than three feet deep. The back settlers (says the Gazette) subsisted chiefly on the carcases of the deer found lying around them. Great part of the gang of the horses and cows in the woods also died. * * * Many deer came to the plantations and fed on hay with the other creatures. Squirrels and birds were found frozen to death.' Kalm says that it began to snow on the 10th of December, and that it lay on the ground until the 13th of March, O. S., and that some of the stags came to the barns to eat with the cattle, and became domesticated thereby."

So terribly severe was the winter of 1780, when the great snow drift at Pettaquamscutt rock was formed, that the ice, it was said, made out into the ocean nearly to the edge of the Gulf Stream, some fifty or sixty miles from land, and wood was sledded across both the ferries from Narragansett to Newport with ox teams, a distance on the ice of some six miles. Wood rose to thirty dollars a cord in Newport, and many poor families were driven to the extremity of burning the inside partitions and doors of their houses to keep from freezing.

The British had but the fall before abandoned their possession of the island, and during their long occupancy of Newport, to supply their troops with fuel, every orchard and tree on the southern half of the island, including thousands of fine black cherry trees, that before the coming of the enemy lined the sides of the roads for miles in all directions, were destroyed by them, with two exceptions only. A pear tree, yet partially alive, and standing opposite the house now owned and occupied by Wm. G. Peckham—son of Daniel, deceased—and situated on the Bliss road, about one mile north of the State House, was spared for some cause, after having been partially scarred with the axe. The only other tree left standing was the old historic buttonwood tree that now lies in ruins on the spot where it fell more than twenty years ago, on the Samuel Elam, or Vaucluse, estate.

This place was named Vaucluse by the old English Quaker gentleman from his fancying that a bitter disappointment he experienced in a love affair with Miss Redwood, the then reigning beauty and belle of Newport, bore some resemblance to the torments Petrarch endured through his unfortunate passion for Laura. Hence the name, as Petrarch resided at Vaucluse, in the south-eastern part of France, not many miles from Avignon. Here in Laura's ever pining lover's former study, I once dined on trout that were caught in the sparkling brook that flows from a subterranean lake navigable for boats lighted with flambeaux—beneath a huge perpendicular mountain rock of granite eight hundred feet in height, and holds its murmuring course directly by the poet's door. Even this old, time-honored tree at Vaucluse, it would appear from a scar on one side, the semi-barbarous Hessians quartered in the neighborhood attempted to fell, but abandoned their design, probably in despair because of its immense size.

Quite a number of these Hessian soldiers lie buried on the Allen estate near by, and among them the commanding officer of a regiment, who met his death very strangely. An official dinner was given at the old Jew house, so called, that stood until within a few years on the site of the house now owned and occupied by Mr. Borden Lawton, on the east side of the Wapping road, and among the guests was the Hessian officer. Amidst the revelry of the hour, some time after the event occurred, he was discovered stone-dead, sitting, in true military attitude, bolt upright in his chair, with his unconscious servant standing behind him, having been choked with a mouthful of steak that had been taken from the tough round of an old Rhode Island cow.

The old buttonwood tree, above named, the trunk of which used to be covered with hundreds of the initials of strangers and others, who visited it from motives of curiosity, was said to be the largest tree on this side of the Alleghany mountains. It measured about forty-two feet in circumference where it entered the ground, and more than twenty-two feet in the smallest part of the trunk, before it came to where it spread out, some ten feet from the roots, into two forks of nearly equal size. One of these forks I measured as it lay dead, entirely bereft of bark, and found it to be exactly thirty-six inches in diameter, fifty feet from where the tree entered the ground. The "big buttonwood" sickened and died with the "buttonwood blight" that commenced in 1842, simultaneously with the "potato blight." This tree has been several times described in the public prints. It seems that its memory has been thought worth preserving as a Revolutionary or historic relic, as, a few years ago, by a written request of the faculty of the Smithsonian Institue, I forwarded, through their friend in Providence, a small block riven from the heart of a huge limb, to be inserted with other relics into a mosaic-made table that it was proposed to exhibit at the Centennial Exhibition. When I first purchased Vaucluse, in 1837, there were blocks fastened to a big limb of this tree, seventy feet from the ground. These Charles De Wolf got a sailor to put in the dizzy position, from which a swing was suspended.

While Mr. De Wolf owned and occupied the place, some fifty years ago, I used to hear a good deal of talk about a magnificent evening entertainment he gave, in compliment to his daughter now living in Newport. At this time all the pleasure grounds, comprising many acres in extent, were lighted up with hundreds of lights placed amid the branches of the trees and shrubbery. There were then a multitude of avenues, intersecting paths and labyrinthian walks in the picturesque hill and dale grounds of Vaucluse, extending several miles, in the aggregate, in length. When these were thus lighted up with stars in miniature, and promenaded by scores of tastefully dressed votaries of fashion, passing and winding to and fro, with here and there a pair of Cupid's gentle votaries seated in some secluded rustic arbor, or rose and honeysuckle entwined bower, the whole enlivened with instrumental music and dulcet song at every turn, the scene presented might well bewilder the imagination and lead the enraptured beholders to deem their senses were beguiled by a fairy scene brought into existence by the magic wand of some sylvan goddess, rather than by beings of mere mortal mould.

Samuel Elam, an English gentleman of fortune, inherited the Vaucluse estate from his uncle, Jarvis Elam, and laid out and commenced the embellishment of the grounds shortly after the British left the Island in 1779. Nearly all the multitude of trees and shrubbery planted were imported by Mr. Elam from Europe. To perfect the whole required an immense outlay of money even in those days when labor cost but twenty-five cents or less per day, the day's work being from sun to sun. The late Isaac Gould, of Newport, told me that he once had Mr. Elam's books of expenses in his possession, and that the debit side showed an outlay of about eighty thousand dollars on the building and ornamental portion of the estate alone.

Mr. Elam lived in generous old English style, having his winter house on South Main street, Newport. This was the same that was owned and occupied by the late Dr. Theophilus Dunn at the time of his decease. On each Thursday of the week he kept open house for his personal friends, all of whom were furnished with a *carte blanche* to bring with them to dinner any strangers from abroad they chose to invite. His cellar was stored with the choicest wines and liquors, which, though a Quaker himself pledged to "temperance in all things," his politeness and good-breeding could not permit him to compel his guests to indulge in without the convivial assistance of their host. Mr. Elam's habit in this respect so grew upon him that Friends of his religious persuasion at last felt required by their book of discipline to deal with him as an offender, because of his lack of sufficient abstinence from the intoxicating fluid. He was, in accordance with the society's usage, notified that on a certain fourth day of the week a committee appointed by the monthly meeting of Newport would call at his house on business deemed of importance, in the way of counsel and reproof.

David Buffum, Sr., father of the late David Buffum, Jr., of Middletown, was one of the committee announced. Friend David was called "the bishop," not because he looked like a bishop, but because he looked as it was thought a bishop *ought* to look. He was tall and portly in person, and no one who ever met him, clothed in his neat and capacious suit of dove-tinted, drab-colored broadcloth coat, short breeches, waistcoat and all, with his becoming, not to say commanding, hat of the same color, silver-buckled, glossy shoes and flesh-colored stockings, could fail to perceive that he was a man of no common mould. In fact, he was one designed by nature to be a leader, in whatever position in life he might be cast. Friend Buffum, too, knew what was good, whether in the way of eating or drinking, and enjoyed it as much as any other man. Of all these things the culprit, Samuel Elam, was perfectly aware, and he felt sure that if he could get friend David on his side, all would yet pass off well.

It was in the month of November, and, luckily, the fourth day of the week designated proved very blustering and chilly. To welcome the coming of his friends, brother Samuel, who was skillful in the preparation and mixing of the juice of the grape, had carefully prepared with his own hands quite a large bowl of metheglin, or, rather, sangaree, concocted largely of the richest and most delicious wines imaginable, and pervaded with *quite* an ingredient of some forty-year-old cognac, of such captivating flavor that a man, though a saint, who could be once induced to put it to his lips would be quickly rendered unable to resist the fascinating, not to say intoxicating, tempter.

When the committee arrived at Vaucluse, Mr. Elam met them at the door, and after courteously and heartily welcoming them to the hospitalities of his house, expressed his tender concern lest they might have taken cold by their long exposure to the raw wind that was blowing, adding that he had prepared especially for them a hot sangaree, made of such harmless materials that they might each one of them drink of it largely without its affecting their health injuriously. In a most especial manner the courtly old gentleman addressed his entreaties to partake freely of the innocent decoction to his friend David, reminding him that there were several bad cases of influenza abroad, and that nothing was so good a preventive of the complaint, after being exposed to the cold, as a hot sangaree!

After friend Buffum had taken a few sips he seemed fully to agree in opinion with his friend Sammy, that the cordial prepared had something almost divine in its flavor, whatever might be its medicinal qualities. From sipping, Mr. Elam was delighted to notice that his genial friend commenced to take full swallows of the tempting fluid, and from that absolute draughts of half a tumbler or more each. When the minor Friends of the committee—Jonathan D. and Benjamin F.—had got sufficiently warm to proceed to business, and made a move to that effect, they were horror-stricken to perceive that their chairman had been smitten with a dizziness or vertigo, and was unable to perform the duties of the commission. Mr. Elam manifested great concern, and insisted upon placing his valued guest in bed and sending for a doctor. This arrangement did not, however, meet the views of the majority of the committee, and by their advice and assistance friend David was supported to his carriage by Mr. Elam; nor—such was his concern—would the host suffer his friend to depart without being accompanied by a faithful servant on horseback, to see him safely home.

David recovered from the attack, though the effect of the vertigo was observable in his countenance for many weeks afterwards, imparting to it a depressed, or, if it might be so said, a crestfallen look. Especially was this true while he was occupying his accustomed seat at the head of the gallery in the Friends Meeting, and still more noticeably when he turned to shake hands with his friend Clark Rodman, who sat next to him, by which the close of the meeting was announced. On such an occasion there seemed to be a furtive expression in the old man's eye, a shrinking, as it were, from honest Clark's steady gaze, as if the former invalid suspected his friend might be thinking of *vertigo* or some of its kindred associations.

Samuel Elam was not called upon again by any disciplinary committee of Friends, but he finally got to indulging so freely in wine, not always without pretty copious infusions of cognac, that the coating of his stomach began to manifest such alarming symptoms that he summoned to his aid the most eminent physicians of Boston. They all recommended abstinence from wine, brandy and highly seasoned dishes.

These prescriptions did not at all agree with their patient's long-indulged tastes, and he at last made a voyage to London for the express purpose of consulting Abernethy. When that crabbed old medical stick had finished his examination and questioning, he bluntly exclaimed, in the language of his nature, "Foundered, by G–d!" The old gentleman returned home soon after this discouraging diagnosis had been pronounced by the greatest and rudest of all living physicians, and shortly after his arrival took to his bed in the south-east lower room at Vaucluse, where he died not many weeks afterward. As "the ruling passion is ever still strong in death," I have heard it said by persons who were acquainted with the facts that, after Mr. Elam had reached a condition where he could not enjoy in the least the pleasures of the table, he used to summon his housekeeper to his sick room every morning and make her state to him minutely what she had provided for dinner, insisting to the last that his table should be bountifully supplied with the best the market afforded. Mr. Elam was buried in the Friends burial ground in Newport.

CHAPTER XII.

Between the magnificent beach, more than once before alluded to, that extends from the mouth of Pettaquamscutt river to Narragansett Pier, and the coast of Africa, there is not in all the broad Atlantic a solitary shoal, reef, rock or island intervening to break the force of the south-easterly gales that sometimes prevail and convey, many miles into the interior, the roar of the mighty billows, that at such seasons thunder against the shore. Nay! in the September gale of 1815, such was the terrific violence of the hurricane that the foam was rifted from the crests of the mountain waves that lashed the sounding shore, and borne by the wind into Connecticut in such volume that vegetation was saturated, and glass windows encrusted with the salt spray full thirty miles from the sea.

There stood, since my memory, a house near the mouth of Pettaquamscutt river, on its south-west bank, twenty rods back of the sand hills, that was tenanted at the time of this gale by the families of James Philips and William Weeden, a colored man. It was said by those who were near the beach that at an early stage of the storm gale an enormous tidal wave, twenty feet or more in height, came rolling in before the wind, and swept, at one blow, this house entirely away. The huge stone chimney alone stood the first shock, and to this Weeden was seen clinging for a few minutes until it, too, disappeared.

I have heard it said in my younger days, by old people, that one cause why the early settlers of New England built such huge stone chimneys, and used such heavy timber for the frames of their houses, was from the fact that shortly after the country began to be settled by Europeans one of these periodical gales occurred that made sad havoc with the frail tenements they at first erected.

Weeden's wife succeeded in getting on a part of the roof with a child under each arm, whom she was forced to drop in succession, reaching the shore herself alive, a mile farther up the river. Weeden and every other person in the house were drowned, except "Old Jim Philips," who, by clinging to a buttonwood limb, was also landed alive.

William Knowles, with his oldest son and three of his work people, went down to the Sand Hill Cove beach, in Point Judith, to draw up a boat, and were all five washed across the beach into the salt pond and drowned. Knowles was found some days after on Ram Island—probably "Narragansett Island," before referred to—a mile and more from the beach, with his hands clenched into a hassock of coarse grass, showing that he had reached the shore alive, but was too much exhausted to arise.

Surpassingly grand is the view of the ocean from the summit of McSparran Hill, stretching in unlimited space in an easterly and southerly direction, and bearing on its broad expanse scores of vessels, large and small. Following the sea-coast with the eye, a mile or so south from the Pier is seen an elevated promontory, now crowned with a turreted stone house, called "Hazard Castle." This building is almost hidden amidst many acres of evergreen and other planted trees that seem to have formed a close alliance and to have uniquely intermingled their branches for mutual defence against the storm elements that in the winter continually battle around and threaten the existence of every living thing.

This headland would doubtless soon be washed away, were it not protected from the ravages of the devastating waves that beat eternally against the bleak coast, by a rock-bound coast, and especially by two huge blocks of granite called severally the "Indian Rock" and "Flat Rock." The first was so named because an Indian was washed from it and drowned while fishing; and the other was called the "Flat Rock" because of its peculiar formation. Visiting this shore a few days after the September gale of 1815, a simple hearted old man named Stephen Champlin, who lived near by, asked me to go with him, a little north of the Flat Rock, to the shore of his farm, that he might show me, as he said, "the power of Almighty God." Complying with his request, he pointed out for my observation some dozen or more square and oblong rocks of from two to three feet in thickness and as many and more yards in their other dimensions, weighing, as I guessed, from one to twenty or more tons each. These, through the force of the wind and waves, had been riven from their foundations in a huge mass of granite, wherein the larger blocks I found by close examination had lain closely embedded after the manner of mosaic work or bricks in a pavement, almost level with the horizon, with a crevice scarcely an inch wide left between them and the parent rock. And yet, such was the tremendous force the wind and waves brought to bear, through some hydraulic power, or other pressure or leverage, applied through these little crevices only, that the huge masses were torn from their rock-bound foundations and cast upward and along the shore as if they had been blocks of cedar.

A landmark that I was acquainted with at the time, a large rock called "Peaked Rock," which old people said was placed upon its firm pedestal in a similar gale some fifty years before, was toppled from its elevated position, and now lies at the foot of the "monarch's former throne."

The boulder near which Mrs. Simons requested her litter to be rested, and which may have been wrenched from some drifting iceberg that came in collision with the firm granite rock on which it lay during the glacier period, stands on the apex of an elevated range that, beginning a mile or more to the north, extends almost due south to the old village of Rochester. This was the capital of King's Province—afterwards called Tower Hill—, where, probably next to " Smith's Fort," on the site of the present Updike house in North Kingstown, the first house was built in the Narragansett country.

Potter, in his History, page 290, says: " Tower Hill was probably the place in the purchase first settled. At that place are traces of a fortification still remaining, which mark with sufficient exactness, the site of Bull's garrison house, which was burnt in the war of 1676. The land on and around Kingston Hill was probably settled next."

When I was a boy there were eight very large houses standing in the village. The court-house and jail were removed to Little Rest Hill, the new county seat, I think, a short time before my remembrance. The first of these, which is still standing, stood on the north side of the road running east. It was built and occupied by Chief Justice Rowse J. Helme, a man of great firmness and unquestioned integrity, and admitted to be such even by his political enemies, of whom he had a full share. The Helme house was bought, put in good repair and occupied, some sixty years ago, by William Gould, from the island of Rhode Island. Mr. Gould, however, became after a time so involved in his pecuniary concerns, that he was obliged to part with the Helme estate and hire a small house that stands on the south side of the road, nearly opposite to it. It was here that I happened once to be present at a most afflicting family scene. In passing over the "Hill" one day, I heard such lamentable sounds issuing from the open window of a lower room in Gould's house, that I was led to dismount and enter the door. The poor man was sick unto death, and partially demented under the fearful prospect of soon having to leave his family of little children totally destitute. He lay in bed, holding in his right hand, the hand of his daughter, a girl of perhaps twelve years of age, and that of a little son in his left hand, while he continued to repeat, in heart-rending tones, "poor children! poor children!" without intermission or variation, until, as I was told, he died a short time after my visit.

The second house was the old Rowland Brown house, which stood on the west side of the north road, at its junction with the east road. The third was the Robert Brown house, that stood a little south of the house just named. The fourth was the Arnold Wilson house, that stood on the south and west corners of the roads leading to Little Rest Hill and the old post-road. The fifth was the John Nichols house, still standing on the east side of the old post-road, near the junction of the road running west. The sixth was the Andrew Nichols house, that stood not far from the corner south and east of the junction of the old post-road and the road running east. The seventh was the old Joseph Hull house—built by his father, John Hull—that stood a little east of the last named—a very large, wide house. The eighth was the old 'Squire John Case house, where Doctor Franklin used to stop over night on his journeys to and fro between Philadelphia and Boston. This house was occupied for some years by the family of Christopher Raymond Perry, father of Commodore O. H. Perry, where the latter spent several years of his boyhood. Commodore Perry was, however, born in a house that formerly stood on his ancestor's homestead estate, situated on the borders of the "hill country," some two miles or more south and west of Wakefield. I remember well the hero of Lake Erie calling and dining at my father's house shortly after the conclusion of the war of 1812 with Great Britain. On that occasion he took the dimensions and drew a plan with his own hand, of the house built by Joseph Congdon, of Peacedale—which is yet standing—agreeable to which he had a new house erected on the site of that in which he was born. After the war of 1812, Commodore Perry used to make frequent visits to Narragansett. On one occasion in returning to Newport on a bitter cold evening, the ferry-boat stuck on what is called the "Saddle Back Rock," just off Rose Island fort. The tide was falling, and he and the ferryman—old Polydore Gardner—were forced to pass most of the night in an open boat, and were it not that the commodore compelled the old negro to dance most of the time, he would, with his scanty clothing, probably have perished with the cold. Sometime after this, a passenger on the boat asked Polydore to show him where the "old Saddle Back" lay, which the ferryman consented to do, but failed to point out the exact spot, although repeatedly requested to do so, until the keel of the heavy ferry-boat grated as it passed over the rock." That's old Saddle Back!" said Polydore.

A couple of furlongs or so west of Tower Hill lies a pond of a few acres, from which flows "Indian run," so called because of an Indian having been pursued on its banks and there killed by a white man. The brook flows southerly and westerly until it unites with the Saucatucket at Peacedale. From this point the range continues in a southerly direction two miles farther to a deep fissure called "Dorothy Hollow," from the circumstances of an old negro woman of that name having perished therein, under a snow-drift during a violent storm many years ago.

About one mile south and east of the village used to stand the house of Thomas Hazard, my grandfather, in which the writer of these papers was born, who was perhaps the first man of much influence in New England who labored in behalf of the freedom of the African race. My father used to relate how his father's mind first became imbued with the conviction that it was wrong to hold negroes in bondage. When a young man, on coming home from college (Yale), my grandfather's father, Robert Hazard, who owned and leased probably the largest landed estate farmed by any one individual in New England, set his son to oversee his negroes, whilst they were engaged under a scorching sun in cultivating a field of corn. As my grandfather sat reading in the shade of a tree, his mind went out in sympathy toward the poor slaves who were thus forced to labor for others in the heat of the sun, when he himself could scarcely keep comfortable while quietly sitting in the shade. This led to a train of thought that finally resulted in a conviction that it was wrong to hold slaves, and when, some time after, he wedded Governor William Robinson's eldest daughter Elizabeth, and his father was about to establish the newly-married couple in life by placing them on a large and well-appointed farm, with a suitable number of negro farm and house servants, he was shocked on hearing his son declare that he could not conscientiously hold his fellowmen in bondage, but must conduct his farming and household affairs entirely with the aid of hired labor. After striving in vain to dissuade his son from this resolve his irritated father, in his anger, threatened to disinherit him. On this account a coolness existed between them for several years. My grandfather, however, continued to adhere strictly to his convictions, and labored faithfully in freedom's cause, in unison with the late Moses Brown, of Providence, and especially with his personal friend, that great light of the eighteenth century, John Woolman, of Mount Holly, New Jersey, and others, among whom was Jeremiah Austin, who after heroically manumitting his one and only slave, labored at day wages on my grandfather's farm, for the maintenance of his family. Nor did Thomas Hazard relax his efforts in behalf of freedom until long after a law was enacted by the General Assembly abolishing slavery in Rhode Island.

Finally the father also became convinced of the soundness of his son's views, and though one of the largest slaveholders in New England, left, by provision in his will—many years previous to the passage of the emancipation act—all his slaves free at his death, and divided his property equally among his children.

CHAPTER XIII.

Robert Hazard, my great-grandfather, was the fourth in descent from Thomas Hazard, one of the original purchasers of Aquidneck, whose remains lie interred in an old burial ground near the west shore of the island, a little north of Lawton's Valley, on the farm now owned by the town of Portsmouth.

Tradition says that Thomas Hazard had two brothers, one of whom, for military services rendered the British government in Ireland, received from the Crown an extensive grant of land situated near Enneskillen, where several wealthy and inflential families of the name yet reside. A son of the brother, it was said, emigrated to Georgia or Carolina, and was the ancestor of the extensive southern branch of the Hazard family.

The earliest land records in the town of Portsmouth, R. I., I think, were commenced in the year 1640. In these the following entries, transcribed therefrom by my son, Barclay Hazard, appear: "June 30, 1658, Thomas Hazard bequeaths to Stephen Wilcock, as dowry of his (T. H.'s) daughter, Hannah, thirty-four acres of land;" "1675, January 11, inventory of estate of Thomas Sheriffe (lately deceased);" "1675, May 29, Thomas Hazard under promise of marriage with Martha Sheriffe, but disclaims any interest in or control of her estate."

There are also several other records of land transfers by Thomas Hazard, and by Robert Hazard, his son, and Mary, his wife, on the books dating from 1665 to 1675, not far from which latter date it is probable the Robert Hazard mentioned emigrated to Narragansett, and first built and settled, as I used to hear old people say in my youth, on or near the site of the old John Rose house, a little to the west of what is now called Moresfield, in South Kingstown. The tradition seems to be fortified in part by documentary testimony. Potter, in his History, p 292, says: "The purchasers [of Pettaquamscutt], in 1671, conveyed to Robert Hazard five hundred acres, bounded north by road, east by Saucatucket, south by Edward and Sampson Sherman and west on purchaser's land. This tract is now owned in part by Rowland Hazard, R. F. Noyes, Peleg Weeden and the heirs and assigns of John Rose." Again, says Potter, p. 291 : " Lot No. 1, of about two hundred acres, was laid out to Mumford, and is that part of the Judge William Potter farm, now chiefly owned by E. R. Potter, bounded north and west by roads, east by Robert Hazard and south by lot No. 2."

I formerly owned about two hundred acres of the Judge William Potter farm, and know that it was bounded largely both east and south on the John Rose farm, where tradition says Robert Hazard, son of Thomas—the earliest immigrant of the name to Rhode Island—first settled in Narragansett, and where one of the oldest burying grounds of the family is yet to be seen.

While I owned the eastern portion of the old Judge William Potter estate, there lived, in a dilapidated tenement on the premises, a colored woman named Sherman who had five children, all of whom were under eleven years of age, and dependent solely on their mother for maintenance. Through hard work and exposure, Mrs. Sherman's health broke down, and the seeds of consumption developed so rapidly that she became conscious she had not many weeks to live. In this debilitated state the heroic mother walked some three miles to a manufactory, and obtained what was called "a piece to weave; that is, some thirty pounds of yarn to be returned from the hand loom in cloth. With this load on her back the woman started for home. A neighbor of mine passed her on the road. The over-wearied creature was then sitting on a stone to rest, with the bundle of yarn beside her. In answer to queries, Mrs. Sherman confessed that she feared the task would prove too great for her in her feeble state of health, but said, that, although conscious she must soon die, she still hoped to be able to weave " the piece," and get with the proceeds of her labor enough " cotton chambra" to make each of her children a dress, so that they might be taken to the poor-house, after her death, " looking kind of decent."

The noble martyr *did* live to weave the yarn into cloth, and again managed to get it back to the store, and returned with the chambra. This she made into garments for her children, and soon after got an old colored woman who occupied the other end of the house, to go to James Knowles, the keeper of the town's poor, and ask him to come to her. Knowles lived in a brick house—some miles away, not far from Worden's pond, commonly called the great pond—that stood on the Major Brenton estate and near old Brenton's large mansion-house, which I remember well. When Mr. Knowles came to see the sick woman some days after he received her message, he found her near death and too ill to leave her bed. The oldest daughter had just finished roasting some potatoes for dinner, and was then in the act of mashing the biggest one in the lot with a pewter spoon for her mother.

In scarcely audible accents, the dying woman told the overseer of the poor that she knew he must take her poor children away, but begged of him to allow them to stay in the house with her until her body was carried to the grave, adding that she had made each one of them a new chambra dress and had provided for them a little meal and enough potatoes to last them until their mother was gone. "And oh," said she, "you will be good to the poor fatherless and motherless things, won't you, Mr. Knowles?" No stone now marks, or ever marked, the spot where the perishable remains of the poor widow were laid away, nor can it, amidst the briers and bushes that have overgrown the grave, be discerned by the keenest mortal eye, though it is doubtless eternally impressed on the memory of legions of loving angels.

Thomas Hazard, the eldest son of the above named Robert, owned the six farms on Boston Neck extending from the north line of the Jenks farm south to the terminus of the point where the Pettaquamscutt river joins the sea. Probably his eldest son, Robert, the great farmer, improved at one time all of these farms, containing in the aggregate nearly fifteen hundred acres, in addition to the great tracts of land he himself owned in his own right, lying on and to the westward of the Tower Hill and McSparran range, and about the Great, or Worden's, pond.

Miss Emily Hazard, daughter of Benjamin, and Dr. Henry E. Turner, both of Newport, have in their possession copies of many antique documents, and among others that of the last will and testament of the first Thomas Hazard, in which he disinherits his only son Robert and his two daughters, because, as it would appear, of their opposition to his contemplated or accomplished marriage with Martha Sheriffe, the widow of Thomas Sheriffe, to whom he bequeathed all his real and personal property. I extract:

"Imprimis, I give unto my son, Robert Hazard, one shilling, to be paid in silver coigne, one month after my death." The same to his daughter, Hannah Wilcox. Again, "I give and bequeath unto my loving daughter, Martha Potter, wife of Icabod Potter, of Portsmouth, one shilling, to be paid one month after my death." "Witness whereof I have hereunto set my hand and seal the thirteenth day of November, one thousand six hundred and seventy-six.

(Signed)   his
                     THOMAS (T. H.) HAZARD.
   Witness,   mark
THOMAS GOULD,
JOHN COGGESHALL,
JOHN HEATH."

It seems it was the custom at the time to sign documents in monograms or initials, in like form as is exhibited in this will. It is perhaps worthy of remark that wherever in the old records of Portsmouth, so far as I have observed, the name is used as a signature, it is spelled " Hazard," while in the body of the documents, it is as uniformly spelled " Hassard." In a very elaborate English genealogical table I have before me, up to the fourth generation the name is spelled " Hazard." Then comes Robert " Hasard" in the fifth and again Thomas " Hassard" in the sixth. From this time down to the twenty-first generation—in the year 1852 inclusive— the name, in both the English and Irish branches of the family, is uniformly spelled " Hassard."

The fact that the name is not spelled alike by different branches of the American Hazards might lead one to suppose there was more truth than poetry in an answer said to have been given by the late Benjamin Hazard, of Newport, to a question wherein he was asked why my grandfather—Thomas Hazard—was called " College Tom." " Because," replied the astute and witty lawyer, " he was the only Hazard who could write his name!" By far the greater number of the American Hazards spell their name as I have last written it, though some, as for instance the family of the late Nichols Hassard, conform to the English method in this respect.

Robert Hazard, son of Thomas, is alluded to in the old records as having surveyed certain tracts of land. Again, there is deeded " to Robert Hazard, of Portsmouth, shipwright, for twenty pounds sterling, 560 acres in King's Province [Narragansett]." It was either this Robert Hazard, or his grandson Robert, the great farmer, who imported a fine stud-horse from Tripoli, called " Snip," whose progeny were much celebrated for their native stamina, high spirit and power of endurance. In time the qualities of the horse became associated with those of the family, and where a member proved deficient in the characteristics of the self-willed race of independent thinkers, he was said not to be of the genuine

"Snip breed," but to have inherited his qualities from the family of his mother rather than from his father's side.

Robert Hazard, my great-grandfather, who lived in a house that stood since my memory nearly opposite the Tower Hill bridge on Boston Neck, was the father of three sons, Thomas, Jonathan, and Richard, and one daughter. The daughter married Job Watson, who occupied and improved the Dyer and Bull farms and other tracts of land lying south and west of Tower Hill village. Job, after his marriage, purchased several farms on Conanicut and removed to that island. He was the most extensive and opulent farmer that ever lived on Conanicut. It was said that he sometimes had fully one hundred men engaged in his numerous hay fields at the same time. He used to occupy with his family, a portion of the year, the Park House, at the head of the Mall, which I have heard represented as being, in his day, one of the fine mansions of Newport. Job Watson was the father of five sons, all of whom I used to know. They were Job, Walter, Robert, Borden, and John; and each and all exemplified, in their stalwart mould of body and mind and uniform gentlemanly demeanor, the characteristics of their "snip" descent.

My grandfather, Thomas Hazard, was large in person, fully six feet in height, and remarkably strong in body, mind and will. He was, for nearly or quite half a century a preacher among "Friends," one of whose cardinal doctrines is an entire subjugation of the will to the teachings of the "inner light." In his latter days, to illustrate the deceitfulness of the human heart, he used to say that although he had sought to inculcate this point of doctrine in his preaching from the beginning, he at last discovered that he himself had "ruled South Kingstown monthly meeting forty years, in his own will, before he found it out!" The late William T. Robinson, of New York, a gentleman of the old school and of world-wide acquaintance, knew my grandfather intimately, and used to say that in general appearance and deportment he came the nearest, in his estimation, to the standard of a truly noble man of any person he ever met with. The estimation in which Thomas Hazard was held by his father-in-law may be gathered from tradition that has come down through a member of the Robinson family. On the occasion of the dinner given on the day that he was wedded to Governor Robinson's eldest daughter, Elizabeth, the father of the bride said to the guests at the table, " This day, by the marriage of my daughter to Thomas Hazard, I have ennobled my family." That this sentiment was prompted purely on grounds of personal worth, there can be no doubt, as both families were of a like honorable and respected ancestry. I may just say here that Thomas and Robert appear to have been favorite names in the family of Hazards, both in England and America. My grandmother used to reckon thirty Thomas Hazards, all living, and not, as she used to say with pride, a drunkard among them all.

Mrs. Mary Hunter, in the diary before quoted from, which is in possession of her daughter, Mrs. Eliza Birckhead, of Newport, says that Mrs. Dr. Mann, formerly Mrs. William Robinson, son of Rowland, had in her possession "a stick," that had come down to her former husband as a family heir loom, "that was cut in the West Riding of Yorkshire, in 1737, by the Right Reverend Thomas Robinson, Earl of Rokeby." June 14, 1856, Mrs. Hunter enters in her diary, "I have been this morning to see two very old and infirm persons, Thomas Hornby, aged 91, and his sister, Polly McClish, aged 84. Mr. Hornby told me that the old house that James Atkinson, the printer, then lived in, was built by our ancestor, Rowland Robinson the first, who came to this country about the year 1654. Also that the Rogers land, situated at the foot of Mary street, was a part of Mr. Robinson's farm, and that on his wife going into the garden one day to cut a cabbage, she was frightened by some animal near the house, and giving the alarm, the work-people rushed out and killed a wolf!"

It was while residing in the house now owned and occupied by ex-Mayor Atkinson, that Rowland Robinson, as tradition holds true, chancing one day to go to the head of Long Wharf, on the arrival of a ship from England, observed among the passengers a young man who so strikingly resembled his elder brother who, in consequence of a quarrel regarding a question of family succession, had been the cause of Mr. Robinson's leaving the parental roof in a fit of passion—that he was led to inquire the stranger's name. On learning that it was his eldest brother's son, Mr. R. asked him home and tendered him the hospitalities of his house, but never spoke to him during his stay of a week or longer thereafter, although he gave his nephew, on his departure, enough money wherewith to buy three thousand acres of land in Virginia. Before these papers are concluded, it may be seen that Rowland Robinson, the father of the "unfortunate Hannah," inherited this trait of his grandfather's character.

Mrs. Hunter, in the same authority, continues in her diary, "The Hunter estate, now owned by James H. Taylor, was built by a man named Hardin, who sold it to Dr. Hunter. The Gibbs house on Thames street was built and occupied by Gov. Samuel Cranston, of whom Governor Gibbs' father (George Gibbs, the great Newport merchant) bought it and carried on the baking business on the wharf. That *our* house on the Point—the Governor Nichols house—was owned and occupied by Col. Joe. Wanton, the same to whom Queen Anne presented the silver bowl as a reward for his prowess in capturing the pirates." Probably these were the fifteen pirates who were hanged at one time, below high water mark, on Gravelly Point, near the junction of Washington street with Long Wharf.

This fine house, with its solid mahogany balustrades, was built by Governor Nichols, whose daughter married Judge Stephen Hassard, of Point Judith—called long Stephen, from his great height—, the father of the late Nichols Hassard, of Newport, who inherited in a remarkable degree the upright, tall, large form and gentlemanly carriage of his ancestors, and was also a man of generous and noble instincts. I personally knew an instance wherein a distinguished citizen of Newport was reduced to such straits, through misfortune, that he applied one day to Mr. Nichols Hassard for the free gift of a dinner at the bounteous table he always spread at the Park House. "Come, Mr. ——," said Mr. H., "and take dinner at my table every day! You will always receive from me and my family a hearty welcome."

The Governor Nichols house was owned and occupied for many years before his death by the late Hon. William Hunter, United States Minister to Brazil, who was probably as accomplished a man in classical literature, polite breeding and general ability, as any other diplomatist that has represented the United States at a foreign court.

CHAPTER XIV.

The Hon. William Hunter married Mary, daughter of William T. Robinson—son of Thomas—, a partner of the great mercantile house of Franklin & Robinson, in New York, the magnitude of whose business transactions—before their still greater losses—may be guessed at from the fact of the house having lost in the Indian seas the ship Ocean, with a cargo of teas, silks, etc., valued at six hundred thousand dollars, on which there was no insurance, without its injuriously affecting their world-wide credit. Of the three prominent mercantile houses of New York, at that time—"Franklin & Robinson," "Minturn & Champlin," and "Franklin & Minturn—," four of the merchant princes comprising the firms, Robinson, Champlin, and Benjamin and Jonas Minturn, were of Narragansett ancestry. It was in the heyday of William T. Robinson's prosperity, when he occupied two fine houses, one in the city, and the other outside its limits situated on the East river, at which period several of his beautiful daughters were in succession reigning belles, that Miss Mary Robinson, then engaged to be married to a New York gentleman, chanced to see for the first time while on a visit at the house of her grandfather, Thomas Robinson, in Newport, William Hunter at Trinity Church.

I may just here remark, in parenthesis, that of the four most beautiful and graceful women I ever knew, or, I may say, ever saw, three of them were from New York City, and, singularly enough, all of the Narragansett Robinson descent. They were Abby Robinson, fourth daughter of

William T. Robinson, who married a Mr. Pierce and was lost at sea; Anna Hazard Barker, eldest daughter of Jacob Barker who married Samuel G. Ward, of New York, American Financial Agent of the Barings of London; and Frances Minturn, second daughter of Jonas Minturn, the deceased wife of the unworthy writer of these papers. The fourth I will leave nameless, to avoid being brought in conflict with a score or more of other beauties, each of whom may have been led, from some inadvertency of mine, or other cause, to suppose that she of all others should be selected to fill the vacant place.

When the church services were ended, and the exuberant spirited girl passed down the broad aisle, she asked of a friend who that portly, fine looking gentleman was? Upon being told that it was William Hunter, she ejaculated, " I mean to marry that man!" The speech was reported to the happy swain, and he lost no time in calling with his sister on the fascinating damsel, on whose susceptible heart he had at first sight made so favorable an impression. What "love darts" may have passed between the eyes of the two mutually smitten, at the first introduction, I have never heard, but probably nothing to greatly dampen the ardor of the aspiring lover, although the coyness of the sex had to be of course overcome by the pressure of a longer or shorter siege, the conducting of which no gay deceiver better understood than the accomplished gallant, William Hunter. After many passages of flirtation, greatly to the annoyance of Mary's Quaker aunts, Abigail, Mary and Amy Robinson—the three most talented and accomplished women, Mr. Hunter used to say, he ever knew in one family—the love affair culminated under the following circumstances. As Mr. Hunter was walking up Washington street, one afternoon, with his sister, who afterward married into a titled family in France, he espied Miss Mary Robinson a short distance in advance of them just as she turned out of Bridge street, on her way to her grandfather's, and with the keen perception of a practiced adept in the art of bewildering the dear sex, he snatched a shawl off his sister, and hastening on, pressed it about the neck and shoulders of his inamorata, with the half whispered reproof, "You imprudent creature!" That was all, and yet that little act and the few words expressed in a half reproachful tone, suffused in tenderness, and the manner, and all, sufficed to soften the heart of the obdurate beauty, and ere the love-cooing pair had reached the door of "Quaker Tommy Robinson," her affianced lover was forgotten and the fickle, giggling "belle of the Newport season," had more than half consented to become the bride of another. I say of the " Newport season," for the reason that Newport was then, as now, the chief summer resort of the *elite* of the land, largely, in that day, from the Carolinas, Georgia and Virginia.

I knew the Hon. William Hunter tolerably well, and have had him in my house as a guest for many days together, but I can not recall to mind a single instance wherein I observed him to swerve in the least degree from the standard of a high-bred gentleman, or speak disparagingly of others, whatever cause he might have had to complain of their conduct toward him. Mr. Hunter made no formal profession of religion, and yet in his last sickness he manifested not the least fear of death. On the contrary, I remember calling to see him when he lay in a dying condition in his house on "the Point,' when he told me, with a serene and happy 'expression of countenance, that it was but a few hours before that his feelings under the prospect of a speedy death had been of so ecstatic a nature that he was constrained to request his wife and family to leave him alone, lest his joyous emotions might prompt him to do or say something that might appear to them unseemly.

Singularly enough, I also sat up with William Vernon, called Count Vernon, the night before he died, in the house of his brother, Samuel Vernon, at the corner of Mary and Clarke streets—the house occupied by Count Rochambeau as headquarters most of the time the French troops were in

Newport during the Revolution. The count was a man who so totally disregarded the prescribed "ordinances" that he was held by most pious neighbors to be a " brand" peculiarly destined for "the burning," and yet when he came to die he manifested no fear of the event. Count Vernon had spent a large portion of his life in Paris and mingled in the court circle of Louis XVI. So completely Frenchified in manners had he become that even the discerning populace of Paris would not be convinced that he was not a Frenchman, and were one day, in the Robespierre and Murat bloody period, dragging him by a rope round his neck to a lamp-post to hang him, when he was fortunately recognized by a passer by and released upon the assurance that he was really what he claimed to be, an American by birth and citizenship. The count lay in a very suffering state, and through the night I probably wiped from his lips the mucus he was constantly raising, many scores of times, but never, in a single instance wherein the courtly old gentleman did not, with quite an effort, bow his head and falter out the words, " Thank you, sir !"

Count Vernon received from his deceased father's estate, eighty thousand dollars, and when he returned to America all he had to show for his fortune ample in that day, was fifty-two oil paintings, all by the old masters, which he had abundant opportunities to purchase during the French Revolution at mere nominal prices. On one occasion the count sent twelve of these pictures to Boston, on exhibition, and had them insured for twenty thousand dollars. After his death the entire collection was sold in Newport at auction, and netted but a trifle over two thousand dollars. This sale, I think, was made in 1834 or 1835. Of them, I purchased three paintings, " The Dying Seneca," said to be by Vandyck, " The Saint Roque and his Dog," and a small landscape, all of them considered to be among the very best in the gallery, and I have since regretted that I had not bought the whole collection.

Mrs. Hunter's diary continues : " Colonel Wanton finally

lost everything, his vast estates being confiscated, a part of which was two large farms on Conanicut. His wife died of a broken heart in New York. The Zenas Hammond house on Bridge street on the Point, was owned and occupied by the father of the Simons who married the beautiful Hannah Robinson, daughter of my uncle Rowland." Mrs. Hunter says also: "There were two young men taken prisoners on board an English vessel of war then in the harbor of Newport. They were the sons of a Quaker friend of my grandparents, and their being arrested was through some mistake. Their parents applied to my grandfather [Thomas Robinson] in great distress, knowing his influence with the English party. He was ill at the time with a periodical attack of asthma, and could do nothing but write, which he did." This, however, failed to procure the release of the two prisoners, and, continues Mrs. Hunter, " My grandmother [Sarah Robinson] then decided to go on board Wallace's ship, and in a personal interview see what female influence could effect. She was received at the gangway with great form and courtesy by every officer on board. She asked for Captain Wallace, was shown into his cabin and made herself known, stating simply her errand and wishes. The commander at once gave orders to have the irons stricken from the two young Quakers, and they were placed in the boat that brought Mrs. Robinson to his ship, and she had thus the great pleasure and triumph of restoring them to their parents."

I have heard Mr. George W. Carr, of Jamestown, relate an anecdote wherein female Quaker influence probably saved a house that is yet standing, a little north-west of the East Ferry on that island. Some "rebels," whose valor appears not to have been tempered with what Falstaff deemed to be "the better part," "discretion," were in the habit of discharging their fowling-pieces, or other small-arms, at night, from the eastern shores of Conanicut, in the direction of the British vessels lying in the outer harbor of Newport, though of course without producing the least effect beyond that of annoying the enemy. Captain Wallace obtained the names of some of these indiscreet "rebels," and sent an officer with a squad of men to burn the culprits' houses. The husband of Abby Greene, who lived in the old Joseph Greene house, yet standing north of the East Ferry, was, if not a participant, a sympathizer with the guilty men, and his house was marked for destruction. After firing quite a number of buildings, the party approached the Greene house, flourishing a fire-brand to keep it alive. Mrs. Abigail Greene, the wife of the owner of the house and mother of the late Anna Greene, the Quaker preacher, persuaded her excitable husband to keep in the background while she herself went out to meet the incendiaries. As they approached she addressed the officer in command, firmly but kindly saying, " I hope you have not come to do us any harm. Come, walk in and I will set you something to eat." The officer regarded Mrs. Greene's placid features a moment and answered, " Dear old mother, we won't hurt a hair of your head," and ordered the brand of blazing wood to be carefully stamped upon until every spark had expired. The party then came into the house, and after taking a cup of tea retired with their blessing, instead of executing their meditated curse. Verily, Solomon spoke truly when he said, " A soft answer turneth away wrath."

The remains of the first Rowland Robinson were removed by Attmore Robinson, of Wakefield, R. I., a lineal descendant of his in the fifth degree, from the Friends' burying ground on Tower Hill and re-interred in the Wakefield cemetery. The headstone bears the following inscription: " Rowland Robinson, born in Cumberland, England, 1654, came to America, 1675, married Mary, daughter of John Allen, died, 1716, interred in Friends' burying ground, Tower Hill, South Kingstown, and removed to this place in 1845."

Under date of November 12, 1877, Mr. Attmore Robinson writes: " I would state, from tradition, that the first house built by Rowland Robinson, of Cumberland, England [in

Narragansett], was near the only short turn in the Point Judith road, a little east of the old Natt Armstrong residence. The chimney and cellar walls I recollect seeing, with some of the old timber lying partly in the cellar walls, which was of pine."

Gov. William Robinson built three houses, all of which are yet standing. They were the old Christopher Robinson house, near " Kit's pond ;" the John Robinson house, on the Narragansett Pier estate, and the Sylvester Robinson house, that is merged or built into the Governor Sprague castellated mansion.

CHAPTER XV.

I remember when, on the spacious kitchen being removed from the old John Robinson house, above mentioned, there were sixty ox-cart loads of beach sand taken from beneath the sleepers which had been used to sand the floor, a large portion of which no doubt had been *danced* through the cracks by the jolly darkies of the olden time, who, in some instances, permitted their masters' families to be present at their Christmas and other holiday pastimes as a matter of favor only.

The annual corn huskings of Narragansett were in the olden time greatly enjoyed by the negroes. Since my remembrance some of the large farmers had many hundred bushels husked of an evening. The refreshments provided consisted mostly of new cider, apple and mince pies, huge loaves of gingerbread, and the never-to-be-dispensed-with fiddle. I remember that Dinah Hawkins, a colored woman, who lived not far from the famous devil's ring in the Wilson woods, lost two infants at one of these night huskings. Dinah had a fine pair of twin boys that she was extremely proud of, and took them one evening to a husking at Wat Watson's farm on which the Tower Hill Hotel now stands, that she might, with a mother's fondness and pride, exhibit them to her assembled friends. After all had got through petting and praising the babies, Dinah laid them down side by side asleep on a pile of corn husks. In the meantime, amidst the hilarity inspired by the cider and the music, Dinah forgot her twins until the heap of corn-stalks on which she had laid them was stacked up, babies and all. After tearing down two or three stacks the infants were found, both smothered to death. Black Cato said he heard something squeal two or three times whilst he was making the stack, and, supposing the noise to come from a nest of young rats, he "stamped on the varmints" till they stopped squeaking.

Updike, pages 177-78-79, speaks as follows of these negro merry-makings: "In imitation of the whites, the negroes held an annual election on the third Saturday in June, when they elected their governor. When the slaves were numerous each town held its election. This annual festivity was looked for with great anxiety. Party spirit was as violent and acrimonious with them as among the whites. The slaves assumed the power and pride and took the relative rank of their masters, and it was degrading to the reputation of the owner if the slave appeared in inferior apparel, or with less money than the slave of another master of equal wealth. The horses of the wealthy landholders were on this day all surrendered to the use of the slaves, and with cues, real or false, head pomatumed and powdered, cocked hat, mounted on the best Narragansett pacers, sometimes with their master's sword, with their ladies on pillions, they pranced to election, which commenced generally at 10 o'clock.

"The canvass for votes soon commenced, the tables with refreshments were spread and all friends of the respective candidates were solicited to partake, and as much anxiety would manifest itself, and as much family pride and influence was exercised and interest created, as in other elections, and was preceded by weeks of *parmateering*—parliamenteering. About one o'clock the vote would be taken by ranging the friends of the respective candidates in two lines under the direction of a chief marshal with assistants. Guy Watson, who distinguished himself in the black regiment under General Greene, at Red Bank, and also at Ticonderoga [and in the capture of Prescott, Updike might have added], acted as chief marshal after the Revolution until the annual elections ceased. There was generally a tumultuous crisis until the count commenced, when silence was proclaimed, and after that no man could change sides or go from one rank to the other. The chief marshal announced the number of votes for each candidate, and in an audible voice proclaimed the name of the governor elected for the ensuing year. The election treat corresponded in extravagance in proportion to the wealth of the master. The defeated candidate was, according to custom, introduced by the chief marshal, and drank the first toast after the inauguration, and all animosities were forgotten. At dinner the governor was seated at the head of the long table, under trees or an arbor, with the unsuccessful candidate at his right and his lady on the left. The afternoon was spent in dancing, games of quoits, athletic exercises, &c. As the slaves decreased in number, these elections became more concentrated. In 1795, elections were held in North and South Kingstown, but in a few years, one was held in South Kingstown only, and they have for years ceased.

" The servant of the late E. R. Potter was elected governor about the year 1800. The canvass was very expensive to his master. Soon after the election, Mr. Potter had a conference with the governor, and stated to him that the one or the other must give up politics, or the expense would ruin them both. Governor John took the wisest course, abandoned politics and retired to the shades of private life.'

Notwithstanding what Mr. Updike says, I feel pretty sure that the colored people of South Kingstown held their elections long after slavery was abolished. I think I can remember when the last came off, which was after the war with Great Britain in 1812. It took place in the Potter woods on Rose Hill, when I think Aaron Potter, who was brought up in the Hon. Elisha R. Potter's family, was elected governor, and Abram Perry, who was born under my father's roof, officiated as chief marshal. Aaron commenced taking lessons in the science of government at an early age. Mr. Potter being a tall and large framed man, nearly twice as heavy as either of his sons, used to ride a very big, strong horse, and sometimes when going about his farm he would take Aaron, when a boy, up behind him to open and close bars, as he rode from lot to lot. On these occasions Aaron used sometimes make his master ride in zigzag directions that he might see what a variety of " funny pikters he and the horse and master Potter made on the ground in the sunshine."

The twelve days of Christmas, were almost wholly devoted to festivities, by both master and slave in the " Olden-time Narragansett." " But the wedding," says Updike, page 186, " was the great gala of olden time. The exhibition of expensive apparel and the attendance of numbers almost exceeds belief. The last of these celebrations was given about the year 1790, by Nicholas Gardiner, Esq. It was attended by six hundred guests." I knew Mr. Gardiner. He dressed in the rich style of former days, with a cocked hat, full bottomed white wig, snuff colored coat, and waistcoat with deep pockets, cape low so as not to disturb the wig, and at the same time display the large silver stock buckle of the plaited neck cloth of white linen cambric, small clothes, and white topped boots, finely polished. He was a portly, courteous gentleman of the old school. " The fox-chase, with hounds and horns, fishing and fowling, were objects of enchanting recreation. Wild pigeons, partridges, quails, woodcocks, squirrels and rabbits were innumerable. Such were the amusements, pastimes, festivities, and galas of ancient Narragansett."

Governor William Robinson's remains lie in the old family burying ground near the Governor Sprague house before alluded to, under a heavy slab of stone with the following inscription: " In memory of the Hon. William Robinson,

Esq., late deputy governor of the colony, who departed this life Sept. ye 19th, 1751, in the 58th year of his age."

Rowland T. Robinson, of Ferrisburgh, Vermont, an octogenarian and lineal descendant of Governor Robinson, in the fourth degree, writes me under date of December 5, 1877: "Governor Robinson was a man of talent, gentlemanly in bearing and of noble stature. His son Rowland—father of the 'unfortunate Hannah'—was six feet high and of symmetrical proportions, but his father was larger than he. Rowland used to lament the gradual diminution in stature of the Robinsons. He would say, 'My grandfather was larger than my father,—my father larger than I, and my Bill!—why, he's nothing!'" This "Bill" married a daughter of George Scott, granddaughter of Peter Ayrault, a French refugee, and lived and died in the Dr. Mann House, at the south-east corner of Broadway and Mann avenue, Newport, R. I.

To return to the main subject once again from this lengthy digression. Just before reaching "Dorothy's Hollow," before described, Tower Hill—here sometimes called Chimney Hill from the old Carter and Jackson chimney—rises to an altitude almost equaling that of McSparran, and from its summit in a clear sky portions of four different States may be seen, and there is spread before the beholder an ocean and landscape view of surpassing beauty and sublimity.

A short distance south of Dorothy Hollow now stands the "Tower Hill house," from near which the hill turns to the south-west and gradually falls until it slopes entirely away near "Kit's Pond," into what was popularly called since my remembrance, "The Crying Bog," from the doleful sounds of weeping and wailing, as tradition asserts, that were often heard to issue therefrom at night, uttered by the ghost of Manouna, an Indian squaw of the Narragansett tribe, through the dire promptings of a remorseful conscience for having, whilst in earth life, cruelly murdered her two helpless children and secretly buried their bodies in the bog. Nor did the wretched spectre always confine its visitations to that immediate locality. Since my memory it used to be said, that the unhappy ghost was at times to be seen sitting under some old willow trees that, until recently, stood on the east side of the Point Judith road, some twenty rods south from the Crying Bog, and half as many east of Kit's Pond—thus called from the abbreviated Christian name of Christopher Robinson. I remember hearing of a stranger, who came late on a moonlight evening to Christopher Robinson's, and requested lodgings, under the plea that he was on his way to a friend's house who lived on the "Point," but that as he approached these willow trees he saw an old Indian squaw sitting on the ground beneath them, rocking herself backward and forward, and moaning and weeping most dolefully. Nor would she take the least notice of what he said until he rode up and took a stone from a wall and rolled it against her feet, when she suddenly vanished from his sight, uttering such unearthly shrieks as she went that he could not force his horse to pass the spot.

It was said that after passing most of the night in woeful lamentations the ghost of the wretched murderess used to leave towards morning in the direction of a little wooded island that stands in the south-western part of Kit's Pond, apparently keeping in her rapid course close to the surface of the water, and screaming as she went until the horrifying sounds reached the island, when all was again still. Many other stories analogous to these used to be told in connection with "the ghost of the Crying Bog," in my younger days.

Some thirty or more rods east by south of where the old willow trees, before mentioned, formerly stood, the site of which is now marked by a buttonwood tree and a bar-way a rod or so from the tree, there is still to be seen the stone foundation and tumble-down chimney of a house on the border of a big bog, that was, more than a century ago, occupied by an old shoe-maker by the name of Drew. In one of the periodical violent snow-storms of early times, this house with the exception of the top of the chimney was entirely buried in a snow-drift. Old Drew, happening to have a good supply of fuel inside the premises, made no effort to make a way out through the snow-bank. When some days after the storm, Christopher Robinson, son of Governor William Robinson, was informed of the circumstances, he sent his negroes to open a passage way through the snow to Drew's door. When they reached the door, the old man was found sitting contentedly at work by the light of a tallow candle; and he did not express much gratitude for being relieved, as he said it did not take so much fuel to warm his room while it was banked up as it did when the snow was away. Old Drew once went to Newport and hired himself out to do journeyman's work. The overseer came into the shop in the afternoon, and noticing for the first time the peculiar workmanship of his newly hired man, remarked that the shoe he was just finishing off was the worst looking thing that was ever made in his shop. "What will you bet on that," queried Drew. "Five dollars," was the reply. "Done," said Drew, and opening a drawer, drew out the mate of the shoe he was just finishing, that he made in the forenoon. The man merely glanced at it and paid the five dollars without demur, telling Drew as he handed him the money that he might also keep the shoes he had made, in lieu of wages.

Opposite the base of Chimney Hill on the east, there lies an irregular arm of Pettaquamscutt river, about a mile in length called "the Cove," in which rises very abruptly a high pile of rocks covered with forest trees, known as "Gooseberry Island." Since my remembrance a French recluse or hermit made his home for some time in a granite cleft on this island. From his martial bearing and dignified demeanor, he was thought by some to have been one of Bonaparte's officers, who had been compelled, from some unknown cause, to flee his country, and whose brain had become shattered through the pressure of dire misfortune.

A furlong further north-west of the picturesque island

bordering a salt marsh on the Cove may be seen the "Robert Hunnohill Meadow," so named from the following appalling circumstance. A negro boy ran away from his master of that name, who gave out word among the blacks, "that if the boy returned home he would not whip him!" The boy came back on this promise, when his master said to him, "I will not whip thee, Peter, but I will tie thee up and let the mosquitoes bite thee!" The poor boy was accordingly tied just at night to a stake driven firmly into the salt marsh, where in the morning, his thoughtless or hard-hearted master, found him stone-dead, having been bitten to death by innumerable mosquitoes that infested the marsh.

CHAPTER XVI.

To return again: looking from McSparran Hill, Block Island is plainly to be seen in all its breadth, some twenty miles to the south, with Montauk Point, the eastern extremity of Long Island, lying some few leagues to the westward of it. From this point, too, if unbroken tradition can be relied upon, there was formerly seen occasionally at night the "Palatine ship" all in flames, hovering about the island, where the legend asserts a ship freighted with emigrants and their effects from Germany in the first half of the eighteenth century was purposely—as some said—run on shore by her captain and crew, for the sake of plunder, whilst others said that the vessel was decoyed one dark stormy night by means of false lights arranged by the islanders with like intent. I remember hearing, when quite young, of an islander by the name of ———, who was generally well and in his right mind except at the season of the year when the Palatine ship was wrecked, and after being stripped of everything of value was set on fire by the land pirates and burned with all the crew and passengers on board. At this particular season this old man, it was said, always became madly insane, and would rave about seeing a ship all ablaze, with men falling from her burning rigging and shrouds, and ever and anon shrink in horror from the spectres of two women, whose hands he cut off or disabled by blows from a cutlass, as they sought to cling to the gunwale of the last boat that left the burning ship and all on board to their fate that not one might remain alive to bear witness of the terrible catastrophe and crime. Whether the legend is true or false I know not, though I do know that many Block Islanders, in my early days, firmly believed that the burning Palatine ship was often seen near the island.

My father became possessed, by will of his uncle, Rowland Robinson, of two or more farms on Block Island, which he leased for some years, and finally sold to several different purchasers. This gave occasion for some of the leading and most intelligent men, as well as others from Block Island, to visit our house in Narragansett, and sometimes pass the night. Of course I was always curious to hear about the old Palatine ship, and I do not remember an instance wherein these several visitors did not bear testimony to the verity of the phenomenon. On one occasion I remember asking the late George Sheffield, who had just arrived at our house from Block Island, what he thought the weather would be, to which he replied that it would continue fair, but directly hesitated, and said to Shedrick Card—a venerable old patriarch, who happened to accompany him—, "Mr. Card, the old Palatine loomed up high last night, didn't she?" Mr. Card answered in the affirmative, when the other rejoined, addressing his words to me, "I was mistaken; it will be stormy soon." It was evident that neither of these men, both of whom were very intelligent, had the least doubt of their having seen the ship all in flames the night before, and that her *bona fide* appearance was no more than an ordinary occurrence.

Since the conclusion of these papers in printed form, I have received a very interesting letter from Mr. Benjamin Congdon, who, I remember, lived many years ago in a house that stood north of the Walcott farm and west of the road in Point Judith. Mr. Congdon is now in his ninetieth year and was considered by all who knew him in Rhode Island to be a man of unusual intelligence and probity. I make the following extracts from his letter which is dated "Napoli, Cattaraugus Co., New York, March 4, 1878."

"In 1800, my elder brother attended Robert Rogers' Academy in Newport. I was then twelve years old. My father had a school kept in a small house, on our farm, for a number of years, by the late Thomas Perry, who kept the best school I was ever in. Mr. Perry afterwards moved to Westerly, and was chosen cashier of the Washington Bank, which position he retained until his death, when his son Charles succeeded him, who, I think, remains cashier of the same bank still, now seventy years since his father first assumed the same position. I can recollect well when Washington's second term expired, in 1797; when John Adams became President, followed by Jefferson, and then Madison, who was President during the War of 1812. About the burning Palatine ship you speak of in your interesting papers, I may say that I have seen her eight or ten times or more. In those early days nobody doubted her being sent by an Almighty Power to punish those wicked men who murdered her passengers and crew. After the last of these were dead she was never more seen. We lived when I was young, in Charlestown, directly opposite Block Island, where we used to have a plain view of the burning ship."

Nearly the whole of the southern coast of Narragansett, extending from Point Judith light to Watch Hill, a distance of twenty miles, in almost one continuous beach, against which the Atlantic waves never cease to roll, can be both seen and often heard from the point on McSparran Hill where the party rested. Looming up some ten miles to the south-west may also be distinctly seen " Broad Hill," the highest point in the district called " the Hills," which embraces some thirty square miles or more of territory, bounded partly on the north and west by the shores of Worden's Pond, a lake several miles in circumference, the northern and north-western extremities of which approach what is called the " Great Swamp," where the terrible Indian fight took place in 1675, that was instigated solely by the Puritan and other bigots of Massachusetts and Connecticut.

This lovely region of hill and dale is dotted throughout with elevated lakes of pure and sparkling water—some of them perched on the very summit of conical hills—whose gravelly shores and mossy banks are fringed and studded with numerous trees, festooned with long pendant moss, with countless evergreens of laurel, rhododendron and the all glorious kalmia species, which in early summer, while in full bloom, might well, when added to the wild, sweet solitude and wierd, heath-like aspect of everything around, lead the beholder to fancy he was trespassing on the charmed domain of some fairy queen. Looking more than twenty miles over the country lying to the west and north-west, the eye rests on many objects of interest, "Bernuse Neck Hill," the highest elevation in the southern half of Rhode Island, among others.

As her kind conductors repeatedly changed the position of the litter, Mrs. Simons was enabled to see in succession, within a short space of time, most of the lovely landscapes and ocean scenery I have endeavored to portray—in what readers must accept as one long parenthsis—, with hundreds of other objects of interest that went to fill up the lovely picture that can be described but partially in detail.

"Old Benny" told me that Mrs. Simons was observed to fix her eyes with interest on a withered bunch of what is called life-everlasting, that grew a few feet from the big boulder on the north side, and that she finally sent Hannah to pluck a sprig of it and pin it on the bosom of her dress.

From the hill the poor invalid looked down toward the east, directly on the enchanting river that winds its course below. On its western bank stood the glebe manse, where she had passed so many happy days in her girlhood at her Aunt McSparran's. Directly in the valley beneath the precipitous declivity grew a thickly-planted orchard of wide-spreading apple-trees, intermingled with the peach, pear, cherry and sweet-smelling locust, all in full bloom, and made vocal by the songs of thousands of birds, humming insects and murmuring bees, that seemed in the *tout ensemble* like some gigantic fairy nosegay, embowering in its midst the mystic harp of a thousand strings, each toned by angel fingers, the rich, ascending incense and melody of which were almost too enrapturing for finite senses to partake of and endure. A little copse of wild honey-suckle and native roses were growing within a few yards of the litter, amidst which a pair of heavenly-tinted humming-birds were buoying themselves in the air with rapid wings, invisible like those of the angels, while with their little bills they gathered sweets as they imperceptibly sped from flower to flower. All around the same rocky pasture in which the party was gathered, lay scattered here and there groups of sheep listlessly chewing the cud, while scores of romping lambs, as is their wont at the sun declining time of day and early summer-tide, gathered ever and anon, on an adjoining ledge, and, at a signal known only to kind nature and themselves, would scamper away at their utmost speed across the field to another mound, where, after gamboling awhile and caressing each other in playful sport, they would bound again and again back and forth to their self-appointed goals.

From old Benny Nichols' account, Mrs. Simons' last return to her parental home must have chanced on one of those rare, halcyon days, in which nature's elements are so nicely attuned that the senses of sight and hearing seem to vie with each other in their respective powers, and the one takes cognizance of sounds almost as readily as the other of objects at like distance. It is recorded that somewhat such a state of the atmosphere prevailed at the time a great fire occurred at Ceuta, in Africa, when the cries of the firemen were heard across the water at Gibraltar, eleven miles distant. I have heard, too, old people relate how some men who were engaged in mowing on the eastern shore of Boston Neck all at once heard another gang of workmen conversing in their natural tone of voice on the opposite shore of Conanicut, full two miles away, and that then the two parties engaged in conversation as readily as if they had been but a few rods apart. Suddenly, however, no answer was returned from the opposite shore, even when their voices were pitched at the highest key.

As has been said before, Narragansett, and especially Boston Neck and the Tower Hill country, were famous in those days for the extent and excellence of their dairies. It was about time for the evening milking, and in almost every direction for miles around herds of idly lowing cows were lazily wending their way to the farm-houses, followed by loitering boys who ever and anon sauntered out of their way, hither and thither, to an isolated bush or hassock, to spy out some blackbird's eggs, or mayhap peek closely about the sides of moss-covered stones or old imprints of cattle's feet for the nests of eggs or younglings of meadow-larks or little ground sparrows, and then, to help redeem lost time, hurry up their charges with renewed vigor. Old Nichols used to tell me that he could hear these boys halloo to their herds when two miles or more away, and what seemed strange to him, the sounds reached his ear with equal distinctness, come from what quarter they might, whether "Get up, old bug-horn" came from the north of the hill, "Go along, you old Daisy" from the east, "Why don't you hurry, old Crumple" from the south, or "Move along, old Full-pail" from the west.

Two fishermen who had gone down in separate canoes from the bridge to the river's mouth to catch tautog—the Indian name for blackfish—, and were lazily singing a roundelay to while away time as their boats floated slowly homeward on the incoming tide, could be seen and their voices heard with equal distinctness as they sang their alternate parts, although the nearer boat was a mile distant from the hill and the other more than half as much further down the river.

Mr. Robinson's house stood a mile and more, on an air-line, in an easterly direction from where the party rested, and yet Nichols plainly identified old black "Scip" chopping wood near the door, and could see the glimmering axe fall on the log some seconds before the sound of the blow reached the hill, which was seemingly conveyed through the air in a packet that exploded with a sharp clap directly as it reached his ear. What seemed stranger to the old man than all was the barking of a big watch-dog some two miles away, across the river, at the old brick house then owned and occupied by Amos Gardiner, and which is yet standing. Nichols said that the watch-dog to the east of the hill, apparently, never barked but in response to the baying of a foxhound that was roaming in a big wood lying not less that two miles to the westward and northward of where he stood, making the distance between the two animals some four miles, with the McSparran elevated hill intervening. Of this fact he felt tolerably sure, as there were occasionally lengthy invervals when both dogs were quiet, which were never broken until the hound uttered his howl, which was on the instant replied to by the hoarse bark of the distant watch-dog.

Directly after the party rested, the old man observed a wanton stripling in the valley beneath, fire his gun at a kill-deer—a species of snipe—that was winging its way toward the summit of the hill, and soon it wavered in its flight, as if wounded, and fluttered to the ground in an adjoining field. Some half hour after this occurrence he heard " every now and then" a faint peeping over the wall in the next field, followed by a rustling as if made by agitated straw, which he could not account for. Mrs. Simons' quick sense of hearing soon caught the unusual sounds, when she sent the old man on a reconnoitering expedition to find the cause. Following the direction of the sounds, after getting over a high wall, Nichols soon came to a nest on the ground beside a rock, in which were four half-fledged birds, a few feet from which lay on its side the kill-deer that the thoughtless boy, had hurt. It was the mother of the young brood, that had been striving to reach and convey to her nestlings a slug which was yet held in its beak, but had fallen on the way from exhaustion, just as it was about to reach them and minister to their wants. The poor bird, however, still continued to utter occasional plaintive notes that were always answered by a shuffling or rustling sound made by the half-feathered wings of her brood in the nest. This could not last, and after making two or three more struggles, each succeeding one weaker than the last, the mother-bird in its latest agonies dropped the slug from its bill and died.

On the old man's return he told Mrs. Simons that he could not learn the cause of the noises they had heard, and as neither the plaintive cry nor the answering rustling sounds occurred again, she was apparently satisfied. On my asking old Benny how he could tell Mrs. Simons such a falsehood the considerate old man replied that "if he told her all about the old kill-deer and her young'uns, he was afeard it would made the poor sick lady feel kinder bad!"

As the sun declined Mr. Robinson again and again tenderly suggested to his sick daughter the danger to be apprehended from the evening air, but still he had not the heart to resist the pleading look she always gave him in response. The party lingered on the rock, and it was not until after the booming evening gun from Fort George, in Newport harbor, had met and mingled its roar with the dirge-like note of the less distant fern owl, that always begins its mournful song exactly as the sun goes down, that the reluctant invalid seemed willing to depart. Even then she motioned to the carriers of her litter to pause while she turned her face from the golden-tinged horizon in the west, and once more followed with her eyes the rich plumaged summer ducks and other water-fowl, as they winged their way up the river to seek their nightly repose in the sequestered nooks of the lake above, where, even after these were lost to sight in the evening shades, their whizzing wings could be heard, as each new arriving bevy circled around for a while in the air, as if for the purpose of reconnoitering, and then dashed into the wave billing and cooing to each other ere they composed themselves to rest. At last, after casting one long, wistful look toward the still roseate west, and murmuring to herself, "It is the last time," Mrs. Simons motioned to her attendants to proceed on their circuitous way.

CHAPTER XVII.

With quickened pace, the bearers of Mrs. Simons' litter—so soon to be her hearse—passed onward to the old post-road that lies on the western side of McSparran Hill, and then south to the precipitous road before spoken of in connection with "Crazy Harry Babcock." This hill they descended and soon reached Pettaquamscutt bridge. Here, at Mrs. Simons' request, the litter was again set down for a few minutes, that her ear might once more drink in the low, sweet murmurings of the now gently surging billows on the distant beach, borne by the calm summer air on the unruffled waters of the river that washed her father's shore, where in happy childhood's days she had so often laved her hands and feet, and which was rendered by a thousand tender recollections more precious in her memory than all the helicons of ancient or modern lore.

The moon, which was little past the full, had just begun to cast its light above the eastern horizon as the party reached the top of the hill that rises in Boston Neck less than a mile east of Pettaquamscutt river and lake. Here, too, the party again halted, that the sick lady's wish might be gratified in once more beholding the moon rising from beyond the sea. As it began to emerge from the ocean its first beams of light were reflected from the top of McSparran Hill where the party had previously rested, and, as the orb ascended in the horizon, its advancing rays chased before them the shadows downward on the eastern slope of the hill, and again through the valley and over the river below, and still again upward on the western side of the elevated ridge where the party now were, until hills, valley, river and lake were all aglow with its mellow beams. This beautiful phenomenon the nearly exhausted invalid, with her quick perception of all that is lovely in nature, particularly noticed and contrasted with what she had observed less than an hour before when on the summit of McSparran Hill, wherein, as the setting sun gradually sank beneath the western horizon the shadows, on the contrary, seemed to chase its retreating light up the hill, where the party now rested, from the river and valley below, until the last gleam of sunshine fled away before them. Looking over the ocean, now lighted up with a silvery sheen, the spread sails of the vessels, lying in the distance—becalmed and heedlessly rolling on the everlasting swell of the sea, waiting for a breeze—that had so recently glistened under the reflected rays of the setting sun in the west, were now reflected and cast into shadow by the rays of the same god of day reflected from the moon as it rose from its watery couch in the east.

As the party drew near the house, which was not until late in the evening, they were met by the whole family, every member of whom was anxious to see the returning invalid, who had in years past been its light and joy. The meeting of the servants, and especially of Mrs. Simons' old nurse, Mum Amey, with their beloved young mistress, was affecting to behold. The poor invalid, however, now too weak to respond to their affectionate and tearful greetings, was, with as little delay as possible, tenderly carried in her father's arms and placed in her own chamber and bed, and everything done for her comfort that mortal love could suggest.

But all was without avail, and it soon became apparent that a marked change had taken place in her condition. The long journey, added to the excitement with which it was attended, proved too much for her weakened vital powers to sustain. Before the hour of midnight arrived, a raging fever set in, in the delirium of which her mind reverted to the days when her unworthy husband, under vows of everlasting love, beguiled her from her home and friends, and afterward abandoned her to misery and despair. But now it seemed as if the months and years of sorrow she had experienced because of his cruel neglect, were blotted from her memory, and she in her distempered fancy again beheld him as in by-gone days, when, from the window of the same chamber, she dropped tender billet-doux into her false lover's hand, as he stood at even-tide, hidden from view amidst the branches of the lilac tree. She called wildly on his name that he would come and defend her from her—now, alas, wretched—father's wrath and vengeance, incurred by her for the true love she had ever cherished in her heart for him alone.

At about the hour of midnight a whip-poor-will, called by the Indians muck-a-wiss—*come to me*—,perched on the eave of the house, opposite the lilac tree, and commenced its mournful cry of " Whip-poor-will, whip-poor-will !" This bird of the night, though common in Narragansett, is seldom known to visit the islands. Not long since I asked a Quaker lady, who had lived more than seventy years on Rhode Island, if she had ever heard a whip-poor-will on the island. " Never but twice," she replied; " once on the night that my father died, and again on the night preceding the day on which I lost my mother." The ominous cry of the bird for a short time seemed to change the current of the poor sufferer's thoughts. Pausing and listening for a few moments, she exclaimed, " Hark ! mother ! do you hear the death angel calling ? He is out in the lilac tree, mother ! He has come to take me away and marry me, mother ! It will be a sad wedding day, but not so sad as that other, dear mother !" Then turning her attention to the withered flower on her bosom, she said, " He told me, when he gave it me, that we must call it, not life everlasting, but love everlasting ! Lay it with me in my grave, mother, that I may take it to the land where life is everlasting and where love never dies!"

As the sun rose in the morning, the malady in the poor sufferer's brain subsided, and left her weak and helpless. With faltering breath and feeble accent she asked to have the different articles of dress in her scanty wardrobe, and the few trinkets and keepsakes she had not been obliged in her extremity of poverty to part with, to be laid upon the bed that she might distribute them with her own hand, or indicate to whom they should be severally given; but the task was too much for her fast failing strength, and the utmost she could accomplish was to place in her mother's hand a cambric handkerchief she had embroidered especially for her, with a family watch-seal for her brother, then absent at school, and lastly, a pair of gloves, the latest work of her own hands, into those of her father. She then intimated with the aid of signs that she wished all her other little effects to be distributed among the servants of the household. This done, with a feeble, ineffectual outstretch of her arms, first to her mother and then to her father, as they by turns pressed the last kiss on her lips, the exhausted invalid settled back on her pillow and resigned herself to die.

Quicker and quicker grew her gasping breath, as she lay partly raised and supported in her mother's arms on the one side, while her agonized father, kneeling beside the bed on the other, held her extended hand in his. A few minutes before she breathed her last, she cast her penetrating eyes upon her mother with an unutterable expression of affection, and then fixing them on her father, she continued to look lovingly and steadfastly in his, until they closed in death.

The struggle is nigh over! Faster and still faster the sufferer draws her labored breath; the fell death-rattle gives its fatal warning; a distressful tension of the muscles of the face from the sides of the nostrils downward; a corrugation of the cuticle between the eyebrows; a convulsive parting of the lips; a spasmodic writhing "contrawise" of the jaws; a wider opening of the mouth; one long, last sigh; one!—two!—three!—four faint breaths!—fainter!—*fainter!* still fainter—yet fainter still!—'tis!—yes; the light has gone out of the sunken eye; the tension of the poor pale cheeks has ceased; the cold dew is on the marble brow; the hue of death is stamped upon the temples; its pale blue lines are penciled around the mouth; the feather placed upon the violet lips " makes no sign;" the glass gathers no moisture; 'tis the last: the " silver cord" that binds the immortal to the mortal is broken, and the freed soul, borne in angel arms, has sped its way to heaven.

Just before the close, old nurse Mum Amey, who had been in tearful attendance ever since the arrival home of her young mistress, and who was held by Dr. McSparran, on account of her fortune-telling pretensions, to be uncanny, raised her eyes from the face of her dying mistress and with a look of devout admiration exclaimed, " De angels is come." Mrs. Simons' favorite little spaniel Marcus had lain in her litter throughout the whole journey from Providence, nor could the affectionate creature be pacified after the arrival of its mistress home, until it was permitted to lie on the foot of her bed. It, too, just before Mum Amey made her singular exclamation, raised itself on his fore feet and gazed earnestly by turns, first into the face of its dying mistress and then apparently on the ceiling of the room just over her head, as if there might be some weird-like impression made on the wall so like its mistress that the loving animal found it difficult to decide to which her proper identity belonged. If it be true, as it is held by some, that the lower animals, and especially those of the canine species, are instinctively gifted with the extraordinary faculty of " second sight," as it is termed in Scotland, the actions of the little spaniel, when viewed in connection with the exclamation of old nurse Mum Amey, might be very suggestive.

Dr. Robert Hazard, the family physician, who had been sent for at an early hour the night before, expressed his belief that the death of his lovely cousin was not the result of any organic disease, but was caused simply by a deep-seated, consuming sorrow. Old nurse Mum Amey evidently coincided with the doctor's views in these respects, for when asked a few days after the funeral, " What ailed her young mistress when she died?" she answered, " Nothin' ail Missus Hannah. Dis world wer eny jes too hard for her, an' de poor chile die ob de heart break!"

While listening to the mournful surge of the sea when her litter was set down on Pettaquamscutt bridge, the evening before her decease, Mrs. Simons, as if aware of her impending fate, expressed a wish to her father that in the event of her death her remains might be carried to the family vault in the litter she was then lying in, and by the same four affectionate man-servants who had borne her from Providence. This request was strictly complied with. The funeral was conducted after the order of the society of Friends, Mrs. Simons' uncle and aunt, Thomas Hazard and his wife, being present. The former, as has been before said, was an eminent preacher among Friends, and he delivered, on the trying occasion, a pertinent and consoling discourse to the bereaved friends. The remains were placed in the old family vault.

The grief of Mr. Robinson on the occasion of the early death of his dearly loved and favorite child could not be described in language by the most gifted pen. For weeks after her remains were laid away in the family vault, the wretched father passed a large portion of his time in sitting on a stone near its entrance, or in wandering to and fro in its vicinity. Not an evening passed that he did not go to the vault, and there, if his countenance and eyes afforded a fair index on his return to his house late at night, he passed hours in weeping. As in life so in death the little dog, Marcus, refused to be separated from its mistress, nor could the faithful creature be induced by any proffers of kindness to leave the spot where the remains of its loved mistress were deposited. It alike refused to partake of food or drink, but there lay for days and nights until the poor thing died from sheer starvation in a cavity it had scratched, and from day to day deepened, in the ground just beneath the door-way of her tomb. In this grave of the affectionate brute's own digging it was one morning found dead by Mr. Robinson, and was therein buried with its master's own hands, after being carefully wrapped in the linen case from off the pillow on which its mistress' head last lay.

On the evening preceding the morning on which Marcus was found dead, Mr Robinson paid his usual nightly pilgrimage to the vault and sat down on the accustomed stone to weep. Hitherto the little dog had never greeted the coming of its master otherwise than by a feeble moan. On this occasion, however, the emaciated creature with difficulty made its way, reeling through weakness, to its master's feet. Then, after resting its head against the sorrowing father's knees and fixing its eyes for several minutes steadily in his, the dying brute faltered its way back to the door of the vault, and with one prolonged, wailing howl, so melancholy, so desparing, again threw itself into its self-appointed grave.

On his speedy return to the house the distracted mourner recited the incident to his wife, and in words rendered almost unintelligible through emotion, declared to her that if he ever looked into Hannah's eyes, he was sure he had just now seen them gazing into his through those of her little dog, with exactly the same loving expression with which she had regarded him at the moment of her death. He also said he was sure that the last howl of the poor animal was mingled with wailing accents, in which he could distinguish poor Hannah's voice, and that it must have come from her tomb. Nor would the half-crazed father be satisfied until, accompanied by Prince with the key and a lantern, he entered the vault and had the lid of the coffin unfastened and lifted, when the calm, rigid features of his idolized child, yet beautiful in death, conveyed to the grief-riven heart of the father unmistakable evidence that the spirit which so late gave them life had indeed taken its eternal departure from its mortal tenement.

A new and larger vault, which had been for some time previous to Mrs. Simons' death in the process of building, was, shortly after the sad event, completed, into which the remains of Mrs. Simons were temporarily placed, while those of the affectionate little spaniel were removed and reinterred at the foot of its mistress' grave.

Some days before this last sad ceremony was performed, Mr. Peter Simons, who had for some months been absent in distant parts, returned to Providence, when he for the first time learned the decease of his heart-broken wife. A regard for decency, and perhaps some remorse of conscience, or it may have been some lingering sentiments of affection, prompted him to call at his father-in-law's, to be present, if permitted, at the removal of the body of Mrs. Simons to the newly erected tomb. On his arrival at the family mansion, Mr. Robinson received him with courtesy, but after asking him to partake of the hospitalities of the house while he remained his guest, he never after, during the days Mr. Simons stayed, spoke a word to him, until the morning on which his daughter's remains were removed, and then only to notify him briefly of his intentions in that respect.

The following communication from a lady, Miss E. G. H., a family connection of Rowland Robinson, of Narragansett, appeared in the Newport Mercury some score or more years ago:

THE DEATH OF HANNAH ROBINSON.

In Mr. Updike's entertaining miscellany, entitled a "History of the Narragansett Church," among other attractive narratives, is a short biographical sketch of the Robinson family, and particularly of a granddaughter of Gov. William Robinson, celebrated in her time for her unequaled beauty and the unhappy consequences of a romantic and ill-starred marriage. Mr. Updike represents her father, Rowland Robinson, as possessed of a relentless, unforgiving spirit, which even the dying hours of his unfortunate daughter could scarely propitiate. This we are assured, is altogether incorrect, and does great injustice to the character of Mr. Robinson, who, though impetuous and overbearing in temper, was far from being vindictive. In the following lines, by a fair descendant of Governor Robinson, the reverse of this picture is presented, uniting, as will be seen, in no ordinary degree, the attractiveness of poetry to the strictness of historical truth.

It was a lovely evening, and the golden light of summer
Was on the hill, and on the plain, and on the flowing river.
The blue and silver gleams, that checker'd o'er the bay,
Had passed from off the waters, that in sombre shadows lay.
The mother, from the lattice, looked to the distant road,
And blessed the coming footsteps that neared her proud abode.
Soft pillowed on a litter, on sturdy shoulders borne,
Slow came the much-loved daughter, a wreck on her return.
Stately, on a courser, did her father slowly ride,
With look of love and anxious care still watching at her side.
And now the home of childhood uprose before her view,
The panes of gold bright shining, the shading branches through,
The fields spread soft and verdant where in infancy she played,
And all the air seemed whispering of hope and love betrayed.
"Now set me down, my father, upon the much-loved ground,
Now set me down, my father, and let me look around.
'Tis beautiful! 'tis beautiful! what visions o'er me hover!
Oh, days of love and peace and joy, how have you passed forever!
Now ask me all, my father! now ask me all thou may:
Thy sorrow-stricken daughter shall not now thee gainsay."
Fast fell the tears and faster upon that beauteous head,
Strong feeling swayed within his breast but not a word he said.
"Father, I know that sorrow has crushed thy spirit strong;
I know my blighted love has wrought thee mighty wrong,
But oh! be kind, my father, to him who called me bride.
Remember that I loved him, and oh, forget thy pride.
Forgive the wrong he wrought me, my early death and woe,
And in all his troubles, still kindness to him show.
Remember me, thy daughter, thy blessed and early pride,
Remember that I loved him, although through him I died."
The golden sun, uprising, shone on a beauteous corpse,

There stood the father in his grief, the spouse in his remorse;
And through the pitying multitude, the busy murmur ran,
As they looked upon the smitten sire, and conscience-stricken man;
But keen reproach, or bitter taunt, the father's lips ne'er spoke,
Tho' from that day the cheerful smile on the mother's face ne'er broke.
And when the moon had filled her horn and the crescent shone again,
And the finished vault had ope'd its doors, its first fair dead to claim;
"To-morrow," said the sorrowing sire, "our daughter, we'll remove,
Again we'll look upon the face of her, our dearest love."
And early when the morrow came, the grave they then unclose,
And from the face the veil remove, lo! beautiful it glows,
The bloom of beauty from her cheek had not yet passed away,
Nor on the graceful moulded form, the signet of decay,
But calm and beautiful as sleep had folded in her arms
The treasure of the parents' heart in all her early charms.
Then passed the husband from the roof, a wand'rer on the sea,
And in daring, bold and cruel strife closed his dark destiny.

  Newport, R. I.   E.

Genealogy of the Robinson Family.

CHAPTER XVIII.

The following genealogical facts have been mainly furnished by Jeremiah P. Robinson, Esq., of New York, with an elaborate chart of the Narragansett Robinson Family, to the compilation of which his friend and kinsman, the late Stephen Ayrault Robinson, of Wakefield, R. I., devoted much time during the latter years of his life. With revisals and some additions as will appear, the following is a transcript of the chart, including the caption and preface attached by its compiler. Mr. S. Ayrault Robinson collected a vast amount of interesting reminiscences of the ancient family, which, it is to be hoped, will be embodied in a volume and given to the public.

GENEALOGICAL CHART OF THE

Robinson Family of Narragansett, as arranged by the late Stephen Ayrault Robinson, of Wakefield, formerly of Newport, R. I.

ROWLAND ROBINSON, the primitive of our family in this country, was born in 1654, at or near a place called Long Bluff, in Cumberland, England. He came to this country in 1675, married Mary, the daughter of John and Mary Allen, in 1676, who were from Barnstable, England. Her mother's name before marriage was Bacon, who was born also in Barnstable. Rowland Robinson died at his residence, situated near the pond or cove of Pettaquamscutt river, in 1716, aged 62 years. His wife was born in 1656, and died in 1706, aged 50 years. They were both buried in the Narragansett Friends—called Quakers—burial ground, Kingston—now South Kingstown—, about two miles south of Tower Hill village. Their graves are in the north-east corner of the burial ground. Mr. Robinson purchased lands of the Narragansetts soon after he came into their country; here he settled and improved the land until his death. He also purchased largely in the Pettaquamscutt and Point Judith lands. On these lands he built several houses and lived in one of them for some years. In the records of the town of Westerly for 1709, is recorded a deed of three thousand acres of the Wood River lands, purchased by Rowland Robinson. These lands he sold in farms containing from one hundred and fifty to three hundred acres each. Portions of his Pettaquamscutt and Point Judith estates have descended uninterruptedly from father to children until the present time, 1870.

Rowland Robinson's children were as follows:

1. JOHN, born in 1677; married Mary Hazard in 1703; died in 1711, aged 34 years. His wife died in 1722, aged 46 years. He left four daughters, all of whom were brought up in Gov. William Robinson's family. One of them married a Hazard, and was the mother of one of the Stephen Hazards. Another married a Babcock.

2. JOSEPH, born in 1679; died in infancy.

3. ELIZABETH, born in 1680; married William Brown in 1698. She died in 1745, aged 64 years. Mr. Brown died in 1749, aged 73 years. They left children, Thomas Brown and others.

4. MARGARET, born in 1683; married Thomas Mumford in 1703. She died in 1707, aged 23 years. Mr. Mumford died in 1745, aged 66 years. They left children, James among others.

5. SARAH, born in 1685; married Rufus Barton in 1712. She died in 1760, aged 76 years. Mr. Barton died in 1743,

aged 70 years. They left children, Rowland, Rufus, and others.

6. ROWLAND, born in 1688; died in 1693, aged 5 years.

7. MERCY, born in 1690; married Col. John Potter in 1714. She died in 1762, aged 72 years. Colonel Potter died in 1739, aged 50 years. They left children.

8. WILLIAM, born in 1693; married Martha Potter in 1717. She died in 1725, aged 33 years. He married his second wife, Mrs. Abigail G. Hazard—widow of Caleb Hazard and daughter of William Gardiner—in 1727 or 1728. William Robinson died in 1751, aged 58 years. His second wife died in 1773, aged 76 years.

9. MARY, born in 1705; married Thomas C. Hazard in 1727. She died in 1756, aged 51 years. Mr. Hazard died in 1750, aged 47 years. They left children.

10. ROWLAND, born in 1706; died in infancy.

11. SARAH, born in 1707; married Charles Babcock in 1725. She died in 1744, aged 37 years. Mr. Babcock died in 1755, aged 55 years. They left children.

12. RUTH, born in 1709; married Robert Underwood in 1728. She died in 1758, aged 49 years. Mr. Underwood died in 1763, aged 58 years. They left children.

The children of GOV. WILLIAM ROBINSON—eighth son of ROWLAND—by his first wife, Martha Potter, were:

1. *Rowland*, born in 1719; married Anstis Gardiner in 1741. " December 3. 1741, the bans being duly published in the church of St. Paul's, Narragansett, Rowland Robinson, son of William, was married to Anstis Gardiner, daughter of John Gardiner, by the Rev. Dr. McSparran." *Updike's History of the Narragansett Church, page 188.* Mr. Robinson died in 1806, aged 87 years. Mrs. Robinson died in 1785, aged 68 years. The children of Rowland Robinson were: 1. Hannah, born in 1746; married Peter Simons. Mrs. Simons died in 1773. Soon after her death Mr. Simons went to Europe, and never returned to America. Miss Robinson

was celebrated for her beauty. 2. Mary, born in 1752; died in 1777. 3. William R., born in 1759; married Ann Scott, 1784; died 1804, aged 45 years. Mrs. Robinson afterward married Doctor John Mann, and died in 1839, aged 76 years, without issue.

2. *John*, born in 1721; died in 1739.

3. *Margaret*, born in 1722; married William Mumford in 1745. She died in 1768, aged 46 years. Mr. Mumford died in 1790, aged 69 years. They left children. [Benjamin R. Smith, of Philadelphia, writes me that in a memorandum in his possession, enumerating by name and order of birth the children of Gov. William Robinson, the name of Margaret does not appear The memorandum is in the handwriting of Thomas Robinson—Mr. Smith's grandfather—a son of Gov. William, and this fact renders it the more probable that there is some mistake in the names.]

4. *Elizabeth*, born in 1724; married Thomas Hazard in 1745. She died in 1804, aged 79 years. Mrs. Hazard died at the Doctor Senter house, south-east corner of the Parade and Thames street, and was buried in the Friends' burial ground in Newport. Mr. Hazard died at his homestead in South Kingstown in 1795, aged 76 years, and was buried in the Friends old burying ground in South Kingstown.

5. *Martha*, born in 1725; married Latham Clarke in 1747. She died in 1768. Mr. Clarke died in 1776, aged 60 years. They left children: Martha, who was the second wife of John Hazard, of North Kingstown, and a woman of strong intellect and sterling character; Samuel; Louis Latham; Hannah, born April 19, 1760. Hannah married Peleg Gardiner—his second wife—, October 26, 1791. Her children were: Martha Clarke, born September 10, 1795, who married Rowland F. Gardiner and died December 19, 1837; Hannah Robinson, born June 3, 1798, married Robert Morey, and died June 3, 1869; Mary Ann, born November 15, 1800, who married Timothy Clarke Collins and died in October, 1860. Peleg Gardiner owned the Rowland Robinson farm,

and there died. The family now have Rowland Robinson's family Bible containing among many other entries in his own handwriting, the following: "William Robinson, died 19th Sept., 1751, aged 57 years, 7 months, 27 days;" "Martha, wife of William, diep November, 1725;" "My daughter, Hannah Robinson, departed this life the 30th October, 1773, aged 27 years, 5 months, 9 days [Hannah Gardiner Morey, daughter of Robert Morey, has now in her possession four silver spoons that belonged to the 'unfortunate Hannah Robinson']"; "Anstis Gardiner, wife of Rowland Robinson, died November 24th, 1773;" " Mary, my daughter, died April 5th, 1777, aged 25 years, 1 month, 21 days;" "William, my son, died 29th October, 1804, aged 45 years;" "My beloved brother, John Robinson, died October 5, 1739." The foregoing extracts from Rowland Robinson's family Bible were kindly furnished me with others by William G. Caswell, of the State of New York, who married Sally C. Gardiner, daughter of Rowland F. Gardiner and Martha Clarke Gardiner, a lineal descendant by the mother's side of Gov. William Robinson.

6. *Christopher*—the first child of Gov. William Robinson by his second wife—, born in 1728; married Rhuhama Champlin in 1752; died in 1807, aged 79 years. Mrs. Robinson died in 1783, aged 52 years. Their children were: 1. Abigail, born 1754; married Stephen Potter 1772; died 1803, aged 49 years. Mr. Potter died in 1793, aged 43 years. The children of Stephen and Abigail Potter were: (a) Captain Robinson Potter, who married and had children. The first child, Elizabeth, married Dr. Theophilus Dunn, whose children were: Professor Robinson Dunn, Thomas, Theophilus, Elizabeth, Anne, who married Joscan Bennet and has children, and Frances, who married Dr. Keith. (b) Abigail, died unmarried. (c) A daughter, who married Captain Gardiner, of Newport, whose daughter married Silas H. Cottrell, and one other daughter who married a Chadwick. 2. Christopher Champlin, born 1756; married Elizabeth Anthony,

1790; died 1841, aged 87 years. Mrs. Robinson died in 1849, aged 79 years. The children of Christopher C. and Elizabeth Robinson were: (a) George C., born 1791; married Mary Niles Potter 1812; died at Canton, East Indies, 1827, aged 36 years. Mrs. Robinson died in 1870, aged 75 years, 10 months and 18 days. (b) Thurston, born 1793; married Sarah Perry 1823; died 1875, aged 82 years. Mrs. Robinson died 1874, aged 85 years. (c) Mary, born 1794; married John Brown 1815; died 1866, aged 72 years. Mr. Brown died 1834, aged 42 years; left children. (d) Harriet, born 1795; died 1796, aged 21 days. (e) Rhubama C., born 1797; married John Robinson 1821; died 1869, aged 71 years. Mr. Robinson died in 1841, aged 47 years. No children. (f) Elizabeth, born, 1799; died 1799, aged 3 months and 5 days. (g) Rodman G., born 1800; died 1841; unmarried. (h) Elizabeth A., born 1801; married Wm. B. Robinson 1830; died 1876. (i) Sally, born 1803; died 1816. (j) Elisha A., born 1804; married Mary Hull 1837. (k) Harriet, born 1807; married Wm. B. Robinson—his second wife—; died 1828. Mr. Robinson died 1875. (l) Frances Wanton, born 1809; died December, 1876; married Thomas Hazard Watson, son of Walter. The children of Thomas H. and Frances W. Watson were: Walter Scott, George Robinson, Caroline, Elizabeth and Thomas H. (m) Christopher, born 1810. (n) Albert, born 1812; married Hannah Pierce 1844; died 1856, aged 44 years. The children of Albert and Hannah Robinson were Albert C., born 1854, and George P., born 1856. Mrs. Robinson married for her second husband, William G. Kenyon. (o) William H. Robinson, born 1814; married Eliza Hazard 1841.

7. *William*—seventh child of Gov. William Robinson—, born 1729; married Hannah Brown 1752; died 1785, aged 56 years. Mrs. Robinson died in 1791, aged 60 years. The children of William and Hannah Robinson were: 1. Philip Robinson, born 1754; married Elizabeth Boynton 1779; died 1799, aged 45 years. Mrs. Robinson died in 1785, aged

26 years. They had one child, Samuel Boynton Robinson, born 1785; died 1794, aged 9 years. 2. Hannah, born 1756; married George Brown 1774; died 1823, aged 67 years. Lieut-Gov. George Brown died in 1836, aged 80 years. They left a large family of children, William, George, John, and several daughters, one of whom married Rowse Babcock, of Westerly.

8. *Thomas*—eighth child of Gov. William Robinson—, born 1730; married Sarah Richardson 1752; died 1817, aged 87 years. Mrs. Robinson died in 1817, aged 84 years.

9. *Abigail*, born in 1732, married John Wanton 1751; died 1754, aged 22 years. Mr. Wanton died in 1793, aged 65 years. They had only one child, which was buried in the same grave with the mother.

10. *Sylvester*, born in 1734; married Alice Perry in 1756; died in 1809, aged 75 years. Mrs. Robinson died in 1787, aged 50 years.

11. *Mary*, born in 1736; married John Dockray in 1756; died in 1776, aged 40 years. Mr. Dockray died in 1787, aged 56 years. Their children were: 1. John Bigelow; 2. James Dockray. John Bigelow Dockray married a daughter of William Congdon, and was the father of John, Nancy and Mary. The last named John Dockray married Mercy Peckham. Their children were: John, William, James, and Mary—all now living. Nancy married William Brown, a son of Governor George Brown. Their children were: Mary, Nancy, John, Hannah, Edward, and Susan.

12. *James*, born 1738; married Nancy Rodman.

13. *John*, born 1742; married Sarah Peckham 1761; died 1801. Mrs. Robinson died in 1775.

The children of Thomas Robinson—eighth child of Gov. WILLIAM ROBINSON—were:

1. William T., born 1754; married Sarah, daughter of Samuel Franklin, of New York City; died 1835, aged 81 years. Mrs. Robinson died in 1811, aged 52 years.

The children of William T. and Sarah Robinson were: 1. Esther, born in 1782, married Jonas Minturn, of New York—son of William Minturn, who married Penelope Greene, a near relative of General Nathaniel Greene. The late Robert Bowne Minturn, of the firm of Grinnell, Minturn & Co., New York, was the grandson of the above named William, and the son of William Minturn the second and Sally Bowne, daughter of Robert Bowne, of New York City. The children of Jonas and Esther Minturn were: (a) Elizabeth, born 1801; died young. (b) William, born 1802: drowned in a sailboat near New York, September 21, 1821. (c) Rowland, born 1804; died 1839; unmarried. (d) Caroline, born 1806, married David Prescott Hall, of New York. Their children were: John Mumford, Rowland Minturn, Caroline Minturn, Elizabeth Prescott, Frances Ann, and David Prescott. David Prescott Hall married Florence Howe, daughter of Dr. Samuel G. Howe, of Boston, and has children— Samuel Prescott, Caroline Minturn, and Henry Marion. (e) Thomas, born 1808; died unmarried, aged about 70 years. (f) Lloyd, deceased, born 1810, married Julia Randolph, of Newport, R. I.; second wife, Anne K. Robinson, of Ferrisburgh, Vt., whose children are named elsewhere. (g) Frances, born 1812; married Thomas R. Hazard, of Vaucluse, R. I. Their children were: Mary, died aged 27 months, Frances, Gertrude, Anna—the last three named all died in early womanhood—, Esther, who married Dr. E. J. Dunning, of New York, and Barclay, born in 1852. (h) Niobe, married Duncan Ferguson, of New York; had one child; Lucy, who died, aged 2 years; married, second, Ward H. Blackler, of New York, whose children were: Mary—who married Theodore Wright, of Philadelphia, and has one child—, Minturn, Gertrude, who died in early womanhood, and Edith Belliden. (i) Jonas, born 1819; married Abby West, of Bristol, R. I. Their children were: Rowland, Mary—married Charles Potter, of Newport, R. I., and has children, Charles,

20

Mary Minturn and Aracelia—, Thomas, Gertrude—married Captain George Sanford, U. S. Army, and has one daughter, Margaret—, Madeline, and James. (j) Agatha, married Edward Mayer, of Vienna, Austria, and has children, John, Lloyd, and William. (k) Gertrude, married William H. Newman, of New York City. All the above named daughters of Jonas and Esther Robinson Minturn are deceased.

2. Thomas—second child of William T. and Sarah Robinson—, attached himself to the fortunes of Aaron Burr, and died in Paris in early manhood, unmarried.

3. Samuel, unmarried, lost in a sailboat near New York, September 21, 1815.

4. Sarah, married Joseph S. Coates, of Philadelphia. Their children were: Joseph H. and Sarah R. Coates. Joseph H. married, first, Elizabeth W. Horner, who died without children; second, Sarah Ann Wisner. Their children were: Alma W., Ellen W., Arthur R., and Joseph S. Coates. Sarah R. Coates married Joshua Toomer, of Charleston, S. C., and has one child, Mary Ann.

5. Mary, married William Hunter, United States Minister to Brazil. Their children were: (a) William, married Sally Hoffman, daughter of General Smith, of Georgetown, D. C. The children of William and Sally H. Hunter were: Walter, Mary—married Richard H. Jones, of Cumberland, Md.·, Blanche, Irene, William, and Godfrey. (b) Eliza, married James Birckhead, of Rio Janeiro, Brazil. Their children were William, and Katherine. William Birckhead married Sarah King, of Newport, R. I., and has children—James, Philip, and Hugh. (c) Thomas R., married Mrs. Frances Wetmore Taylor, of New York City. Their children are: William, Elizabeth, Augusta, Mary, and Charles. (d) Mary, married Captain Piers, of the Royal Navy of Great Britain. (e) Charles, Commander U. S. Navy, married Miss Rotch, of New Bedford. Their children are: Catherine—married Thomas Dunn, of Newport, R. I.—, Caroline, Mary—married Walter Langdon Kane, of New York—, Anna Falconet. (f)

Catherine, married William Greenway, of Rio Janeiro, Brazil, whose son was Charles. (g) John, died in youth.

6. *Abby*—daughter of William T. and Sarah Robinson—, married Mr. Pierce ; both lost at sea.

7. *Franklin*, married and died in Alabama, leaving Mary, who died while at school in Newport, R. I., and other children.

8. *Nancy*, married John Toulmin, of Mobile, Ala., and left one child, Agatha.

9. *Rowland*, married and settled in Ohio, where he died highly respected, leaving several children.

10. *Eliza*, died in early womanhood, unmarried.

11. *William*, died in mature manhood, unmarried.

12. *Emma*, married John Grimshaw ; died 1878. They had a daughter, Emma, who married Benjamin Haviland, and had children—William Robinson, Gertrude, Ellen, and Frances.

2. *Thomas*—second son of Thomas Robinson, the eighth son of GOVERNOR WILLIAM—born 1756 ; died young.

3. *Mary*, born 1757 ; married John Morton, of Philadelphia, 1793 ; died in Philadelphia 1829. Mr. Morton died in Philadelphia 1828. Their children were : Esther, born 1797, Robert, born 1801 ; died unmarried 1848. Esther married Daniel B. Smith 1824. The children of Daniel B. and Esther Smith were : Benjamin R., born 1825, John, born 1828, died 1836, Mary, born 1830, died 1854. Benjamin R. Smith married Esther F. Wharton, 1859. Their children are : Robert Morton, born 1860, died 1864, William Wharton, born 1861, Anna Wharton, born 1864, Esther Morton, born 1865, Deborah Fisher, born 1869, died 1877, Edward Wanton, born 1875. Benjamin R. Smith inherited and now occupies as a summer residence the old homestead of his maternal ancestors in Newport, R. I.

4. *Abigail*, born 1760 ; died at an advanced age, unmarried.

5. *Thomas Richardson*, born 1761; married Jemima Fish 1783; died 1851, aged 90 years. Mrs. Robinson died in 1846, aged 85 years. They left children: 1. Abigail, married Nathan C. Hoag. Their children were: Rachel—married, no children—, Amy, unmarried, Thomas, married Huldah Case, Huldah, married Louis Estis, Jane, married Henry Miles, Joseph, Nathan, died young, Mary, married Daniel Clark. 2. Rowland T., married Rachel Gilpin, of New York. Their children were: (a) Thomas R., married Charlotte Satterly, and had children, William G., and Sarah R., who married William Harman. (b) George G. (c) Anne K., married Lloyd Minturn. Their children were: Rowland R., Agatha Barclay—married William R. Haviland—, and Frances. (d) Rowland E., married Anna Stevens.

6. *Rowland*, born 1763; lost at sea in early manhood; unmarried.

7. *Joseph Jacob*, born 1765; died at an advanced age, unmarried.

8. *Amy*, born 1768; married Robert Bowne, of New York. Their children were: George, who died unmarried, and Rowland, who left a daughter.

The children of Sylvester Robinson, son of Gov. WILLIAM ROBINSON, were:

1. *James*, born 1756; married Mary Attmore, of Philadelphia, in 1781; died 1841, aged 85 years. Mrs. Robinson died 1856, aged 86 years.

2. *Mary*, born 1763, married Jonathan N. Hassard, 1783; died 1837, aged 74 years. Mr. Hassard died 1802 in the West Indies, aged 42 years. He left children, Stephen, James, Alice, Jonathan N., Robinson, and Mary, and numerous grandchildren.

3. *Abigail*, born 1769; married Thomas H. Hazard 1789; died 1818, aged 49 years. Mr. Hazard died 1823, aged 61 years, and left children.

The children of James Robinson—ninth child of Gov. WILLIAM ROBINSON—were:

1. *Abigail*, born 1768; married John Robinson 1794; died 1805, aged 37 years. Mr. Robinson died in 1831, aged 64 years; left children.
2. *Ruth*, born 1769; was never married; died in 1839, aged 70 years.
3. *Mary*, born 1771; married John Bowers 1792; died 1826, aged 55 years. Mr. Bowers died 1819, aged 53 years; left children.
4. *Ann*, born 1772; died 1790, aged 17 years.
5. *James*, born 1774; died 1781, aged 7 years.

The children of John Robinson—the tenth and youngest child of Gov. WILLIAM ROBINSON—were:

1. *Benjamin*, born 1763, married Elizabeth Brown, daughter of Gov. George Brown, 1801; died 1830, aged 66 years. Mrs. Robinson died in 1855, aged 86 years.
2. *Sarah*, born in 1764; married John Taber 1789; died 1837, aged 73 years. Mr. Taber died in 1820, aged 62 years. They left children.
3. *William*, born 1766; married.
4. *John J.*, born 1767, married Abigail Robinson 1794; died 1831, aged 64 years. Mrs. Robinson died in 1805, aged 39 years. Mr. Robinson was at one time a partner with Rowland Hazard in the mercantile house of Hazard & Robinson, of Charleston, South Carolina.
5. *Sylvester*, born 1769; married; died in 1837, aged 68 years.
6. *Thomas*, born 1771; died 1786, aged 14 years.

3. George C.—third child of Christopher, son of Gov. WILLIAM ROBINSON—, born 1758; died 1780, aged 22 years. He was taken prisoner in the privateer Revenge in 1778, carried into New York and placed on board the prison-ship Jersey at the Wallabout, Long Island, N. Y., where he died with the prison fever, and was buried at that place.

4. Elizabeth—fourth child of Christopher—, born 1760; married Mumford Hazard, son of Simeon, 1786; died 1822,

aged 62 years. Mr. Hazard died in 1811, aged 55 years. They left no children.

5. William C., born 1763; married Frances Wanton 1794; died 1803, aged 40 years. Mrs. Robinson died in 1816, aged 43 years.

6. Jesse, born 1764; married Hannah T. Sands 1789; died 1808, aged 44 years. Mrs. Robinson died in 1848, aged 82 years.

7. Robert, born 1765; married Sarah Congdon 1795. She died in 1802, aged 26 years. Married Ann Deblois 1807. Mr. Robinson died in 1831, aged 66 years. Mrs. Robinson, his second wife, died in 1850, aged 68 years.

8. Hannah, born 1769; married John Perry 1787; died 1849, aged 80 years. Mr. Perry died in 1834, aged 69 years. Left children: Robinson Perry, of Wakefield, John G. Perry, of Kingston, Oliver Hazard, of Peace Dale, and several other sons and daughters.

9. Matthew, born 1772; married Mary S. Potter 1797 She died in 1801, aged 24 years. Married Mary Potter in 1802. Mr. Robinson died in 1821, aged 49 years. Mrs. Robinson, second wife, died in 1836, aged 54 years.

The children of William C.—fifth child of Christopher and grandson of Gov. WILLIAM ROBINSON—were:

1. *Edward Wanton*, born 1797; died 1818, aged 21 years.
2. *Stephen Ayrault*, born 1799; married Sarah H. Potter 1822, at Wakefield, R. I.; died in South Kingstown, April 7, 1877, aged 78 years. [NOTE by T. R. H.—He was a most amiable man and a true gentleman of the old school.]
3. *Frances W.*, born 1800; died 1802, aged 2 years.
4. *George C.*, born 1802; died 1820, aged 18 years.
5. *William C.*, born 1803; married Abby B. Shaw 1827; died 1871, aged 67 years.

The children of Jesse—sixth child of Christopher and grandson of Gov. WILLIAM ROBINSON— were:

1. *Robert*, born 1790; died 1809, aged 19 years. Mr.

Robinson was killed by falling from the mast-head of the ship Resolution, of Newport, R. I., while in the harbor of Charleston, S. C.

2. *William J.*, born 1792; married Rebecca Ann Gould 1822; died 1852, aged 60 years, without issue. His widow married in 1859, Isaac Jacques, of Elizabeth, N. J.

3. *Matthew*, born 1794; married Mary D. Shields 1828; died 1833, aged 39 years; left issue. His widow married Dr. DeForrest, of Baltimore, Md., 1843.

4. *Samuel Perry*, born 1798; married Alzada R. Willey 1824; died 1868, aged 70 years.

5. *Edwin*, born 1801; married Mary Connor 1833; died 1843, aged 42 years.

6. *Mary Ann*, born 1803, married Elijah Johnson 1825. Mr. Johnson died 1875, aged 74 years; left children.

7. *Abby*, born 1805; married Samuel Clarke 1828; died 1847, aged 42 years; left children.

8. *John Ray*, born 1808; died 1818, aged 10 years. He was drowned in the Pettaquamscutt river near the foot of Tower Hill.

9. *Sarah Ann*, born 1807; married William Bailey 1832. Mr. Bailey died 1854, aged 45 years. Mrs. Bailey died 1865, aged 58 years. They left no children.

The children of Robert—seventh child of Christopher and grandson of Gov. WILLIAM ROBINSON—were:

1. *Alexander S.*, born 1797; died 1819, aged 22 years.

2. *Samuel W.*, born 1799; never married; died 1862, aged 63 years.

3. *Robert*, born 1802; never married; died 1869, aged 67 years.

4. *Sarah Ann*, born 1808; never married; died 1864, aged 56 years.

The children of Matthew, ninth and youngest child of Christopher and grandson of Gov. WILLIAM ROBINSON, were:

1. *John P.*, born 1799; died 1801, aged 2 years. He was twin brother to Rowland.

2. *Rowland*, born 1799; married——, 1834; died 1859, aged 60 years; left children.

3. *Samuel S.*, born 1801; married——, 1825; died 1874, aged 73 years; left children.

4. *Maria*, born 1803; died 1831, aged 27 years; was never married.

5. *Frances W.*, born 1804; married Benjamin Balch 1842; died 1845, aged 41 years; left no children.

6. *William C.*, born 1806; died 1827, aged 21 years.

7. *Sarah Ann*, born 1807; died 1832, aged 25 years.

8. *Edward W.*, born 1809, married——1835; has children.

9. *Hannah*, born 1811; married Edward Larned 1841.

10. *S. Ayrault*, born 1814; not married.

The children of James Robinson—son of Sylvester and grandson of Gov. WILLIAM ROBINSON—were:

1. *William A.*, born 1797; married Dorcas B. Hadwen 1828; died 1872, aged 75 years. The children of William A. and Dorcas B. Robinson were: 1. Mary A., married Jacob Dunnell. 2. James, married Anna Balch. 3. Edward H., married Grace M. Howard. 4. Caroline, died 1845. 5. Anne A. 6. William A., Jr., married Marian L. Swift.

2. *Edward Mott*, born 1800; married Abby S. Howland; died 1865. The children of Edward M. and Abby S. Robinson were: 1. Hetty H., married Edward H. Green. 2. Isaac H., died in infancy.

3. *Anne A.*, born 1801; married Stephen A. Chase. Mr. Chase died in 1876.

4. *Sarah*, born 1804; died in infancy.

5. *Attmore*, twin of Sarah; married Laura Hazard. The children of Attmore and Laura Robinson were: 1. James A., married, first, Mary E. Alger, second, Mary Ring. 2.

Jane H. 3. Sylvester, died 1874. 4. George H., married Sarah Delamater. 5. Anne C. 6. William H. H.

6. *Rowland*, born 1806 ; died 1819.

7. *Sylvester C.*, born 1808.

The children of Benjamin Robinson—son of John and grandson of Gov. WILLIAM ROBINSON—were :

1. *George*, born 1792 ; died 1795, aged 3 years.

2. *John*, born 1794 ; married Rhuhama Robinson 1821 ; died 1841, aged 47 years. Mrs. Robinson died 1868, aged 71 years. No children.

3. *George B.*, born 1796 ; married Mary R. Wells 1832. She died 1838, aged 27 years. Married Julianna Willes 1839. Mr. Robinson died 1872, aged 76 years.

4. *Sylvester*, born 1798 ; married Eliza Noyes 1822 ; died 1867, aged 69 years. Their children were : 1. Ann B., married Nicholas Austin. 2. B. Franklin, married Caroline Rodman. 3. Hannah.

5. *William B.*, born 1800; married Harriet Robinson 1827. She died 1828, aged 21 years. Married Eliza A. Robinson 1831. She died 1874, aged 72 years. Mr. Robinson died 1875, aged 75 years. His children were : 1. Caroline H., born 1828 ; died 1829. 2. Caroline E., born 1842 ; married Benjamin Sherman 1875.

The children of John I. Robinson—son of John and grandson of Gov. WILLIAM ROBINSON—were :

1. *James*, born 1796 ; married Maria Gibbs 1832 ; died 1874, aged 78 years. Mrs. Robinson died 1875, aged 70 years. Their children were : 1. John C., born 1835 ; died 1865, aged 30 years. 2. James, born 1837, died 1838. 3. Virginia, born 1839 ; died 1846. 4. Arabella, born 1845 ; married John A. Cross 1871.

2. *Mary Ann*, born 1798 ; married Mr. Shotwell 1825 ; died 1870, aged 71 years, leaving one child.

The children of William C. Robinson—son of William C.—were:
1. *Frances W.*, born 1829; died 1851, aged 21 years.
2. *William A.*, born 1834; died 1837, aged 3 years.
3. *Ann Maria*, born 1836; married Albert J. S. Molinard 1863. Captain Molinard died 1875, leaving two children. Mrs. Molinard married Mr. Pendall, for her second husband, 1875.
4. *Edward Ayrault*, born 1838; married Alice Canby 1871; has children.
5. *George Francis*, born 1843; married Ellen F. Lord 1869; has children.

The children of George B. Robinson—son of Benjamin and great-grandson of Gov. WILLIAM ROBINSON—were:
1. *Maria*, born 1833; died 1848.
2. *Elizabeth B.*, born 1835.
3. *John W.*, born 1836; died 1837.
4. *Mary W.*, born 1838; died 1838.
5. *Hannah W.*, born 1840.
6. *George B.*, born 1842; married.
7. *Thomas W.*, born 1843.

The children of Samuel Perry Robinson—son of Jesse and great-grandson of Gov. WILLIAM ROBINSON—were:
1. *Anna R.*, born 1824; died 1853, aged 29 years.
2. *William J.*, born 1828; died 1829.
3. *William*, born 1830.
4. *Hannah T.*, born 1832; died 1834.
5. *Edwin M.*, born 1834; died 1861, aged 26 years.
6. *Sarah Jane*, born 1837; died 1841.
7. *Alzayda R. W.*, born 1839.
8. *Rebecca*, born 1842; married Alfred Gregory 1870.
9. *Alvira Weeden*, born 1843.
10. *Samuel P.*, born 1844.
11. *Kingston Goddard*, born 1846.

The children of George C. Robinson—eldest son of Christopher C. and great-grandson of Gov. WILLIAM ROBINSON—were:

1. *Jeremiah P.*, born 1819; married Elizabeth DeWitt 1843. Their children are: 1. Mary N., born 1844; died 1845, aged 1 year, 4 months and 17 days. 2. Jeremiah P., born 1846; married Margaret D. Lanman 1867. 3. Elizabeth D., born 1851; married Lewis H. Leonard 1871. 4. Harriet W., born 1853. 5. Isaac R., born 1856.

2. *Sarah H.*, born 1821; married William Rhoades Hazard 1851; died 1860, aged 38 years.

3. *Elizabeth A.*, born 1823; married James Stewart 1854.

4. *George C.*, born 1825; married Mary L. Arnold 1852. Their children are: 1. George C., born 1854. 2. Louisa L., born 1856. 3. Mary N., born 1858. 4. Richard A., born 1860; died 1862, aged 1 year and 10 months. 5. Margaret, born 1864. 6. Anna D., born 1870; died 1871, aged 1 year, 6 months and 12 days. 7. Edward Wanton, born 1872.

5. *Mary N.*, born 1827; married George G. Pearse 1849.

The children of Thurston Robinson—son of Christopher C. and great-grandson of Gov. WILLIAM ROBINSON—were:

1. *Morton*, born 1825; married Ann E. Collins 1854. Their children are: 1. Annanth, born 1855; married Sylvester Cross 1875. 2. Harriet E., born 1858. 3. Fanny W., born 1859. 4. Benjamin A., born 1862. 5. Morton P., born 1864.

2. *Harriet*, born 1828; married Samuel Robinson.

3. *Benjamin*, born 1832; died 1834.

The children of Elisha A. Robinson—son of Christopher C. and great-grandson of Gov. WILLIAM ROBINSON—were:

1. *Sarah Hull*, born 1838; married John Eldred, of Newport, R. I., 1869. They have one son, John Robinson.

2. *George I.*, born 1840; married Jane Porter 1864.

3. *Christopher C.*, born 1842; married Alvira A. Blanchard 1867; died February 8, 1879.

4. *Elisha A.*, born 1845; married Abby A. Proud 1874.

5. *Mary Anna*, born 1847; died 1848, aged 5 months and 16 days.

6. *Benjamin Hull*, born 1849; died 1850, aged 6 months and 8 days.

7. *Francis Warner*, born 1852; married Mary Nichols 1875.

Arms of the Hassard's of Garden Hill—of Watesford, of Parkmore, County Antrim, and Skea House, County Fermanagh.
Gules, two bars argent, on a chief, or, three escallops of the first.
Crest. *An escallop or.*
Motto. "*Vive en Espoir*" above the crest, and "Fortuna viam ducit" beneath the shield.

Genealogy of the Family of Hazard, or Hassard.

CHAPTER XIX.

"When," says Gibbon somewhere in his "Rise and Fall"—I write without the book—"we see a long list of ancestors so ancient that they have no beginning, so worthy that they ought to have no end, we feel an interest in all their fortunes; nor can we blame the generous enthusiasm or harmless vanity of those who are allied to the honors of the name."

I have before me a neat quarto volume of seventy-two pages, printed at York, England, "H. Southeran, book-seller, Coney street, 1858," entitled "Outlines of the History and Genealogy of the Hassards and their Connections." The work is by "John Hassard Short, Esq., of Edlington Grove, County Lincoln," who assumed the surname of Short to entitle him to the Edlington estate.

In his preface, which is addressed to "My Dear Children," the author says: "The origin of surnames is various; many are taken from trades and professions—many are mere nicknames—probably the best are from the places in which families resided and where they possessed property. It seems that the Hassards, or Hazards, took theirs from the place in which they first settled in England. The Manor of Haroldesore, in the parish of Ingleborne, in the county of Devon, is in old deeds called the Manor of Hardiswardshore, otherwise Hardwardshore, otherwise Hasworth, otherwise Hazard. *Lyons, Magna Britannia, Devonshire.* From this place they apparently branched off. One purchased lands in Derbyshire and Notts, in the reign of John, A. D. 1199, whose pedigree—as I have had the labor of collecting it from the 'Rotuli Hundredorum,' 'Chancery Suits,' and wills in the record office of York—I insert. The other—our branch of the family—removed to Bristol."

After adverting to some of the virtues and peculiarities that characterized their ancestors, the preface thus concludes: "In conclusion, I exhort you, my dear children, ever endeavor to maintain the same honorable position in society; to show the same patriotic zeal, and to devote an equal portion of your time and talents to the temporal and spiritualistics; be ashamed of anything which will bring a slur upon your good name; take warning from the few unfortunate examples we have recorded, to avoid evil—that your names and examples may one day be handed down with credit, to your posterity. Especially if the blood—as we are informed—of the noble and mighty Plantagenets, 'the men of iron and mailed breast and gauntleted hand and jewel crest,' flows in your veins, do not disgrace it. Prove that you are worthy of such honor, by your manly and christian conduct, your perseverance, your zeal in serving your country; and above everything, by your heart's devotion to your Saviour and your God."

Accompanying the book is an elaborate genealogical chart, bringing down the senior male members of the family in regular unbroken succession for twenty-one generations. Under the caption of "History and Lineage," the compiler says: "The family of Hassard, Hassart, or Hazard is of Norman extraction, and of considerable antiquity. At the time of the Conquest they were living on the borders of Switzerland, and distinguished by the ancient but long extinct title of Duke de Charante. Two bearing this title visited the Holy Land as crusaders.

"The cause of their first coming to our island is thus related: In one of the early troubles of France, the Duke de Charante, being in rebellion and outlawed by the monarch, placed his duchess and youngest son, a boy of ten years of age, on board a vessel in a neighboring seaport, under the protection of Dr. Foulke. Intelligence having come to them that the duke and his two eldest sons had been defeated and slain in a great battle, their castles leveled and estates confiscated to the crown, the duchess, under Dr. Foulke's care, sailed for England, accompanied by her son, who became the first English ancestor of the family.

"The duchess died in London. Probably at her death her son took his surname of Hazard or Hassard, from the manor of that name, and soon after settled in Gloucestershire, where his descendants continued to reside for more than a century. During this period two of them held important offices in Bristol, one of whom, Rainald, or Reginauld was appointed, A. D. 1216, one of the prepositors, under circumstances which threw considerable light upon his character. The term [prepositor], it seems, signifies both 'the chief magistrate of a city' and 'the head or chief officer of the King in a town'. Sayer, in mentioning Mr. Hassard's appointment, represents him as a grave and worshipful man, who was chosen to the office by the King—Henry III.—on his coming to Bristol, with his counselors and tutor, as to a place of safety." It seems that London was then in the possession of Louis, the King of France.

The genealogical chart commences with the Duke de Charante in the eleventh century, and gives the several generations of the family as follows:

First Generation.—DUKE DE CHARANTE, living on the borders of Switzerland, circa 1060.

Second Generation.—DUKE DE CHARANTE, crusader, killed in battle against king of France. Duchess fled to England.

Third Generation.—1. DUKE DE CHARANTE, killed fighting by the side of his father. 2. DUKE DE CHARANTE, also killed. 3 HAZARD OF HAZARD.

Fourth Generation.—REGINAULD HAZARD, of Bristol, 1216, married granddaughter of Dr. Foulke.

Fifth Generation.—ROBERT HAZARD, of Bristol, possessed property in Essex.

Sixth Generation.—JOHN, coroner of Bristol, in the reign of Edward II., A. D. 1312; mentioned by Sayer in his History and Antiquities of Bristol. Coroner was an officer of the King of great importance in that day, none under the rank of Knight being allowed to fill it.

Seventh Generation.—THOMAS, of Bristol, held lands in the county of Stafford.

Eighth Generation.—ALEXANDER HASSARD, of Lyme Regis, 1377, whose name appears, A. D. 1377, as witness to a deed amongst the archives of Lyme Regis in the county of Dorset. From this period some of the family resided in and around Lyme for the next three centuries.

Ninth Generation.—First THOMAS HASSARD, settled himself for a time in Wiltshire, where he is mentioned as among the worthies of the county..

Tenth Generation.—JOHN HASSARD, Esq., lord of the fine manor of Seaton, resident there A. D. 1465.

Eleventh Generation.—ROBERT, member of Parliament from Lyme in the reign of Henry VIII. Lyme was as early as the reign of Edward I., one of the one hundred and forty-five places in England that sent members to Parliament.

Twelfth Generation.—JOHN, Mayor of Lyme in the reign of both Edward VI. and Mary for many years, extending from 1498 to 1557-8 inclusive. Mr. Hassard appears to have been a man of many sterling qualities and of great influence. Several pages are devoted to him. His children were: 1. Gilbert, rector of Trusham 1541. 2. Robert, Lord de Beer and Bridport; will registered A. D. 1543. 3. Ann, married

John Yonge, Esq., of Collyton, son of the Member of Parliament for Plymouth.

Thirteenth Generation.—ROBERT, of Charmouth, member of Parliament 1589-90. Robert's fourth son was John, Lord de Beer, member of Parliament 1616, born 1555.

Fourteenth Generation.—JOHN, son of John, Lord de Beer, Charmouth, Lyme, &c. For many years mayor of Lyme, also member of Parliament.

Fifteenth Generation.—JOHN, of Charmouth, born at Bridport; baptized there 1625. "To him was bequeathed by his father lands in Lyme Regis, also in great Bridport, Allington, Charmouth, Axminister, Waldich, and Parson's Holme near Lyme." He was mayor of Lyme and member of Parliament. Says the author, "Before leaving the member of Parliament we may give a single proof of the esteem in which the family was held. In comparing several of the accounts of the different members for their journeys, we find that those of the Hassards exceeded all others by their being allowed an extra horse for their servants, wine at their meals, separate bedrooms, etc., all of which, while they seem necessaries now, were luxuries neither expected nor granted in those early times to others."

Sixteenth Generation.—JOHN, of London, born circa 1650, like his brothers left the country of Dorset for that of Middlesex, where he purchased land, and a house in London.

Seventeenth Generation.—JOHN, of Bloomsbury Square, in the county of Middlesex, sole heir to his father, born 1680, married A. D. 1714, Elizabeth, daughter of Joseph Short, Esq., lord of the manors of Edlington, East Keal, Belleau and Claythorpe, in the county of Lincoln, and of the moiety of Clerkenwell in the county of Middlesex; and his wife, Elizabeth, daughter and heir of George Longue, of Clerkenwell and East Kirby, Esq. Belleau and Claythorpe fell before his death, probably by purchase, into the hands of his godfather, the then Duke of Ancaster, and are yet possessed by his descendant, the Lord Willoughby D'Erseby. Mr. Hassard left one son.

Eighteenth Generation.—HENRY HASSARD, of Bloomsbury Square, London, Esq., who married Anne, daughter of Valentine Fitzhugh of Mile End House, county of Middlesex, Esq. He died in 1796, aged 75 years, and was buried in the Church of St. James, Clerkenwell. Mrs. Hassard, after the death of her husband, resided with her son, Colonel Short, at Edlington, and was buried there in the family vault, beneath the chancel of the Church of St. Helena, A. D. 1809.

Nineteenth Generation.—COL. HENRY HASSARD, J. P. and Dep. Lieut. for Suffolk, assumed the name and arms of Short only on taking possession of Edlington Grove.

Twentieth Generation.—RICHARD SAMUEL HASSARD, born at Castleford, county of York, of Great Bealings, in the county of Suffolk, Esq. On the death of his brothers he became sole heir, assumed the surname and arms of Short, and took up his residence at Edlington Grove.

Twenty-first Generation.—JOHN HASSARD SHORT, of Edlington Grove, J. P. and Dep. Lieut. for the county of Lincoln, the present senior representative of the family of Hassard. His children were: 1. Fitzhugh Hassard, born October 27, 1832; died November 3, 1849. 2. Edward Hassard, born August 22, 1848. 3. Algernon Lawson Hassard, born Feburuary 20, 1852. 4. Agnes Margarette. 5. Marian. 6. Caroline Mary. 7. Henrietta Frances, died in infancy 1839. 8. Frances Adela. 9. Katherine Jane. 10. Gertrude Elmhurst.

The genealogical chart also contains a multitude of the names of members of the family who sprang from senior branches. Many of these held distinguished positions in civil affairs and in the army, ranking from lieutenants, captains and colonels to major general. Although there are but two main branches of the family designated in the genealogical chart, there are several minor offshoots referred to in the history. Each one of these has its own peculiar family crest and coat of arms. The original one was an "escalop shell proper," surmounting a palm, the last indicating that the family had visited the Holy Land as crusaders, and the former suggestive of the fact that in that age of superstition they had also performed pilgrimage to the holy shrine of St. Jago de Compostella, which, says Mr. Short, "at one time partook of the character of a mania."

The branch of the family from which the Rhode Island Hazards claim descent as tabulated in the chart, branches off in the third generation from "HAZARD OF HAZARD."

Fourth Generation.—REGINAULD HAZARD.
Fifth Generation.—HASARD, of Notts, A. D. 1199.
Sixth Generation.—1. THOMAS HASSARD. 2. JOHN, county of Notts.
Seventh Generation.—WILLIAM, married Hawissa, A. D. 1270.
Eighth Generation.—THOMAS, of Radcliffe, county of Notts, 1297.
Ninth Generation.—PHILIP, of Kynson, county of Notts, certified heir at the age of 27, A. D. 1310.
Tenth Generation.—THOMAS, A. D. 1376.
Eleventh Generation.—THOMAS, A. D. 1433.
Twelfth Generation.—1. PHILIP, King's Forester, A. D. 1568. 2. THOMAS, county of Notts, a brother.
Thirteenth Generation.—JOHN, of Stapleford, county of Notts, 1556.
Fourteenth Generation.—WILLIAM, married Ellianor, daughter and heir of Henry Sacheverell, Esq., of Radcliffe, county of Notts. He was living at Radcliffe, on Soar, 1662.

[Here occurs a break in the regular succession of this branch of the family, which is recommenced later with a member of the Irish branch, then of recent origin, as follows:]

Fifteenth Generation.—ROBERT HAZARD ,of Enniskillen, or Enniskeen, buried there May 12, 1668.

Sixteenth Generation.—JOHN of Enniskillen, married Alice. Both were buried at Enniskillen, John 1684, Alice January 15, 1697.

Seventeenth Generation.— JOHN, married Anne, living 1701. His sister Jane was buried at Enniskillen June 3, 1703.

Eighteenth Generation.—JAMES, baptized at Enniskillen June 3, 1703.

Here the genealogical record of this branch of the family pauses.

It is from the Nottingham branch of the ancient family that the Rhode Island Hazards claim to be descended and to have so long perpetuated its favorite names of Thomas and Robert. And certainly the English chart and history compiled by Mr. John Hassard Short affords testimony that goes to confirm the truth of the tradition. He says: "The first Thomas Hassard, of Rhode Island, was a brother of the Hassard who first settled in Ireland." The only error is that instead of the latter going over as an officer in King William's army, he obtained his first grant of estates in Ireland from King James or Charles I., for military services rendered, and was afterwards engaged in the war under William of Orange.

The author of the history says of Captain George Hassard of the army: "Captain Hassard left three sons, Jason, William, and Robert. The eldest son, Jason [a familiar name among the early Rhode Island family], born A. D. 1617, high sheriff of Fermanagh 1649, the year Cromwell landed in Ireland, is generaly looked upon as the 'Adventurer,' inasmuch as more is known of him than of his father or his brothers, and he certainly lived at and most probably purchased Mullymesker, where the family long resided. This estate appears to have been purchased about 1641." Mullymesker was about three miles from Enniskillen, where several families of the Hassards now reside.

The narrative continues: "The Hassards especially distinguished themselves by taking an active part in the sieges of Enniskillen and Londonderry. The horrors of these sieges were inconceivable. Sir William Cole was at that time Governor and Provost of Enniskillen, and we read that it was bravely defended by the English settlers, among whom our ancestors were eminent. In July, 1689, Mr. Hassard's troop of Enniskillens was again engaged, when we find that the Enniskilleners severally defeated the three divisions of James' army—the first under Sarsfield, the second under the Duke of Berwick, and the third under Macarthy. * * * Mr. Hassard and his nephew were also engaged in the battle of the Boyne—1690—when the Enniskillens behaved with great valor, and at one time turned the tide of battle."

The following account of the Hassards of Garden Hill, Ireland, is attached to Short's history of the family:

JASON, eldest son of Captain George Hassard, first adventurer of Mullymesker, Esq., left two sons. 1. Robert, of Carne, whose branch is now extinct. 2. Richard, born about 1671; married 1706 Mary, daughter of John Emery, of Ballyconnell House, county of Cavan, Esq., and had issue, Richard, of Garden Hill. Richard married Jane, daughter of J. Little, Esq., county of Fermanagh, and had issue: (a) Jason, of Garden Hill. (b) John, of Toam, ancestor of the Hassards of Waterford, of whom hereafter. (c) William, major in the 44th Regiment.

Jason (*Richard, Richard, Jason, Captain George Hassard*), born 1734; married 1777 Ann Montgomery, daughter of Alexander Montgomery, of Clontarf County, Dublin; died 1812, leaving six sons and two daughters. 1. Richard, of Garden Hill, born 1778; captain in the 74th Highlanders and brevet major; died 1812—immediately after his father—

unmarried. 2. Jason, born 1780, died at Garden Hill, 1852, unmarried. 3. William, born 1781; succeeded his brother Jason; treasurer of the county of Fermanagh from 1813 to November, 1847; shot by an assassin in the avenue of Garden Hill. He died unmarried. It was owing to his debts that five thousand or six thousand acres of his estate were sold under the Encumbered Estates act. The remainder of this estate, a yet handsome property, is divided between Alexander Hassard, of Garden Hill, Esq., lieutenant in the 96th regiment of foot, and the family of the late Sir Francis Hazard. Some half century ago I used to hear that William Hassard, of Garden Hill, fatted annually for market three thousand beeves on his Garden Hill estate. 4. Alexander, captain in the 6th Enniskillin dragoons, a Waterloo officer. He was desperately wounded in that battle, and when lying unhorsed and bleeding on the field, was pierced entirely through the body by a Polish lancer; notwithstanding which he recovered and married, in 1836, Elizabeth Bolton Hassard, daughter of his cousin, Captain Jason Hassard, of the 74th Highlanders. He died September, 1845, leaving issue: (a) Alexander, present representative of Garden Hill, Esq., born 1837. (b) John, of Bawnbay House, county of Cavan, high sheriff for the county of Cavan in 1824; married, in 1818 Charlotte Desey, youngest daughter of Robert Desey, Esq., of Ravensdale House, near Maynorth, and Merrion square, Dublin. He was killed by a fall from his horse, in 1830, leaving issue.

JOHN HASSARD, Esq., of Toam, second son of Richard, of Garden Hill, 1767; had issue.

RICHARD, born 1768; a lieutenant in the Royal Artillery, and afterwards captain in the Waterford Militia; left issue.

SIR FRANCIS JOHN HASSARD, barrister-at-law, born 1780; recorder at Waterford, knighted in 1810; died in 1822, leaving issue.

JOHN, captain in the 74th Highlanders, born 1782; died unmarried 1825.

JASON, captain in the 74th Highlanders, born 1785; died in 1842, leaving issue.

WILLIAM HENRY, born 1790, barrister-at-law; recorder of Waterford in 1828; left issue.

MICHAEL DARBIN HASSARD, Esq., residing at Glenville, member of Parliament for Waterford, present representative of this family; married Anne, third daughter of Sir Francis Hassard Knight; has issue.

The following additional items are recorded in Short's History, concerning the Nottingham branch of the family, from which, as before said, the Rhode Island Hazards claim to be descended:

A. D. 1199. Walter Hazard, one the sons of the first Hazard, of Hazard, or Hassart, and Mabel, his wife, we find from ancient Latin records possessed of certain osier lands at Pokinton, in the county of Derby. He appears to have left two sons, Thomas and John.

A. D. 1240. Thomas, we learn from the same manuscript, formed one of twelve jurors on the trial of Burg in Malmesbyr. John seems to have acted as a magistrate in the case of William, son of Ade de Grimeston, who was indicted for theft and taken to York Castle.

1270. We next find William and his wife Hawissa, who had a trial respecting service of land in Radcliffe and Kynston, in the county of Notts, defendants, against Peter Pigot, lord of the Manor of Radcliffe on Soar, plaintiff. Judgment was given in favor of defendants that they they ought to render none. They left issue a son, Thomas Hassard.

1298. In the 27th Edward I., Thomas Hassard, aged 28 years, was found heir of the aforesaid William, who had a house and some land at Radcliffe, held of the king for £3, 8s., 9d. He left a son, Philip.

1310. In the third year of Edward II., Philip Hassard was certified heir of Thomas at the age of 27 years.

1370. Thomas Hassard appears to have been Philip's heir and left a son, 1433, Thomas.

From the Valor Ecclesiasticus of Henry VIII. we find: 1508. Philip and Thomas [most probably their descendants], the former the King's forester, held lands under his Majesty to the value of iijs iiijd. The latter connected with the College of Arundel.

1556. John Hassard was plaintiff in a trial in the reign of Elizabeth, respecting a tenement and sixty acres of land in Sandyacre, county of Derby, and in Stapleford, county of Notts, Roger Columbell, Esq., defendant. We must observe here that William Hassard, son of John, afterwards married the said Roger Columbell's widow. At this period, says the author, the family seem to have branched off again, one possessing property at Kirton and Laxton, county of Notts, the other at Radcliffe, in the same county.

1562. WILLIAM HASSARD, son of the last named John, married Ellianor, only daughter and heiress of Henry Sacheverell, Esq., de Radcliffe, a scion of an ancient and knightly family, and widow of Roger Columbell, Esq. They were living at Radcliffe on Soar at the time of the visitation of that county, A. D. 1662—perhaps a misprint for 1562—and his wife was buried A. D. 1564.

"Having no special object," says the author, "we have not traced this branch farther, nor ascertained whether any of their descendants are now living, but in course of our researches we have examined one or the other of their wills of later date in the record office of York."

Notwithstanding what Mr. Short, the author of the History, says above, the family chart shows that he did nevertheless discover a missing link in the line of succession of the Nottingham branch of the family that connected it with the Enniskillen Hassards, and had he persevered in his researches he might have found two other missing links, the one connecting the family with the Long Island, Georgia and Carolina Hazards, and the other with those of Rhode Island, from whence the prolific race have flowed into and multiplied in nearly or quite every State and Territory in the Union.

I again quote from Short's History: "The late Major General Hassard, who was, from 1830 until he became general, colonel commanding the Royal Engineers in the Ionian Islands, with a salary of £1195 per annum, and who died in Malta A. D. 1848, is supposed to be a descendant of John, the son of Jason, who was attainted, together with his uncle. Jason Hassart, Esq., by James II.'s Parliament, in 1680, for taking the side of William and Mary, and for his firm protestantism. General Hassard left a son, Major Fairfax Hassard, of the Royal Engineers, who is now—1858—in India, and ranks among the heroes of the Alma, Balaklava and Sevastopol."

In addition to the above extracts from John Hassard Short's "Outlines of the History and Genealogy of the Hassards and their Connections," I have taken the following accounts—abridged—from records of several of the Irish branches of the family, in the "Landed Gentry of Great Britain and Ireland," pp. 664, 665, vol. 1. The work in two volumes is to be found in the Astor Library, New York.

Hassard of Garden Hill.—ALEXANDER JASON HASSARD, Esq., of Garden Hill, County Fermanagh, born September, 1837; 76th regiment. The family of Hassard is of Norman extraction, and of considerable antiquity. The orthography was originally "Hassart." The long extinct title of Duke de Charante was in this family Two members thereof visited the Holy Land as crusaders. Soon after the Conquest a branch became seated in Gloustershire and afterwords removed to Dorsetshire. The first English ancestor from whom an unbroken succession can be traced was JOHN HASSART, or HASSARD, A. D. 1469, lord of the man-

23

or of Seaton, seven miles from Lyme. A long line of descendants follow, among whom is the eldest son, JOHN HASSARD, born 1498, mayor of Lyme in 1550 and 1557. ROBERT HASSARD, several times mayor of Lyme and member of Parliament for the borough in 1580 and 1593.

JOHN HASSARD, eldest son of John, born 1531, mayor of Lyme in 1567, 1572, 1578, 1582, 1588, 1594, 1601 and 1606, altogether seven times; was returned to Parliament for the borough in 1585, 1586 and 1603. The gallery at the west end of the nave of the church of Lyme Regis bears the following inscription on its front in capital letters: "John Hassard built this to the glory of Almighty God, in the eightieth year of his age, Anno Domini 1611," and on the north side appears, "John Hassard, seven maior, deceased the 7th day of November, Anno Domini 1612."

JASON and GEORGE HASSARD, accompanied by some of the Caldwells, went over to Ireland in the reign of Charles II., after having previously raised troops in the south of England. They assumed the motto of "*Fortuna Viam Ducit,*" upon landing. They had eventually large tracts of land granted them in Fermanagh and adjoining counties. The Hassards were distinguished at the sieges of Enniskillen and Londonderry.

JASON HASSARD, Esq., of Garden Hill and Toam, born 1617; was mayor of Lyme before he departed for Ireland. His will bears date 21st October, 1690.

JOHN, son of Jason, the supposed ancestor of the family of the late Major General Hassard, of the Royal Engineers.

JOHN, of Toam, ancestor of the Hassards of Waterford.

RICHARD, of Garden Hill, born 1778; captain 74th Highlanders.

WILLIAM, of Garden Hill, born 1781; for many years treasurer for the county of Fermanagh; assassinated in the avenue of Garden Hill, 13th November, 1845.

ALEXANDER, captain 6th Enniskillen dragoons.

JOHN, of Bawnbay House, county Cavan, high sheriff for

county Cavan in 1824; killed by a fall from his horse in 1830.

ROBERT DEEY H., born 1822; 2d Bombay European Light Infantry.

The family arms are also given in connection with the record.

Hassard of Waterford (abridged).—MICHAEL DOBBYN HASSARD, Esq., of Glenville, County Waterford, M. P. and J. P. and high sheriff in 1853; born October, 1817; married, August, 1846, Anne, daughter of the late Sir Francis John Hassard. This family is a branch of the Hassards of Garden Hill, county Fermanagh.

RICHARD, son of Michael, born 1768; lieutenant in the Royal Irish Artillery, and afterwards captain in the Waterford Militia.

SIR FRANCIS JOHN, born 1780, recorder of the city of Waterford; knighted in 1810.

JOHN, captain 74th Highlanders; born 1782; died 1825.

JASON, also captain 74th Highlanders; born 1785; died 1842.

JASON, born 1826; major 59th regiment.

WILLIAM HENRY, born 1790; recorder of the city of Waterford in 1828. The family arms are also given.

Hassard of Skea (abridged).—REV. EDWARD HASSARD, rector of Rath Keale and chancellor of the diocese of Limerick; succeeded to the representation of the family of Hassard of Skea, at the death of his father, 10th August, 1847.

The family of Hassard of Skea is a branch of the old English stock of Hassard of Lyme.

GEORGE HASSARD, Esq., of Skea, born May, 1775; J. P.; served as high sheriff of county of Fermanagh in 1818 and 1828.

EDWARD, present head of the Skea family.

HENRY, barrister-at-law.

WILLIAM, of Mountjoy square, Dublin, barrister.

FRANCIS, in holy orders, rector of Fuerty, County Roscommon.

The family arms are also given.

Genealogy of the Hazards of Rhode Island.

CHAPTER XX.

"The Hazards," says Updike, page 320, "are a numerous family, the most so in Narragansett, if not in the State. Watson, in the 'Historic Tales of Olden Time,' says, 'Mrs. Maria Hazard, of South Kingstown, R. I., and mother of the Governor, died in 1739, at the age of one hundred years, and could count up five hundred children, grand-children, great-grandchildren and great-great-grandchildren, two hundred and five of whom were then living. A granddaughter of hers had already been a grandmother fifteen years! Probably this instance of Rhode Island's fruitfulness may match against the world.'"

In the following tables I have copied largely from *data* that have been furnished me by Miss Emily Hazard, daughter of the late Hon. Benjamin Hazard of Newport; from manuscript furnished me by Rowland T. Robinson, of Ferrisburgh, Vt.; from E. R. Potter's "Early History of Narragansett," and from Updike's "History of the Narragansett Church."

From these and other sources, I learn that the first Hassard—pronounced Hazard—that settled in Rhode Island was Thomas Hassard,[1]* or Hazard, who came from England, some say Wales, and settled on the island of Rhode Island

*The small figures affixed to the names of the Hazards mark the generations from Thomas the originator of the Rhode Island Hazards.

about the year 1639, by way of New Jersey or Long Island, and Massachusetts Bay. Tradition says that Thomas was accompanied by a nephew, who was the ancestor of the New York and Southern branches of the family.

Thomas Hazard was one of the first settlers of Aquidneck, and was appointed, with Nicholas Easton and Robert Jeffries, to lay out the town of Newport. The colonial records of Massachusetts contain the following entries, which have been furnished me by Mr. Hazard Stevens, son of the late General Stevens, late Governor of Washington Territory: "September 3, 1634, Mr. Nicholas Easton admitted freeman [at the General Court]"; "May 25, 1636, Thomas Hassard admitted freeman."

Arnold in his history of the State of Rhode Island, vol. 1, page 132, says: "The colony [Aquidneck] had now so greatly increased that a division was deemed expedient. A meeting was held, at which the following agreement was entered into by the signers, by whom the settlement of Newport was commenced on the south-west side of the island:

'Pocasset, on the 28th of the 2d, 1639.

'It is agreed by us whose hands are underwritten, to propagate a Plantation in the midst of the island, or elsewhere; and to engage ourselves to bear equal charges, answerable to our strength and estates in common; and that our determination shall be by major voices of judge and elders, the judge to have a double voice.

"Present:

WILLIAM CODDINGTON, Judge.

NICHOLAS EASTON,
JOHN COGGESHALL,
WILLIAM BRENTON,
JOHN CLARK,   } Elders.
JEREMY CLARKE,
THOMAS HAZARD,
HENRY BULL,

WILLIAM DYRE, Clerk.'"

Three children came with Thomas Hazard to Portsmouth, the northern town of Aquidneck: 1. Hannah[2], married Stephen Wilcox. 2. Martha[2], married Ichabod Potter. 3. Robert[2], a boy of four years of age.

Thomas Hazard married his second wife, Martha, the widow of Thomas Sheriffe, of Portsmouth, about 1675, by whom he had no offspring. His will, signed August 6, 1677, is recorded in Portsmouth, in which he empowers "my loving wife, Martha Hazard, whole and sole executrix of all and every part of my estate." He was buried on the farm lying on the west shore of the island, next north of Lawton's Valley, which farm is now occupied as an asylum for the poor of the town of Portsmouth.

Second Generation.—ROBERT[2] (*Thomas*[1]), born in England, 1635, came with his father to Portsmouth, R. I.; was a deputy to the General Assembly 1664. In 1670 it appears on the records that he was a juror and a commissioner in Portsmouth. In 1671, he purchased five hundred acres of land in Kingstown, of the Pettaquamscutt purchasers, situated between Rose Hill and Saucatucket river to which he permanently removed in 1695. His children were: 1. Thomas[3], born 1658; admitted freeman in Portsmouth, 1684. 2. George[3], admitted freeman of the colony, 1696. 3. Stephen[3]. 4. Robert[3]. 5. Jeremiah[3]. Robert[2] died possessed of a large property, and was buried by his eldest son in Portsmouth.

Third Generation.—THOMAS HASSARD[3] (*Robert*[2], *Thomas*[1]),born 1658; became a very great land-holder. He owned Popasquash in Bristol, and exchanged it for the Jencks and the Gov. George Brown farms in Boston Neck, the two comprising some seven hundred acres of land. April 28, 1698, Thomas Hassard, of Boston Neck, bought for £700 (currency) three hundred acres of the Sewall farm, bounded in part on land of Jahleel Brenton. The records of Kingstown, now South Kingstown, abound with land conveyances to Thomas Hassard, the son of Robert. His children were:

1. Robert⁴. 2. George⁴. 3. Jeremiah⁴. 4. Benjamin⁴, born 1701. 5. Stephen⁴. 6. Jonathan⁴. 7. Thomas⁴. 8. Hannah⁴. 9. Sarah⁴. 10. Mary⁴.

Before his death, which occurred in 1749 at the age of 92, Thomas Hassard deeded to his son Robert, besides other land, two hundred acres lying in Boston Neck, being what is now known as the "Wilkins Updike farm." To his son George he conveyed two hundred acres, lying next south of the above named farm, the same being now owned and occupied by his lineal descendant, Thomas G. Hazard; also to the same two hundred acres, comprising the farm next south, now belonging to Dr. Thomas M. Potter. To his son Benjamin, he conveyed three hundred and thirty acres, now known as "The Jencks farm." To his son Jonathan he conveyed the two farms lying next south of the above, now known as the "Gov. George Brown farm," and the "John J. Watson Boston Neck Pier farm," the first named containing three hundred and thirty, and the last two hundred and nine acres. These six farms, aggregating nearly fifteen hundred acres (old measure), all lay adjoining on the southern part of Boston Neck and used to be noted for their great fertility.

Fourth Generation.—ROBERT HAZARD⁴ (*Thomas³, Robert², Thomas¹*), lived on the Wilkins Updike farm in Boston Neck, and was buried in 1762 in a family burying ground on the farm now owned and occupied by William Nichols, on Tower Hill, which was formerly a part of Robert Hazard's great landed estate. The children of Robert⁴ were: 1. Thomas⁵. 2. Jonathan⁵. 3. Richard⁵. 4. Sarah⁵. Robert Hazard was reputed in his day to be the largest farmer in New England. We used to have in my father's house one of his cheese vats which held nearly a bushel, and it was said that he had twelve cheeses of its size made daily.

Fifth Generation.—THOMAS HAZARD⁵ (*Robert⁴, Thomas³, Robert², Thomas¹*), lived and died on the farm now owned by William Nichols, mentioned before, in the year 1795, aged 76 years, and was buried in the Friends burial ground, situated on the southern extremity of Tower Hill, near where the Tower Hill House now stands. He married Elizabeth, daughter of Gov. William Robinson, who died in the Dr. Senter house, corner of Parade and Thames street, Newport, R. I., in 1804, aged 79 years, and was buried in the Friends burying ground in that town. Their children were: 1. Sarah[6], born 1747; died 1753. 2. Robert[6].

Sixth Generation.—ROBERT HAZARD[6] (*Thomas[5], Robert[4], Thomas[3], Robert[2], Thomas[1]*), born 1753; moved sometime before his death to Ferrisburgh, Vermont, where he died May 3, 1833. He married Sarah Fish 1781. His wife died 1847. Their children were: 1. Thomas[7]. 2. Elizabeth[7], died young. 3. Rowland Robinson[7], married Fanny Carpenter; no issue. 4. David Fish[7], married Sarah B. Rogers. Their children were: (a) Sarah[8]. (b) John[8]. (c) Ann[8]. 5. Robert Borden[7], married and had children: (a) Mary[8]. (b) Martha[8]. 6. Sarah[7], married Nicholas Holmes. Their children were: (a) Robert. (b) Titus. (c) John. (d) Mary. (e) Julia. 7. Lydia[7], married Schuyler Lewis. 8. Mary[7], died unmarried. 9. William[7], married Hannah Rogers; no issue. He married as his second wife Lucia Burroughs. Their children were: (a) William B[8]. (b) Robert[8]. 10. Robinson[7], died unmarried. 11. Stephen[7], married Sarah Odell. Their children were: (a) George G.[8] (b) Henry[8]. (c) Lydia[8]. (d) Robert[8]. (e) Elizabeth[8]. All the above named children of Robert Hazard[6], except the last four, were born in Narragansett, Rhode Island.

Seventh Generation. — THOMAS HAZARD[7] (*Robert[6], Thomas[5], Robert[4], Thomas[3], Robert[2], Thomas[1]*), married Lydia Rogers. Their children were: 1. Robert[8]. 2. Rufus[8], married, first, Sarah Allen; second, Ruth Holmes; no issue. 3. Seneca[8], married, first, Elizabeth Allen. Their child was: (a) Elizabeth[9]. He married as his second wife Persis Hoag. Their children were: (b) Persis C.[9], died unmarried. (c) Seneca[9], married Frances Hand. (d) Pliny,[9] died unmarried. (e) Russell[9], died young. 4. Achsah[8], married —— Taber. Their child was: (a) Richard B.

Eighth Generation.—ROBERT HAZARD[8] (*Thomas*[7], *Robert*[6], *Thomas*[5], *Robert*[4], *Thomas*[3], *Robert*[2], *Thomas*[1]), married Elizabeth Alexander. Their children were: 1. Ezra[9]. 2. Sylvia[9]. Robert Hazard died some years ago.

Ninth Generation.—EZRA HAZARD[9] (*Robert,*[8] *Thomas*[7], *Robert*[6], *Thomas*[5], *Robert*[4], *Thomas*[3], *Robert*[2], *Thomas*[1]), married Catharine Williams. He is living on his own fine paternal farm in North Ferrisburgh, Vermont, and under the same roof tree beneath which his father and grandfather were born, and where his great-grandfather lived and died. He is now the male representative of the senior branch of the Hazard family in a direct line, and from all I saw of him on a recent visit, and can learn, he inherits the like resolute, independent character that the self-reliant race of the true "snip" breed have ever asserted and maintained.

As may be seen, the christian names of the senior sons of the family, for eight generations preceding Ezra, have all been regularly alternated from Thomas to Robert—the two favorite names among their English ancestry.

THOMAS HAZARD [6] (*Thomas*[5], *Robert*[4], *Thomas*[3], *Robert*[2], *Thomas*[1]), third child of Thomas; born 1755; died 1756.

THOMAS ~~Rodman~~ HAZARD[6] (*Thomas*[5], *Robert*[4], *Thomas*[3], *Robert*[2], *Thomas*[1]), fourth child of Thomas; born 1758; married Anna Rodman, sister of Samuel Rodman, of New Bedford, to which city he removed and amassed a large fortune in the whaling business, and afterwards owned and occupied a house at No. 80 Beekman street, New York, where he died about 1829. His children were: 1. Thomas R[7]. 2. Samuel[7]. 3. Sarah[7]. 4. Elizabeth[7]. 5. Ann[7]. 6. Edward[7].

THOMAS RODMAN HAZARD[7] (*Thomas*[6], *Thomas*[5], *Robert*[4], *Thomas*[3], *Robert*[2], *Thomas*[1]). Samuel L. Hazard[8], of

West Castleton, Vermont, son of Thomas R., has furnished me with the following statistics of his father's descendants. Thomas Rodman Hazard[7] married Margaret Every, of Liverpool, England in 1808 or 1809. Their children were: 1. Eliza[8], born 1810; married Allan G. Callom, Delhi township, Hamilton county, Ohio, 1826. Their children were four sons and three daughters. 2. Thomas R.[8], born 1812; lost at sea August, 1842; never married. 3. Samuel L.[8], born June 16, 1813; married Olivia B. Woodman, of Wilton, Maine, February 9, 1840. Their children were: (a) Oliver W[9], born in Boston, January 10, 1841: married Margaret Fulton, of Cambridge, Mass., June 27, 1864; has one child, Anna, born in Cambridge, April 8, 1866. (b) Thomas R.[9], born Boston, April 4, 1843; married Ida G. Shattuck, of Boston, May 24, 1868; has one child, Carrie[10], born in West Castleton, Vermont, June 25, 1869. (c) Samuel Lister[9], born in Cambridge, September 23, 1854. 4. Edward[8], born 1816; married Mary Anderson, of Delhi township, Ohio, 1839. Their children were: Robert[9], born 1840; Maria[9], born 1842; Emma[9], born 1844; William[9], born 1846; Ella[9], born 1848; Elizabeth[9], born 1850; Charles[9], born 1852; Minnie[9], born 1854; Alice[9], born 1855; Thomas R.[9], born 1856. 5. William[8], born 1818; died 1849 unmarried. 6. Robert P.[8], born 1821; married Eliza Mixer, of Delhi township, Ohio, 1842. Their children were: Thomas R.[9], born 1843, died 1861; Eben[9], born 1845; Arabel[9], born 1847; Charles[9], born 1851. Robert P. Hazard died in 1865.

SAMUEL[7]—second child of Thomas Hazard[6]—, married Rebecca Peace, of Philadelphia, and resided in Franklin street, New York, where they both died, leaving no children.

SARAH[7]—third child of Thomas Hazard[6]—married John H. Howland, a leading and wealthy merchant of New York. Their children were: William; Martha, married Mr. Hooker; John, married; Mary, married Mr. Pell; Sarah, married Mr. Osgood.

ELIZABETH[7]— fourth child of Thomas Hazard[6]—married

Jacob Barker, of New York City. Mr. Abraham Barker, of Philadelphia, has kindly furnished me with the following genealogical statistics. Jacob Barker and Elizabeth Hazard were married at New Bedford, Mass., August 27, 1801. Elizabeth Hazard, daughter of Thomas and Anna Hazard, was born in Rhode Island, December 2, 1783. She died in New York September 18, 1861, aged 77 years, 9 months and 16 days, and was buried in the Friends burying ground, Brooklyn, Long Island. Jacob Barker was born on Swan Island, Kennebec, Maine, December 17, 1779, and died in Philadelphia at the residence of his son, Abraham Barker, December 26, 1871, aged 92 years and 9 days, and was buried in Laurel Hill Cemetery. Their children were: 1. Robert, born in New York, June 11, 1802; died in Brooklyn, Long Island, September 28, 1803, aged 1 year, 3 months and 17 days. 2. Robert Hazard, born in Flushing, Long Island, July 20, 1804; died at sea, December 24, 1830, after a long illness, aged 26 years, 5 months and 4 days, unmarried. 3. Thomas Hazard, born in New York, June 21, 1807; died January 14, 1876, at Richmond, Va., unmarried; buried in Laurel Hill Cemetery, Philadelphia. 4. William, born in New York, August 21, 1809; married Janette James, of Albany, N. Y., and is now residing in New York. 5. Andrew Sigourney, born in New York, November 11, 1811; died in New York, August 11, 1846, aged 34 years and 9 months, unmarried; buried in the Friends burial ground, Brooklyn, Long Island. 6. Anna Hazard, born in New York, October 25, 1813; married Samuel G. Ward, of Boston. 7. Jacob, Jr., born in New York, May 23, 1816; died unmarried in New Orleans, Louisiana, April 27, 1842, aged 25 years, 11 months and 4 days; buried in the Protestant Cemetery, New Orleans. 8. Elizabeth Hazard, born in New York, July 4, 1817; married Baldwin Brower; second, Wm. T. Van Zandt; third John J. McCaulis. 9. Sarah, born in New York, July 23, 1819; married John C. Harrison, and, second, Wm. H. Hunt. 10. Abraham, born New York,

June 3, 1823; married, first, Sarah Wharton, daughter of William Wharton, of Philadelphia, and, second, Katherine, daughter of James Crane, of Elizabeth, New Jersey. 11. Mary, died in New York, January 9, 1826, aged 2 years, 6 months and 12 days. 12. John Wells, died in New York, December 18, 1825, a few hours after his birth.

ANN[7]—youngest daughter of Thomas Hazard[6]—married Philip Hone, of New York—son of the mayor—, and left one daughter, Joanna, who married Charles Kneeland, of New York, and left two sons.

EDWARD[7]—youngest son of Thomas Hazard[6]—died as he was entering into manhood, respected and beloved by all who knew him. He was a young man of singular amiability of disposition and irreproachable character.

ROWLAND HAZARD[6] (*Thomas*[5], *Robert*[4], *Thomas*[3], *Robert*[2], *Thomas*[1]), born April 4, 1763; removed in early manhood to Charleston, South Carolina, where he married in 1793, Mary, daughter of Isaac Peace, a wealthy merchant and highly respected citizen of that city. Joseph Peace, father of Isaac, embarked at Gravesend, England, for America, and settled in Pennsylvania, where he became possessed of the Brandywine, the Bristol and the Trenton flouring mills, together with a very large landed estate in and about Bristol and Trenton, including a goodly portion of Penn Manor. He died when his two daughters were minors and his sons, Joseph and Isaac, in infancy. Through the negligence of a fox-hunting guardian—an uncle Allen—the estate was mostly dissipated and alienated, leaving the heirs in comparative poverty. One of the daughters married ———Austin; the second—Sarah—married Sir Richard Chubb, whose gold sleeve-button with coat of arms thereon I have in my possession. I knew both these great-aunts in my boyhood. They lived and died in Philadelphia. Joseph Peace settled at New Garden, North Carolina, where many of his descendants remain and are highly respected.

Isaac Peace married and first settled in the Island of Barbadoes, where he engaged in mercantile pursuits. He afterwards removed to Charleston, where he followed the same business. During the devastating period of the Revolutionary War, he was again ruined in property, but long before his decease retrieved his circumstances. Finally, in his old age, he removed north and settled in Bristol, Bucks county, Pennsylvania. He was a man of great strength of mind and of sterling integrity. Isaac Peace married Elizabeth Gibson, of Barbadoes, July 12, 1770, and died in Bristol, Pennsylvania, December 25, 1818, aged 80 years. His wife died November 30, 1800, and was buried at Speights Town, Barbadoes. Their children were: 1. Joseph, born May 10, 1771; died May 31, 1826; married Anna Maria Rudhall, of Charleston, S. C. Their children were: Elizabeth G.; Ann Maria; Rebecca; Sophia; Isaac; Joseph; William Rudhall; Edward; Carolina; Mary, and Washington. 2. Sarah, born in Charleston, S. C., January 13, 1774; died January 14, 1795. 3. Mary P., born March 6, 1775; married Rowland Hazard. 4. Francis P., born February 16, 1776; died in infancy. 5. Isaac, born May 9, 1777; died July 16, 1780. 6. Rebecca, born August 22, 1781; married Dr. Nathaniel Cole, March 25, 1807; died November 13, 1851. Dr. Cole died July 18, 1848. Their children were: Elizabeth, born July 9, 1808; Sarah P., born October 1, 1810; married Samuel Starr and had children, Samuel and William; Rebecca, born August 10, 1813. Dr. Cole, his wife and children, all lived and died in Burlington, New Jersey.

Rowland Hazard[6] died at Washington Hollow, near Poughkeepsie, N. Y., 1835, aged 72. His wife died in Newport, R. I., in 1853, aged 78. Their remains are interred in the family burying ground at Vaucluse. Rowland engaged largely in mercantile pursuits, but was finally ruined through the operations of Napoleon's Berlin and Milan decrees, under which there were no less than seven ships and other vessels confiscated of which his mercantile firm was sole or part owner. He returned to South Kingstown and engaged in the manufacture of cotton and wool linseys some years previous to 1800. When he commenced the manufacturing business, the cotton used was brought from Charleston in what were called "pockets," containing some six or eight pounds each of cotton in the seed. This was picked by hand since my remembrance, and in the same manner as the wool was carded with hand cards, spun on hand wheels, and woven in hand looms.

For more than three-quarters of a century, Rowland Hazard, his sons, and his grandsons, have persevered in the manufacturing business, pursuing it through all its successive changes and improvements, until their extensive manufactories at Peace Dale, devoted to the manufacture of worsted goods, shawls, and French cassimeres, have reached a point of perfection perhaps not surpassed in the world, giving employment to four hundred and fifty persons, who, with the aid of the wonderfully improved machinery, turn out daily as many or more yards of goods than could have been produced in the infancy of the manufacture by one hundred thousand individuals or more. Nay, not long since I stood and observed a strippling spinning in one of these mills on ten highly improved jennies, and estimated statistically, from personal knowledge of the facts, that the boy turned off as much yarn *daily* as *one hundred* women used to spin for me, some sixty years ago, on the primitive hand spinning wheels, in a full week. Thus, supposing all the hands in the Peace Dale mills to be engaged in spinning with the present improved machinery, they would turn off as much yarn per week as two hundred and seventy thousand would have done since I commenced business in the same locality. Then, a spinner on a hand wheel earned twelve cents per day, only, while cotton sheeting was worth sixty cents and more per yard. Now, one woman will earn seventy-five cents per day, and pay ten cents, only, per yard for cotton sheeting, and other manufactured goods in proportion. Then a woman's work for a full week would buy one and one-quarter yards of sheeting; now, her week's wages will purchase forty-five yards, and most other manufactured articles in like proportion. This reads like romance, but it is nevertheless true.

The children of Rowland[6] and Mary Peace Hazard were: 1. Isaac Peace[7], born in South Kingstown, R. I., January, 1794; is now living in Newport, unmarried, aged 85 years. 2. Thomas R.[7], born in South Kingstown, R. I., January 3, 1797; married Frances Minturn, daughter of Jonas Minturn, of New York, October 12, 1838. Their children were: (a) Mary Robinson[8], born in Newport 1839; died 1842. (b) Frances Minturn[8], born at Vaucluse 1841; died 1877. (c) Gertrude Minturn[8], born at Vaucluse 1843; died 1877. (d) Anna Peace[8], born at Vaucluse 1845; died 1868. (e) Esther Robinson[8], born at Vaucluse 1848; married Edwin J. Dunning. (f) Barclay[8], born at Vaucluse December 4, 1852. [Thomas R. Hazard, the compiler of these tables, has been an earnest worker in the cause of what is called "Modern Spiritualism," since the year 1856, and whatever may be his merits or demerits otherwise, he has no higher ambition than that his name should be handed down to the coming generations associated with this fact alone.] 3. Eliza Gibson[7], born March, 1799, in South Kingstown, R. I., and now lives at No. 15 Kay street, Newport, where also dwell her brother Isaac and sister Anna. 4. Rowland Gibson[7], born in 1801, in South Kingstown, R. I.,; married Caroline, daughter of John Newbold, of Bristol, Pennsylvania. Their children are: (a) Rowland[8], born August 16, 1829; married Margaret, daughter of Rev. Anson Rood, of New Haven, Conn.; and has children, Rowland G., 2d.[9], Caroline[9], Frederick[9], Helen[8], and Margaret[9]. (b) John Newbold[8], born September 11, 1836: married Augusta Gurloff, of Philadelphia, and has children, Ernest[9], Edith[9], Robert[9], Mary[9], and John Gibson[9].

Rowland G. Hazard is one of the ablest of American writers, and has published many volumes and essays of wide-acknowledged merit. Among others are the following: "Language," 120 pages, 1835, second edition 1857; "The Adaptation of the Universe to the Cultivation of the Mind," 1841; "The Philosophical Character of Channing," written by request of Channing's friends, and first published in Boston soon after Channing's death; "The Character and Writings of the late Chief Justice Durfee, LL. D., of Rhode Island"; "The Duty of Individuals to support Science and Literature"; "Causes of the Decline of Political Morality"; "Public Schools"; "Intemperance"; "Freedom of Mind in Willing, or Every Being that Wills a Creative First Cause," 455 pages, published by D. Appleton & Co., 1864; "Two Letters on Causation and Freedom of Willing, addressed to John Stuart Mill," with appendices on "The Existence of Matter," and " Our Notions of Infinite Space," 300 pages, published by Lee & Shepard Boston, 1869, translated and published in Leipsic, Germany, by B. Westermann & Co., 1875; "Our Resources"—treating of the financial and political situation in the United States—London and Amsterdam, 1864, 35 pages; "Hours of Labor," published in the North American Review, January, 1866; "Relations of Railroad Corporations to the Public", published in Hunt's Merchants' Magazine, December, 1849, 50 pages; and "Animals not Automatic"—a reply to Huxley—published in Popular Science Monthly, February, 1875.

WILLIAM R. HAZARD[7] (*Rowland*[6], *Thomas*[5], *Robert*[4], *Thomas*[3], *Robert*[2], *Thomas*[1]), fifth child of Rowland; of Poplar Ridge, New York; born 1803 in South Kingstown; married Mary, daughter of John Wilbur, of Hopkinton, R. I., 1828. Their children are: 1. John W. Hazard[8], born 1830; married Adelia Hoag, and had children (a) Jarvis[9]; (b) Charles M.[9] His second wife is Sarah E. Raymond. 2. Mary G.,[8] born 1833; married Samuel G. Cook 1863. 3. Lydia

C.[8], born 1835; married Franklin E. Hoag. 4. Elizabeth[8], born 1837. 5. Rowland[8], born 1839; married Phebe Ann Moore 1865, and has children: (a) George[9], died 1875, aged 7 years. (b) William[9]. 6. Anna[8], born 1841; married Thomas Tierney 1867. 7. William W.[8], born 1843. 8. Isaac P.[8], born 1847; married Elizabeth Howland 1871.

JOSEPH PEACE HAZARD, (*Rowland*[6], *Thomas*,[5] *Robert*[4], *Thomas*[3], *Robert*[2], *Thomas*[1]), sixth child of Rowland; born February, 1807, at Burlington, N. J.; now 72 years of age. Joseph is one of the most extensive of American travelers, and is now absent on an overland journey around the world.

ISABELLA WAKEFIELD HAZARD[7], seventh child of Rowland[6]; born in Bristol, Pennsylvania, February, 1807; died 1838. Mary Peace Hazard[7], eighth child of Rowland[6], born in Bristol, Pennsylvania, 1814; died in Newport 1874; buried at Vaucluse beside the grave of her sister Isabella. Anna[7], ninth child of Rowland[6], born in South Kingstown, October, 1820.

JONATHAN HAZARD[5] (*Robert*[4], *Thomas*[3], *Robert*[2], *Thomas*[1]), second child; died young.

RICHARD HAZARD[5] (*Robert*[4], *Thomas*[3], *Robert*,[2] *Thomas*[1]), third child; removed to the West in early manhood. He was the father of George[6], who lived highly respected, near Worden's Pond, on a part of the estate that descended from his grandfather Robert[4]. He here died about 1826-7.

SARAH HAZARD[5] (*Robert*[4], *Thomas*[3], *Robert*[2], *Thomas*[1]), the only daughter of Robert; married Job Watson. At the time of his marriage, Mr. Watson occupied and improved the Dyer and Bull estates on Tower Hill, and afterwards removed to Conanicut, where he became a great land-holder. Their children were: 1. Job Watson, married Phebe Weeden, and had children, Daniel W., Elizabeth E., Sally, and Phebe. 2. Robert H. Watson, married Catherine Weeden, and had children, Isabella, Joseph W., Sarah, Daniel (M. D), Hannah, and Robert H. 3. Walter Watson, married Mary Carr, and had children, Isabella, Nicholas C., Job, Isabella, 2d, Thomas Hazard, William M., Elisha, Walter, and John E. 4. Borden Watson, married Isabella Babcock, and had children, John H., Borden, Sarah, Mary, Abijah B., Albert, and Job S. 5. John J. Watson, married, first, a daughter of Gov. George Brown, and had children, William R., Henry H., and two daughters. His second wife was Isabella Watson. Their children were: Walter S., Job H., Isabella, Emily, Harriet, and Thomas.

GEORGE HAZARD^3 (*Robert^2, Thomas^1*), second son of Robert; died 1743. His children were: 1. Robert^4, "who", says E. R. Potter, "probably died before his father." 2. Caleb^4. 3. George^4. 4. Thomas^4. 5. Oliver^4.

CALEB HAZARD^4 (*George^3, Robert^2, Thomas^1*), married Abigail, daughter of William Gardiner. Mrs. Hazard subsequently became the wife of Gov. William Robinson. Caleb died January 15, 1727, aged 28 years and was buried in the family burying ground, situated to the east of the old post-road, about two miles south and west of Wakefield, R. I., on the farm now owned by Mrs. Mary F., the wife of Rev. Elisha F. Watson. Judging from the length of his grave, Caleb Hazard must have been a man of Herculean stature. The children of Caleb Hazard were: 1. William^5. 2. Dr. Robert^5, died February 12, 1771 [see Updike]. 3. Caleb^5.

GEORGE HAZARD^4 (*George^3, Robert^2, Thomas^1*), deputy governor. His children were: 1. Carder^5, married Alice, daughter of Col. Thomas Hazard, March 5, 1761. Their children were: (a) George^6, doctor; had children: (A) Dr. William Henry^7, of Wakefield, R. I.; married a daughter of the late Governor Lemuel Arnold. (B) Carder^7, died some years ago at his residence in Wakefield. (C) Jane^7, married Dr. Greene, of East Greenwich. (D) Edward H.^{7}, attorney at law, Providence; owns and occupies the John Bigelow Dockray old mansion-house and farm, near Wakefield. (E) George^7. (F) Mary H.^{7}, married Rev. James H. Carpenter, and has children: Esther B.—a fine writer of both prose and verse—, Elizabeth Case—deceased—, James Willett, Laura, and Mary. (G) Laura[7], married Attmore Robinson—for children, see "Robinson Genealogy." (H) Alice[7]. (b) Peter[6]. (c) Robert[6]. By his second wife, Carder Hazard's children were: (d) Thomas C.[6], had children: (A) Joseph B.[7], deceased. (B) A daughter[7], married Nathan Kenyon. (e) Richard[6], had children: (A) Joseph[7]. (B) Daniel [7], who now lives in the old homestead on the farm next north of the Dr. George Hazard estate; a daughter[8] of his married Jonathan Allen, of South Portsmouth, R. I. (C) Joshua[7]. (f) Arnold[6], ship captain, died in early manhood. (g) Edward[6], ship captain; died in early manhood. (h) Alice[6]. 2. George[5].

From a late paper I have cut this slip containing an obituary of Judge Carder Hazard[5]: "*The Providence Journal Eighty-Five Years Ago.*—The sight of a yellow old paper of diminutive size, No. 48 of the Providence Gazette and Country Journal, bearing date of December 1, 1792, suggests many trite but still impressive comparisons between the customs of the old times and the way we live now. * * * A longer notice records the death of a member of one of the Narragansett Families: 'Last Saturday departed this life, at South Kingston, in the 59th year of his age, Honorable Carder Hazard, Esq., one of the Judges of the Supreme Court of this State. In political life he exhibited the honest citizen and the upright judge; subject to Laws, he reverenced them, and invested with Power, he executed it without Intrigue, and without a view of Self-interest. In social Life, the Goodness of his Heart and the Simplicity of his Manners were peculiarly agreeable—but death has closed his Labors! and the Pity of that Death has evidenced the Innocence of his Life. With that of the Public, his particular Friends have united their own private Sorrow.' Judge Carder Hazard was son of George Hazard, Deputy Governor of Rhode Island, brother to George Hazard, Mayor of Newport, and father of the late Dr. George Hazard, of South Kingstown, R. I. E. B. C."

From Updike's History of the Narragansett Church, page 321, I extract the following: George Hazard, the son of Caleb, was elected a member of the General Assembly for Newport many years. The Newport Mercury contained the following obituary notice: 'Died in this town on Friday, August 11, 1791, George Hazard, Esq., for many years a respectable merchant; for upwards of thirty years a Representative from this town in the Legislature; for twelve years Chief Justice of the Court of Common Pleas for this county; a member of the convention which adopted the Constitution of the United States, and formerly mayor of the city of Newport.'

Edward Hazard, the eldest son of Mayor George Hazard, married Sarah Cranston, the daughter of the Hon. Thomas Cranston, grandson of Gov. Samuel Cranston, in May, 1770, and settled on a farm given him by his father in South Kingstown. Thomas Cranston Hazard, only son and child of Edward, graduated from Rhode Island college in 1792, and is now living in Voluntown, Connecticut. Nathaniel Hazard, third son of Mayor George, graduated from Rhode Island college in 1792. He was a Representative in the General Assembly for several years, and was Speaker of the House. In 1818 he was elected Representative to Congress. He died at Washington in 182—, and was interred in the Congressional burial ground. Nathaniel was the father of the late gallant Captain Samuel F. Hazard of the U. S. Navy, who married Martha, youngest daughter of Charles DeWolf, Esq. Their children were: a daughter who died in infancy, and Martha, who married Dr. Sturgis, of New York City.

THOMAS HAZARD[4] (*George*[3], *Robert*[2], *Thomas*[1]), fourth son; colonel; had children: 1. George[5], married Jane Tweedy, July 28, 1769. 2. Penelope[5], married Judge William Potter, youngest son of Col. John Potter, November 18, 1750. 3. Abigail[5], married Rev. Samuel Fayerweather. 4. Sarah[5], married George Hazard, son of Thomas[3].

OLIVER HAZARD[4] (*George*[3], *Robert*[2], *Thomas*[1]), fifth son; his children were: 1. Oliver[5]. 2. Raymond[5]. 3. Sarah[5]. 4. Lucretia[6]. One of his daughters married Freeman Perry, grandfather of Commodore Oliver Hazard Perry.

STEPHEN HAZARD[3] (*Robert*[2], *Thomas*[1]), third son; had a son, Judge Stephen[4], who married Mary Robinson. Their son Stephen[5]—called "Long Stephen"—owned and occupied a large landed estate in Point Judith. He married a daughter of Lieutenant Governor Nichols, who built and lived in the fine Hunter mansion on the "Point" in Newport, as his winter residence, and the house in Middletown where Colonel Prescott was captured, as his summer residence. The children of Stephen[5] and Mary Robinson Hazard were: 1. Nichols Hassard[6], died in Newport, 1848; had children: Alice[7], Mary[7], Phebe[7], Ruth[7], Sarah[7], Hannah[7], Nichols[7], Edward[7]. 2. Jonathan N. Hassard[6], married Mary Robinson, daughter of Sylvester Robinson; died in the West Indies whilst captain of a ship. His children were: James[7], Alice[7], Stephen[7], Jonathan N.[7], Sylvester[7], and Mary[7].

JONATHAN N. HASSARD[7] (*Jonathan N.*[6], *Stephen*[5], *Stephen*[4], *Stephen*[3], *Robert*[2], *Thomas*[1]), grandson of "Long Stephen"; married Mary, daughter of John Congdon. Their children were: 1. Mary Abby[8]. 2. Sarah C.[8], married the late Captain Louis Hazard, and has children. 3. John C.[8] 4. Rowland N.[8], married Sarah Lawrence Suydam, of New York City. 5. William S.[8]. 6. Herbert[8], married Jennie B. Hunter. All four of the above named sons of Jonathan N. Hassard are at present highly respected and prosperous business men in the city of New York.

JOHN HASSARD[6] (*Stephen*[5], *Stephen*[4], *Stephen*[3], *Robert*[2], *Thomas*[1]), son of "Long Stephen"; was an officer in the British Navy, and after the war of 1776 emigrated to Prince Edward's Island, where many of his descendants now reside.

THOMAS HASSARD[5] (*Stephen*[4], *Stephen*[3], *Robert*[2], *Thomas*[1]), a son of Judge Stephen; had a son, Thomas S. Hassard[6]. Judge Stephen Hassard[4] also left daughters, Mary[5], Martha[5], Elizabeth[5], and Sarah[5]. Many of the descendants of Judge Stephen Hassard at the present day write the name with a double *s*, as their ancestors, including the judge, were wont to do.

ROBERT HAZARD[3] (*Robert*[2], *Thomas*[1]), had sons: Geoffrey[4], "called Stout Jeffrey." 2. Robert[4], Deputy Governor of the colony 1750; died February 12, 1771. 3. John[4]. 4. Jeremiah[4], who was, says Potter, "grandfather of Jeffrey Hazard[6], late Lieutenant Governor [1835]."

GEOFFREY HAZARD[4] (*Robert*[3], *Robert*[2], *Thomas*[1]), inherited the northern portion of his father's estate, lying on the east side of Rose Hill, R. I. The remains of the cellar of his house are still to be seen a little north of the family burial ground. It used to be said that "Stout Jeffrey" had the strength of six common men. Rowland Hazard[8], son of Rowland G.[7], has now on his lawn at Peace Dale, R. I., a blue-stone weighing over sixteen hundred pounds, that he had brought from the Governor Brown farm in Boston Neck, once occupied by Stout Jeffrey. Tradition says that this stone was lifted and carried several rods by Geoffrey.

To judge by the length of many of their graves the early Hazards must indeed have been a race of giants in comparison with whom their descendants are mere pigmies. My own family of five brothers—all now living, and averaging over 78 years of age—in early manhood averaged fully six feet and one inch in height, standing in their stockings, and certainly will not require grave-stones to be set more than from six to six and one-half feet apart; whereas, on a visit I lately made to the old Jeffrey Hazard burial ground, I measured five separate graves ranging from seven feet between the head and foot stone to seven feet nine inches.

Stout Jeffrey Hazard[4] had several sons. One son was Jeremiah[5]. His son was Thomas[6], and his son was Arnold[7].

Arnold Hazard lived on Conanicut Island, Rhode Island, and had children : Lucy[8], Jeremiah[8], Thomas A.[8], Job W.[8] —who now lives on Conanicut—, Daniel W.W.[8] Dr. Thomas A. Hazard[8], now of Kingston, is probably as good a specimen of his ancestors, in physique, as can be found. He stands six feet two inches in his boots, and weighs two hundred and sixty-five pounds avoirdupois.

HANNAH[5], daughter of Geoffrey Hazard[4], married Thomas Champlin, who removed into New York State. From them have descended a numerous progeny.

Some years ago there came to Narragansett from the western part of Massachusetts, one of the finest looking men I ever saw, whose name was Rodman Hazard, and whose ancestors emigrated from Rhode Island. From his height and athletic build of person I think he must have been one of Stout Jeffrey's lineal descendants. At another time there called at my house at Vaucluse, Judge Meech, who was the largest farmer, and I think the tallest and most gigantic man every way there was at that time in Vermont. His mother was a Hazard from Narragansett, and I think must have belonged to the Stout Jeffrey branch of the family. Since the above was first printed, I have met a gentleman from Madison, New York, who told me that the late Paul Hazard, a highly respected citizen of that place, was an early settler from Rhode Island. Paul left two sons—now living—who inherit, in an eminent degree, the sterling qualities and strong physique of their father. I think they may have descended from Stout Jeffrey. I also learn by a letter from Mr. Lester Gorton, of Hancock, Berkshire county, Massachusetts, that Rodman Hazard mentioned above was an early settler in that town ; that he was a son of Henry, whose father's name was Thomas; and that Henry with his brother Clark came to Hancock from Rhode Island. Rodman's children were : Wanton, Rodman, Laura—married a Mr. Green and is the mother of four children—, and Eunice, who married a Gorton and is the mother of Lester Gorton mentioned before and four other children. The late Thomas T. Hazard, who represented the town of West Greenwich for a great many years in the General Assembly, was probably a descendant of Stout Jeffrey.

JEREMIAH HAZARD[4] (*Robert,*[3] *Robert*[2], *Thomas*[1]), had either a son or a grandson named Jeremiah. His sons were: John, who lived on Boston Neck near Stewart's snuff mill, Robert, and Rowland, by his first wife, and Wilbur, by his second wife. Ephraim Hazard[4], the father of Robinson Hazard[5] and grandfather of Louis Hazard[6], who is now living on MacSparran Hill in North Kingstown, and Gideon Hazard[4] were brothers of Jeremiah. The children of John, by his first wife, were: George, John, Ruth, Sarah, Patience, Mary, Abby, Hannah, Jeremiah, and Catherine; by his second wife, Cranston, and Elizabeth.

JEREMIAH HAZARD, the son of John, died recently in Newport. He was nearly 85 years of age, but up to within a short time of his death stood as straight and walked with as vigorous and elastic a step as an ordinary boy of twenty. He inherited many of the distinguishing traits of the "snip" breed of Hazards. His children were: James W., and Harriet, who married George H. Wilson, a master builder and highly respected citizen of Newport, Rhode Island.

GEORGE HAZARD[4] (*Thomas*[3], *Robert*[2], *Thomas*[1]), second son; had children: 1. Benjamin[5]. 2. Simeon[5]. 3. Enoch[5]. 4. George[5]. 5. Thomas G.[5].

BENJAMIN HAZARD[5], first son of George[4]; had children: 1. Richard[6], married, on the death of his brother Benjamin, her first husband, his cousin Hannah Hazard, a daughter of Simeon Hazard. Their children were: (a) Joseph Wanton[7], married Mary Potter, of South Kingstown. (b) John. (c) Mary. (d) Richard Joseph. (e) Rowland. (f) Abigail, married Richard Mumford. (g) Mary Ann, married a Snow of Providence. (h) Alice, married William Perry.

26

Richard[6] died in Newport between 1845 and 1850, aged 102 years. The mother of the late John D. Dennis, in Broadway, Newport, was a granddaughter of Richard Hazard[6]. 2. Benjamin[6], married his cousin Hannah Hazard, who after his decease married his brother Richard. 3. Wanton [6].

From all I can learn John Hazard[6]—called "Wickham John" from the fact that his mother's name had been Wickham—appears to have been a son of Enoch[5], or Benjamin[5], both sons of George Hazard[4]. John Hazard[6] owned and occupied, since my remembrance, a large tract of land on MacSparran Hill extending from Pettaquamscutt lake on the east, to Saucatucket river on the west. He married Sarah, daughter of Nathan Gardner. Their children were: 1. John[7]. 2. Nathan G.[7] He married as his second wife, Martha Clarke, daughter of Latham and Martha Robinson Clarke and sister to Lewis Latham Clarke. John[7] married Frances, daughter of ——— Gardiner, a lineal descendant of Col. John Gardner, of Boston Neck, and granddaughter of George Hazard, first and only mayor of Newport of the olden time. Their children were: (a) Martha Clarke[8], married Elnathan Brown, and, second, Ossimus Stillman. (b) Frances Gardiner[8]. (c) John Alfred[8]. Nathan G.[7] married his brother John's widow. Their children were: (a) William R.[8], married a daughter of Benjamin Staunton. (b) Sarah G.[8] (c) Catharine H.[8] (d) John[8]. I was well acquainted with Nathan G. Hazard. He was a thorough gentleman of the old school, inheriting in that respect the qualities of his father.

SIMEON HAZARD[5] (*George*[4], *Thomas*[3], *Robert*[2], *Thomas*[1]), had children: 1. Geoffrey[6], who was the father of the late Dr. Jonathan Easton Hazard[7], of Portsmouth, R. I., a man of the most sterling qualities and a true gentleman. 2. Mumford[6], married, 1786, Elizabeth, daughter of Christopher Robinson. 3. Simeon[6], whose daughter, married a Mumford and had a son, Richard. 4. George[6]. 5. Abigail[6].

GEORGE S. HAZARD[6], fourth child of Simeon[5], born May 15, 1773; married Content Wilbur; died November 29. 1836, aged 63 years, 6 months and 14 days. Mrs. Hazard was born October 8, 1782; died January 16, 1833, aged 50 years, 3 months and 8 days. Their children were: 1. Mumford[7]. 2. Elizabeth[7]. 3. Charles Tillinghast[7]. 4. Arnold W.[7]. 5. Ann Matilda[7]. 6. William Wilbour[7]. 7. Harriet[7]. 8. Henry B.[7]. 9. Simeon[7]. 10. James Lawrence[7]. 11. George Augustus[7].

MUMFORD HAZARD[7], first child of George S.[6], born February 1, 1802; married Sarah Tilley; died November 13, 1876. Their children are: 1. George Mumford[8], born March 25, 1822; married Almira Sweet February 1, 1847. Mrs. Hazard was born June 27, 1823. Their children are: (a) Henry Holt[9], born July 11, 1848; died August 27, 1851. (b) Albert Armstrong[9], born July 25, 1850; died March 2, 1852. (c) Frank Sweet[9], born February 25, 1852. (d) Herbert Gould[9], born November 15, 1853; married Fannie Packard, 1878. (e) Simeon[9], born January 16, 1856. (f) Mary Frances[9], born November 16, 1857; died September 1,1858. (g) Benj. I.[9], born March 11,1860; died August 26, 1860. 2. Charles H.[8], married Sarah Smith. Their children are: Daniel[9], Isaac[9], Maria[9], Henry[9],—deceased—, and Emma[9]. 3. James T.[8], born May 2, 1828; married Phebe Gould, daughter of Thomas Gould March 10, 1851. Mrs. Gould was born June 8, 1828. Their children are: (a) Fanny H.[9], born May 15, 1853; married Gardner S. Perry 1876, and has one child. (b) Eloise P.[9], born June 4, 1858. 4. Benjamin I.[8], of Georgetown, S. C., born March, 1831; married Sarah Ingalls, of Taunton, Mass. Their children are: Allen P.[9], Walter[9], Benjamin I., Jr.[9], Jonathan Ingalls[9], Schuyler[9], Lena May[9], Ruth Tilley[9], and Hattie W.[9]. 5. William T.[8], of Randolph, Mass., born 1834; married Mary Ryan. Their children are: Nellie[9], William R.[9], and Blanche[9]. 6. Sarah E.[8], born 1836. 7. Thomas T.[8], of New York, born 1839; married Margaret Kellogg. Their children are: Leverett

K.[9], Nellie[9], Sallie T.[9], and Thomas T., Jr.[9]   8. Mary S.[8], born 1842.

ELIZABETH HAZARD[7], second child of George S.[6], born January 19, 1804; married William Wilbour April 15, 1827. Their children are: Joseph [8]—deceased—, William Henry[8], Harriet[8], and Caroline[8]—deceased.

CHARLES TILLINGHAST HAZARD[7], third child of George S.[6], born July 31, 1806; married Sarah Cook. Mrs. Hazard was born October 6, 1807; died January 16, 1874. Their children were: 1. George Sullivan[8], born May 18, 1827; married Mary Wilson, and had one child, Annie F.[9] His second wife is Annie Wellman. 2. Charles Godfrey[8], born November 9, 1830; married Mary Warner, and has children, Charles T.[9], and Louie Augustus[9]. 3. John C.[8], born May 16, 1833; died July 29, 1835. 4. Lucretia S.[8], born August 5, 1835; died September 1, 1845. 5. William C.[8], born August 16, 1837; married Mary Peckham. 6. Silas H.[8], born January 27, 1840; married Sallie Burdick, and has one child, Fannie[9]. 7. Edward E.[8], born April 13, 1843. 8. Charles T.[8], born December 30, 1845.

ARNOLD W. HAZARD[7], fourth child of George S.[6], born October 8, 1807; married Sarah Ann Stedman March 14, 1830. Their children are: 1. George A.[8], born August 5, 1831; married Mary Barber, and has children: Sarah Ellen[9], William S.[9], Elizabeth S.[9], and Amelia T.[9] 2. Stephen Stedman[8], born February 2, 1833; died September 3, 1834. 3. Sarah Content[8], born October 14, 1834; married Jethro C. Carr December 1, 1852, and had children, George H., Florence T., Samuel E.; married, second, George W. Sanford and has one child, James Hazard. 4. Mary Elizabeth[8], born November 19, 1836; died October 23, 1842. 5. Harriet A.[8], born June 5, 1838; married Charles F. Palmer, of Randolph, Mass., September 18, 1856; and has one child, Sarah S. 6. James Stedman[8], born January 4, 1841; died November 4, 1842. 7. James Stedman[8], born April 4, 1843; married, first, Sarah E. Harvey, second, Sarah A.

Titus.[8] Elizabeth S.[8], born October 7, 1845; died September 28, 1846.   9. Simeon[8], born December 3, 1847; died January 8, 1848.

ANN MATILDA HAZARD[7], fifth child of George S.[6], born September 20, 1808; married Stephen M. Stedman, November 3, 1833.

WILLIAM WILBOR HAZARD[7], sixth child of George S[6]., born July 4, 1810; married Sarah M. Armstrong, October 27, 1834; died January 11, 1874. Their children are: 1. Isabella Donaldson[8], married Joseph M. Bokee, of Brooklyn, N. Y., October 6, 1855; and has children, Ida Donaldson, Margaret Helena, Joseph Alexander, and Archer Hazard—died October, 1873. 2. Theophilus Dunn[8]. 3. George Armstrong[8], married Josephine Augusta, daughter of Thomas T. Carr, of Newport, December 18, 1871, and has one child, Duncan Armstrong[9], born May, 1875. 4. Mary Estelle[8]. 5. Helen Bannister[8]. 6. Alithea Lenox.

HARRIET HAZARD[7], seventh child of George S[6]. born January, 23, 1813; married George Albert Armstrong November 4, 1833. Mr. Armstrong was born September 30, 1809. Their children are: 1. William Albert, born October 11, 1834; married Carrie Lewis November, 1857, and has children, Minnie and George A. 2. Harriet Augusta, born December 11, 1841; died August 16, 1850.

HENRY B. HAZARD[7], eighth child of George S.[6], born December 23, 1815; married Eunice G. Wilbur, August 11, 1840. Mrs. Hazard was born February 16, 1816. Their children are: 1. Lebbeus Ensworth[8], born July 3, 1841; married Amelia J. Ludlum, of New York, August 3, 1865, and has one child, Lawrence Wilbur[9], born October 17, 1874. Mrs. Hazard died February 13, 1878, in the 34th year of her age. 2. Abby Congdon[8], born October 18, 1843. 3. Henry Bond, Jr.[8], born December 26, 1845. 4. Frank[8], born July 30, 1848; died July 21, 1851. 5. Arthur[8], born November 6, 1850. 6. Emma[8], born January 18, 1853. 7. Rena[8], born July 18, 1856.

SIMEON HAZARD[7], ninth child of George S.[6], born January 7, 1817; married Mary Ann Stevens, November 15, 1838; died August 20, 1855. Their children were: 1. Sarah W.[8], born October 2, 1839; married Edwin G. Spooner June 27, 1864, and has children, Sarah C., born March 12, 1865, George S., born January 1, 1869. 2 Elizabeth S.[8], born October 28, 1841; died September 26, 1842. 3. Elizabeth S.[8], born November 13, 1843; died May 29, 1846. 4. George S.[8], born, June 4, 1846; married Sarah Amanda Stoddard October 20, 1870, and has children: (a) Margie S.[9], born May 11, 1872. (b) George Ashley[9], born April 12, 1875. 5. Annie W.[8], born June 26, 1849. 6. Willam S.[8], born November 5, 1853.

JAMES LAWRENCE[7], tenth child of George S.[6], born February 21, 1818; married Frances B. Irish 1842. Their child is: 1. Martha Simpson[8], born September 30, 1843; married Eben H. Godbold May 31, 1866, and has children, Edwin Joslyn, and Lawrence Hazard.

GEORGE AUGUSTUS[7], eleventh child of George S.[6], born March 26, 1819; married Abby C. Card October 3, 1843, and has children: 1. Charlotte Thayer[8], married Prof. John M. Cross, of Johns Hopkins University, March 27, 1878. 2. Caroline Clark[8].

ABIGAIL HAZARD[6] (*Simeon*[5], *George*[4], *Thomas*[3], *Robert*[2], *Thomas*[1]), fifth and last child of Simeon[6], was the second wife of Robert Rodman, of South Kingstown. Robert Rodman's children—all by his first wife—were: Robert, Samuel, William, Clark, Thomas, James, and Sarah. Sarah married Samuel Curtis, of Peace Dale, one of the truly good men that have lived on earth. Robert Rodman, son of Robert, married a sister of Thomas S. Hazard, who was the father of Augustus Hazard, the great powder manufacturer of Enfield, Connecticut, who supplied the government with most of that material of war used during the late dreadful fraternal strife. A daughter of Augustus married Governor Bullock, of Massachusetts. Robert Rodman the second was the father of Samuel, whose son, Gen. Isaac P. Rodman, was killed at Antietam, whilst his younger brother, Capt. Rowland G. Rodman, was shot through the shoulder with a musket bullet at the Fredericksburg slaughter. Daniel Rodman, who owns the manufactory and a large estate at Mooresfield, in South Kingstown, on which he now resides, and Robert Rodman, who owns the manufactory at Wakefield and several other large establishments in North Kingstown, were sons of Clark Rodman, son of the first Robert.

GEORGE HAZARD[5] (*George*[4], *Thomas*[3], *Robert*[2], *Thomas*[1]), born March 3, 1727; married Sarah Hazard, third daughter of Colonel Thomas Hazard. [See Updike.] George owned and occupied the "Little Neck farm" in Point Judith, situated south of Boston Neck on the Pettaquamscutt river. He was the father of Thomas H. Hazard[6], who was born March 3, 1765.

THOMAS H. HAZARD[6] (*George*[5], *George*[4], *Thomas*[3], *Robert*[2], *Thomas*[1]), married Abigail, youngest daughter of Sylvester Robinson. Their children were: 1. Sylvester R.[7], born March 3, 1791; married Hannah, daughter of Stephen Congdon, of South Kingstown; died in Newport September 16, 1875. Their children were: (a) Christopher C. G.[8], born March 3, 1818; died in infancy. (b) Christopher Grant Champlin[8]. Sylvester married as his second wife Gulielma M., daughter of Caleb and Waite Babcock. Their children was: (c) Abby K.[8], married William Atmore Whaley, of Newport, R. I. Sylvester R. married as his third wife Abby C., daughter of Thomas and Abby Clarke, of Philadelphia, and widow of Mr. Francisco. Sylvester R. Hazard was a tall, strong and a good man. 2. Dr. Rowland Robinson[7], second son of Thomas H.[6], married Anna, daughter of Governor Charles Collins. He died in Newport, September 21, 1874, aged 82 years. He was a gentleman of refined breeding and highly respected. 3. Sally[7], married George Congdon, of Point Judith. 4. George R.[7].

GEORGE R. HAZARD[7], third son of Thomas H[6], married Ann Barnet, an English lady. Their children were: 1. Victoria[8]. 2. Oliver Perry[8]. 3. Rowland R.[8], married Margaret Rhodes. 4. Louis L.[8], married Sarah C., daughter of Jonathan N. Hazard, and had children: (a) Ada [9]. (b) Helen[9]. (c) George R.[9] (d) Sarah C.[9] (e) Louise Holyoke[9]. (f) Jane Hunter[9]. In February, 1876, Captain Hazard sailed from Calcutta, India, for New York, in command of the fine ship Radiant, owned by Thayer & Lincoln, of Boston, and no tidings of the vessel, crew or passengers have ever been received. The voyage was begun under the most favorable auspices, and the sad fate which awaited the ship, was entirely unforeseen. 5. Alice[8], married Joseph Babcock, and has children, Thomas, and Abby. 6. Abby [8]. 7. Mary Ann[8], married Thomas G., son of Thomas G. Hazard, of Newport; had children, Thomas, and Mary Anna.

A most extraordinary succession of coincidences or freaks of nature is associated with this branch of the Hazard family, and until within a few years this has been commemorated by an annual anniversary held by the family on the third day of March for more than three-quarters of a century. I extract from the printed copy: "George Hazard, son of George, was born in South Kingstown, R. I., *March* 3, 1727. Thomas H. Hazard, eldest son of George, the son of George, was born in South Kingstown, *March* 3, 1775. Sylvester R. Hazard, eldest son of Thomas H., was born in South Kingstown *March* 3, 1793. Christopher G. Hazard, eldest son of Sylvester R., who died in infancy, was born in Newport, *March* 3, 1818." Sylvester R. used to speak of remembering being present at one of these anniversaries more than seventy years ago, when Thomas B. Hazard, of South Kingstown —called "Nailor Tom"—, proposed this toast: "Here is

'Health to the sick,
Honor to the brave,
Success to the lover,
And freedom to the slave.'"

ENOCH HAZARD[5] (*George*[4], *Thomas*[3], *Robert*[2], *Thomas*[1]), lived on the farm in Boston Neck now owned by J. M. Potter, and had children: Enoch[6], and two daughters[6], one of whom married Jeremiah Niles Potter, the maternal grandfather of Jeremiah P. Robinson, of New York.

THOMAS G. HAZARD[5] (*George*[4], *Thomas*[3], *Robert*[2], *Thomas*[1]), youngest son of George; married Mary, daughter of Jonathan Easton. Thomas G. was but four years old when his father died, and had nephews older than himself. His patrimony fell into the hands of lawyers, but his sister Mary—called "Molly"—, seeing that they would plunder her little brother of his estate, went into court and contended successfully for his rights in her own person. Molly was a heroine of no ordinary stamp, and made several journeys to and from Philadelphia on horseback. More than one of Thomas G. Hazard's female descendants inherited her spirit in an eminent degree. The children of Thomas G.[6], son of Thomas G.[5], were: 1. John Alfred[7]. 2. William[7]. 3. Thomas G.[7]. 4. Mary E.[7]. 5. George Borden[7]. 6. Enoch[7]. 7. Ruth[7], married Luther Bateman. 8. Benjamin[7]. 9. Isaac[7].

BENJAMIN HAZARD[7] (*Thomas G.*[6], *Thomas G.*[5], *George*[4], *Thomas*[3], *Robert*[2], *Thomas*[1]), born September 9, 1774; married Harriet Lyman October 28, 1807; died March 10, 1841. Mrs. Hazard was born March 6, 1784; died February 23, 1875. Their children were: 1. Emily[8], born October 16, 1808. 2. Peyton Randolph°, born April 9, 1810; died in St. Louis July 2, 1849. 3. Harriet[8], born March 26, 1812; married Rev. Charles T. Brooks October 18, 1837. Their children are: (a) Charles, born July 24, 1830; married, and has had four children, two of whom are living. (b) Harriet Lyman, born July 10, 1841; married George Stevens, of Haverhill, Mass., and has four children. (c) Jonathan Mason, born September 12, 1844; died March, 1863. (d) Mary Elizabeth, born April 6, 1847; married Lieutenant Washburn Maynard, U. S. Navy, and has two sons. (e)

Peyton H., born September 26, 1850; married and has one child. 4. Mary Wanton[8], born December 14, 1813; died April 2, 1814. 5. Mary Wanton[8], born March 5, 1815. 6. Margaret Lyman[8], born April 8, 1817; married General Isaac Ingalls Stevens September 8, 1841. General Stevens was shot through the head with a musket ball, and instantly killed during the late civil war. Their children are: (a) Hazard, born June 9, 1842. He was more than once promoted during the war of the Rebellion, before he was twenty years of age, for his bravery and good conduct. (b) Julia Virginia, born June 27, 1844; died in Bucksport, Me. (c) Susan, born November 20, 1846; married Captain Eskridge, U. S. Army, and has five children. (d) Gertrude Maud, born April 29, 1850. (e) Kate, born November 28, 1852. 7. Nancy[8], born June 4, 1819; married John Alfred Hazard, son of Dr. Enoch, June 11, 1855; had one child, Nicholas Easton, born October 14, 1856; died May 18, 1874, aged 17 years. 8. Daniel L.[8], born July 19, 1821; married Delia Louisa Colton, of Philadelphia, May 20, 1869, and has children: (a) Emily B.[9], born October 20, 1870. (b) Peyton Randolph[9], born April 13, 1873. 9. Thomas G.[8], born March 13, 1824; married Mary King Brooks, sister of Rev. C. T. Brooks, December 8, 1858. Thomas G. owns and occupies the farm in Narragansett that has been in the family since it was purchased by Thomas Hazard[3], the son of Robert[2], the son of Thomas[1]. The children of Thomas G.[8], and Mary King Hazard are: (a) Mary King[8]—called "Molly"—, born February 20, 1860; died January 2, 1874; a child of great promise. (b) Thomas G.[9], born July 20, 1862. (c) Daniel L.[9], born August 26, 1865.

The following just tribute to the memory of Benjamin Hazard[6], son of Thomas G.[5], is from the pen of Hon. William Hunter, formerly United States minister at the Court of Brazil: "There is one individual belonging to this numerous, widespread and highly respectable race, who is deserving of particular notice and regard. We refer to the late Hon. Benjamin

Hazard. His portrait has already been sketched by the skillful hand of Professor Goddard. [See 'Address to the People of Rhode Island,' etc., page 62.] Mr. Goddard's remarks need no correction, and but little of addition. 'The ancient constitution of Rhode Island, formed out of the provisions of the admiral charter, was the most democratic perhaps that ever existed. It required a semi-annual election of Representatives to the General Assembly. Mr. Hazard was a representative from the town of Newport in the General Assembly for thirty-one years, and of course was subject to the ordeal of sixty-two popular elections'—a singular proof of the enlightened stability of his constituents, of his general high desert, and his peculiar fitness for this important office. This fact independent of all others entitles him to claim rank as a distinguished man, and, as it were, demonstrates the possession of those impressive and useful qualities, whose combination renders character at once eminent and enduring. Mr. Hazard's course of reading and study operating upon a mind of genuine native strength and confirming and justifying a native sturdiness of will—the germ and guaranty of greatness—gave to all his literary efforts and political proceedings an air and cast of originality. He read and dwelt upon such books as Rabelais, Burton's Anatomy of Melancholy, Hobbes' Leviathan, Swift's Gulliver, Berkeley's Querist, and latterly, the dramas of Shakespeare and the Romances of Sir Walter Scott. In the middle and latter periods of his professional career, he was employed in most of the important law suits of the day in the courts both of the State, and of the United States. In politics, though his agency in the conflict of parties, if examined in the nicety of details, might betray some seeming inconsistencies, he was in the main true to himself and the system of conservatism.

"His legislative reports on banks, currency, etc., and on the extension of suffrage, are marked by sterling thoughts and true and profound principles. In his style as may have been anticipated from what has been here said, there was nothing gaudy or flashy; he aimed at and hit the mark of a plain, pure and Anglo-Saxon diction. He disdained the ordinary garden flowers, and the glittering, though far from precious, stones of the surface, to refresh and surprise us occasionally with flowers 'of native hue serene,' discovered by explorations in the depths of thought and meditation."

BENJAMIN HAZARD[4] (*Thomas*[3], *Robert*[2], *Thomas*[1]), fourth son of Thomas Hazard[3]; born 1701; married a Miss Redwood, of Newport. Their children were: 1. Jonathan[5]—called "Beau Jonathan" because of his politeness and nicety in dress. 2. Thomas B.[5]—called "Nailor Tom"—, died in South Kingstown 1845, aged 90 years. He married a sister of Robert Knowles, who owned and occupied what is called "Sot's Hole farm" in South Kingstown. Their children were: (a) Benjamin[6], married a Miss Carr for his first wife and had children, Sarah[7]—married Dr. Amos Wilbur—and Hannah[7], who died in early maidenhood. (b) Thomas B.[6], married Ruth Carpenter and had children, Peter[7] and several other sons and daughters. Thomas B. Hazard[5] was a man of intelligence, highly gifted with conversational powers, and of inexhaustible anecdote. 3. Mehitable[5]. 4. Benjamin[5], died on board the Jersey prison-ship.

STEPHEN HAZARD[4] (*Thomas*[3], *Robert*[2], *Thomas*[1]), fifth son of Thomas; had children, Stephen Fones Hazard[5] and others.

JONATHAN J. HAZARD[4] (*Thomas*[3], *Robert*[2], *Thomas*[1]), sixth son of Thomas, in point of force of character and general ability, was second to none of the remarkable sons of Thomas Hazard. In speaking of him, Updike says, page 328-29, "Jonathan J. Hazard was a descendant in the fourth degree from the first settler. He took an early and decided stand in favor of liberty in the Revolutionary struggle. In 1776, he appeared in the General Assembly as a representative from Charlestown, and was elected paymaster of the continental battalion, 1777, and joined the army in New Jersey. In 1778, he was re-elected member of the General Assembly and constituted one of the council of war. He continued a member of the House most of the time during the Revolution. In 1787, he was elected by the people a delegate to the Confederated Congress. In 1788, he was re-elected and attended the old Congress as a delegate from this State.

"Mr. Hazard was a leader of the Anti-Federalist party, and a fiery opponent of the adoption of the Federal Constitution. As a delegate to the convention assembled at South Kingstwon, in March, 1790, to take into consideration the adoption of that instrument, he successfully resisted the measure and upon an informal vote, it was ascertained that there was a majority of seventeen against its adoption. Upon this event, the popular party chaired Mr. Hazard as their leader." It seemed that for some cause Mr. Hazard, suspected of political aspirations, changed his views, and on his forbearing longer to oppose the measure, " the constitution was adopted by a bare majority of one."

"Mr. Hazard," says Updike, "was well formed, sturdy in body and mind, with a fine phrenological development of head. He was a natural orator, with a ready command of language, subtle and ingenious in debate. He successfully contended against Merchant, Bradford, and Welcome Arnold, the debaters of the House at that period. He was for a long time the idol of the country interests, manager of the State, leader of the legislature, in fact, the political dictator of Rhode Island ; but his course in the constitutional convention was the cause of his political ruin. It was a Wolsey's fall, to rise no more. The late Hon. Elisha R. Potter and the late Benjamin Hazard, who knew Mr. Jonathan J. Hazard, in the zenith of his political influence, always spoke of him as a man of great natural power and sagacity. He moved to New York in the latter part of his life, purchased a valuable estate, and settled his children there. He occasionally visited Rhode Island. He died at an advanced age."

THOMAS HAZARD[4] (*Thomas*[3], *Robert*[2], *Thomas*[1]), was the seventh and last of Thomas Hazard's remarkable sons. He was an eminent and successful merchant of Newport, and in 1760 presented to the government a ship of war that he had built and equipped at his own expense. In the Revolution he adhered to the British government and fled the country. His great estate was confiscated and after the war he settled with most of his children at St. John, New Brunswick, where he died in 1804. His son Jonathan[5]— by his first wife, who was a Bowdoin—remained in Rhode Island, and had children: 1. George[6], of Mumford Mill; had children, George L.[7], Hannah, Mary, and others. 2. Samuel[6], died in South Kingstown, and had children, Thomas E.[7], Jonathan, Mary, Esther, Wanton Wilbour, William A., and Job—killed in the battle at Kingston, North Carolina, during the late war. 3. Bowdoin[6], had children, Arnold[7], Alfred, William R., John L., Nathaniel, Isaac, and Edward.

The late Willard Hazard, who died not many years since, was also a son of the grandson of Virginia Thomas Hazard.

Since the genealogies have been in press in book form I have received from a descendant of Thomas A. Hazard, the following table, which I here insert, supposing him to have been a descendant of "Virginia Tom Hazard", though not sure of the fact:

THOMAS A. HAZARD, married Sarah Hazard, daughter of Robert Hazard: died 1862, aged 68 years. Their children were: Thomas G., married Sarah Kenyon, and had one child, Sarah. 2. Hannah, married Stephen Barrow. 3. Sarah, married Benjamin Carpenter; died 1876, aged 62 years. Their children were: Alice S., Thomas A., Wanton R., George A., Benjamin S., Susan A., Sarah E., and Elisha E. 4. Wanton R., married Miss Munroe, and has one daughter. 5. George Walter, died 1879, aged 59 years; married Susan Arnold. Their children were: Susan, Nettie, Annie, and Sarah. 6. Albert Arnold, died November 5, 1868, aged 78 years. Dr. A. A. Hazard established and was chief physician of the first hospital instituted in the city of Sacramento. 7. Rebecca A., married Stanley W. Webb; died 1862, aged 37 years. Their children were: Wanton S., and Joel A. 8. Susan A., died 1877, aged 48 years. 9. Laura E., died 1863, aged 28 years. The sisters of Thomas A., George Bowdoin and Samuel Hazard, were: Patience, married Elam Holloway; Abby, married William H. Nye; Esther, married Robert Champlin; and Ann, married William T. Gardner.

"Thomas Hazard ['Virginia Tom'],"says Updike, page 326, "was a descendant in the fourth degree from the common ancestor. He was a merchant in Newport for many years and acquired a large estate. His first wife was a Bowdoin, a branch of the Boston family; his second wife was Eunice Rhodes, of Pawtuxet, Rhode Island. In the Revolution, Mr. Hazard adhered to the cause of the Crown, fled to the enemy, and his estates were seized and subsequently confiscated. * * After the war Mr. Hazard returned to this State, and the General Assembly, through the influence of his brother, Jonathan J. Hazard, a leading Whig, were inclined to restore his estates, if a satisfactory submission should be made. This he indignantly refused, and the confiscation was consummated." Virginia Tom was beyond a doubt one of the true "snip" breed.

Updike continues, "In 1785, Mr. Hazard repaired to England, and the British grovernment, for his loyalty, his sacrifices, and sufferings, besides other remunerations, granted him a large tract of land at St. John. In 1786, he embarked for his new residence, with his wife, and all his children, except those who had previously married and settled in Rhode Island." One of Mr. Hazard's daughters married Walter Watson, whose daughter Isabella, married John J. Watson, the son of the first Job Watson. Walter's only remaining daughter, Abigail, married Wilkins Updike.

The following detached memoranda may be of some interest to readers interested in the antecedents of the Hazard family: "Jeffrey Hazard, of Exeter, was a descendant from Thomas, the common ancestor, in the sixth degree. He was for many years representative in the General Assembly, Chief Justice of the Court of Common Pleas, Judge of the Supreme Court, and Lieutenant Governor of the State."—*Updike's History.* "Four of the Hazard family have been lieutenant governors of Rhode Island."—*Ibid.* "The late Commodore Oliver H. Perry was a descendant of Thomas Hazard, the first settler, in the sixth degree. Raymond, father of the commodore, was the son of Judge Freeman Perry, who married the daughter of Oliver Hazard, of South Kingstown. The commodore was named after his maternal grandfather, Oliver Hazard."—*Ibid.* "Mr. Hazard, of Philadelphia, together with Dr. Franklin, petitioned the legislature of Pennsylvania to found the great insane asylum, at the corner of Ninth and Spruce streets, Philadelphia, and was a manager of the same for many years."—*Old Philadelphia Paper.* "Hazard was founder of the anthracite coal trade in Pennsylvania. Some coal company published a memorial four years ago concerning him."

A number of the "Book of Beauty" in Redwood Library, Newport, contains this sentence: "*Catharine Van Courtland Field.* In 1838, she married Mr. Benjamin Hazard Field, a descendant of Sir John Field, the astronomer. He is owner of a tract of land in Westchester county, New York, which has been kept in the family about two hundred and fifty years."

E. R. Potter, in his Early History of Narragansett, page 312, says: "It is traditionary in the family that a brother [perhaps, it should be nephew] of the first Thomas Hazard came over with him, and was the ancestor of the New York and South Carolina Hazards." I have always heard that it was a brother's son who came over with Thomas Hazard.

I remember meeting several years ago in New York, the captain of a ship by the name of Hazard—a tall, athletic, fine looking man—, who told me that he was from the southerly and easterly shore of Long Island where there were several families of the name who did not trace their descent to the Rhode Island Hazards. These may have been descended from the first South Carolina settler—whether a brother or brother's son of the first Thomas being immaterial.

As before stated, there is a tradition in the family that the first Thomas Hazard who came to America stopped for a time in New Jersey. My sister Eliza Hazard informs me that she has heard it stated—she thinks by Thomas B. Hazard, called "Nailor Tom"—that Thomas the first came to Rhode Island from Long Island. It may be that his nephew, who probably left England with his uncle, remained on Long Island, and that from this place his descendants branched off to Carolina or Georgia.

From copies of Colonial Records furnished me by Miss Emily Hazard, I quote:

"1671. Robert Hazard, Juror for Portsmouth; also Commissioner."

"1684. Thomas Hazard, of Portsmouth, admitted Freeman of the Colony."

"1696. George Hazard, Stephen Hazard, Robert Hazard, admitted Freemen."

"1712. Robert Hazard, of Kingstown, also George and Stephen Hazard, Deputies."

"1717. Thomas Hazard, Stephen Hazard, sons of Thomas, of Kingstown, admitted Freemen."

"1720. Lieutenant Colonel George Hazard chosen Lieutenant Colonel of the Regiment on the Mainland."

"1723. George Hazard, Jr., Benjamin Hazard, Robert Hazard, Jeffrey Hazard, George Hazard—son of Thomas—, admitted Freemen at Kingstown."

"1730. Thomas Hazard, Freeman."

"1750. Gideon Wanton, Governor; Robert Hazard, Deputy Governor."

"1760. Thomas Hazard, of Newport, equipped a ship of war."

"1775. Colonel Thomas Hazard, Nicholas Easton, Assistants [of the governor]."

From Updike's History of the Narragansett Church, page 247, I quote: "November 7, 1752, Dr. MacSparran at the house of Col. Thomas Hazard, in Boston Neck, married George Hazard—son of George, the son of old Thomas Hazard—to Sarah Hazard, the third daughter of said Colonel Hazard.

"'On the third Sunday of April, 1752, being the 19th day of said month, Robert Hazard, commonly called Dr. Hazard, was married to Elizabeth Hazard, daughter of Robert Hazard, of Point Judith, deceased, at the house of his mother, Esther Hazard, and Col. Joseph Hazard, her son, by the Rev. Dr. MacSparran.'—*Narragansett Church Record.*

"Robert Hazard was educated a physician, by his uncle, Dr. Sylvester Gardiner, of Boston. He settled in South Kingstown, and married Elizabeth, the daughter of Gov. Robert Hazard, of Point Judith, who was Lieut. Governor of the State, in 1750. He was a popular physician, and died in Narragansett, February 12, 1771.

"Esther, the widow of Governor Hazard, was an extraordinary woman, portly and masculine. She was styled Queen Esther and when mounted on her high-spirited Narragansett pacer, proudly traveling through the Narragansett country, the people would almost pay her homage. Colonel Joseph Hazard, her son, inherited all the lofty firmness, the unwavering perseverance, and sterling mind of the mother. He was elected to many important offices by the people, and sustained them with honor. Although a determined partisan, he never permitted his political attachments to sway him from the principles of right. His motto was 'to do right, and let consequences take care of themselves.' He was on the bench of the Supreme Court of the State, when the General Assembly enacted the celebrated 'Paper Money Law' of 1786, and was one of the paper money party. As the party put the judges into office, it was expected that the judges would support the party. But when the question of the constitutionality of those laws came before the court for decision in the case of Trevett *vs.* Weeden, in which cause General Varnum made his great and eloquent effort, this court stood firm in the defence of the cause of law in their country, and declared the paper money tender law unconstitutional and void.

"The fiery partisans of the law in the General Assembly ordered the court to be arraigned before them for a contempt of legislative power, and they were required to give their respective reasons for overthrowing the laws of the legislature that had created them. This novel procedure in judicial history, Judge Hazard met with firmness; and when called on, unmoved, rose and said: 'It gives me pain, that the conduct of the court seems to have met with displeasure of the Administration, but their obligations were of too sacred a nature for them to aim at pleasing, but in the line of their duty. It is well known that my sentiments have fully accorded with the general system of the legislature in emitting the paper money currency. But I never did, and never will, depart from the character of an honest man, to support any measures however agreeable in themselves. If there could have been any prepossession in my mind, it must have been in favor of the act of the General Assembly; but it is not possible to resist the force of conviction. The opinion I gave on the trial was dictated by the energy of truth. I thought I was right. I still think so. But be it as it may, we derive our understandings from God, and to him alone are we accountable for our judgment.'

"This was an instance where the heroic firmness of a few men saved the State." Benjamin Hazard, of Charlestown, and Robert Hazard, also of Charlestown, called "Cold Brook Robert," were sons of Judge Hazard. The latter especially inherited, as Updike observes, "all the firm traits of character of the grandmother and father."

I further quote from Updike: "'March 5, 1771, Mr. Fayerweather married Mr. Carder Hazard to Miss Alice Hazard, daughter of Col. Thomas Hazard, of South Kingstown.'

"'July 28, 1769, on Friday evening Mr. Fayerweather married his brother-in-law, George Hazard, Esq., to Miss Jane Tweedy, at the parsonage house, Narragansett.'

"'On the 12th of February, 1771, Dr. Robert Hazard was buried, having a long and lingering illness. A considerable assembly present, and a funeral sermon preached, and on Sunday, the 24th, preached at the house of mourning of the late Dr. Hazard, on mortality, a large congregation present. The Hon. James Honeyman was present, who came from Little Rest—now Kingston—, where the court had been sitting the whole week.'—*Narragansett Church Record.*"

Before closing, I will remark that there appears to be much uncertainty as regards the proper way of spelling the name of Hazard. In a recent cursory examination of the ancient records of Kingstown, now in the office of the present town clerk of South Kingstown—Mr. John G. Perry—, I found that for about one hundred years including parts of the seventeenth and eighteenth centuries there were on the books no less than four hundred and seventy-nine land conveyances to and from the family of Hazards, and so far as I then examined the name was invariably spelled "Hassard." Since then I have been favored with a note from Mr. Perry in which he writes: "The name of Hassard, spelled 'Hazard,' first occurs on the land records of this town, in a deed from Thomas Calverwell to 'George Hazard,' dated June 6, 1723. The next is in a deed from George 'Hazzard' to Thomas 'Hazard,' dated January 8, 1725. The name is spelled with two z's in the first instance and one in the latter." It would appear by this that the first Hazards who came to Narragansett spelled their name as the English Hazards now do and did at the period the first settlers emigrated to America.

I have heard that, though spelled with a double *s*, the

name is pronounced in England to this day as if spelled with z. It is said there are many of the name in France, and it would seem, by an anecdote I have heard concerning a street in the central part of Paris, that the two different modes of spelling prevail the same there as in America. I have more than once noticed a placard on one end of this street spelled "Hazard" and have heard that, with that nice observance of proprieties so characteristic of the French people, the name is placarded on the other end of the street "Hassard." In French I think the accent is placed on the last syllable. Some years ago I was introduced to the lady of the French Minister at Washington, and was a little surprised on being announced as "Monsieur Ha-*zard.*" I am half inclined to think that notwithstanding what Mr. Short says to the contrary in his history, Hazard or Hassard was the actual family name of the first immigrant to England and that it might have been suppressed for a while in those troublous times, for political or prudential reasons, and afterwards resumed.

In an "Etymological Dictionary of Family and Christian Names," etc., by William Arthur, M. A., published by Sheldon, Blakeman & Co., New York, 1857, the following item occurs under the heading "Hazard:" "*Hazard* (Br.). From *ard*, nature, and *has*, of high disposition, proud, independent."

My father used to say twenty or more years before Mr. Short's history of the family was printed that the Hazards came from Pictou—as we remember the pronunciation—, and singularly enough on turning recently to a gazetteer, I find "Poiter" mentioned as a former province of French now divided among the departments of Vienne, Dux, Sevres, Vendee, Indre-et-Loire, and Charante, the last named department being that from which, by the English historian's account, the family actually emigrated in the eleventh century. Probably we misunderstood our father's pronunciation of the name. My sister Eliza writes me that some years ago whilst she was visiting my family at Vaucluse, a Frenchman came to the house to tune a piano, who told her there were a good many families of our name living in Marseilles and its vicinity in France, that they were merchants and owners of vineyards, but were people who held rank with the first in the community. This Frenchman had the bearing and manners of a gentleman. On looking at a portrait of Napoleon the First that hung in the library, he remarked that he had seen him at his father's, who was a commissary of the army.

My sister writes farther that she once went into a French jeweler's shop in Philadelphia and on giving her name, he told her there were many of her name where he came from in France. She also writes me that a Mr. Hazard who kept a druggist's store in Chestnut street, Philadelphia, wore a gold vignette—an anchor borne upon waves,—on his watch-chain, which he said was the crest of a Hazard coat of arms.

Whichever may be the true way of spelling the name, it is certain that most or all of the Narragansett Hazards spelled their name, for half a century or more after they settled in Rhode Island, with a double *s*, or with an *s* and a *z*, thus; *Haszard*. In looking through the colonial records I find the name occurs very often, perhaps two or three hundred times in all. Up to the close of the Revolutionary war or a little later—say, 1784—, the name is spelled three different ways, Haszard, Hassard and Hazard, generally like the first. In the tenth volume running from 1784 to 1792, the name is uniformly spelled *Hazard*. Without an exception, wherever it occurs, it is spelled in this way, including ten different members of the family—Carder, Eunice, George, Godfrey, Jonathan J., Jonathan, Jr., of Charlestown, Jonathan, Joseph, Thomas G., and Thomas. That some of the English Hazards still continue to spell the name with a *z*, as in the twelfth century, is also probable, as I remember seeing, less than forty years ago, a grocer's sign in Jermain street, London, with the name "Hazard" in large letters, and saw also

"Thomas Hazard" scratched with a diamond on a pane of glass in the window of a hotel in Manchester.

Some forty years ago I used sometimes to meet " Thomas Hassard," an architect and master railroad bridge builder, who strikingly resembled in his features and person many of the Narragansett Hazards. He came from Ireland, married a lady of the General Nathaniel Greene family and settled in this country. His son, John R. G. Hassard, a man of education and fine talents, is now attached to the editorial corps of the New York Tribune. I have learned from personal observation and other sources, that there is at this day a striking resemblance between the Irish, Rhode Island and southern branches of the Hassard family, who, it is believed, all descended from the " Nottingham Hassards."

Since these papers have been printed in the Newport Mercury and Narragansett Times, I have received a letter from my brother, Joseph P. Hazard, dated " Zurich, Switzerland, May 30, 1878," in which he writes : " I met a Mr. Hazard at Lucerne the other day. He spells his name as we do—*Hazard*. He was born near Norwich in Norfolk county. He now lives in Nottingham. He is remarkably handsome, stands six feet in his boots, and is evidently a straight forward man. He has black hair and eyes. He says a characteristic of the English Hazards is dark hair with gray eyes. The upper part of his face is strikingly like Rowland N. Hazard—son of Jonathan—, and so are its expression and his manner of handling himself. All these characteristics are retained in two branches of a family that have been widely separated for two hundred and forty years or more." Subsequently my brother writes from London : " I have seen the names of Hazards in a church-yard near Boar or Beer head, where Hazards were ' Lords of Beer,' that is, ' Lords of the manor,' some centuries ago."

I may just here remark—although I know it will be scouted by many—that some fifteen years before I knew anything of the whereabouts of the European Hazards, the spirits of one John Hazard and his daughter used often to communicate with me. They said they lived a few miles south of Bristol some three centuries before. John drew a plan of his castle through the hand of an entranced medium. This plan I now have. Long since then I learned that Bristol was the most prominent place of residence of the family in England in olden times.

I add in closing the record of the Hazard family a most appropriate though brief notice of an ancestor who preferred death to a recantation of his religion. The record is found on the four hundred and fifteenth page of Samuel Smiles' "The Huguenots; their Settlements, Churches and Industries in England and Ireland," and reads thus:"

"HAZARD or HASAERT, Peter. A refugee in England from the persecutions in the Low Countries under the Duchess of Parma. Returning on a visit to his native land, he was seized and burned alive in 1568. His descendants still survive in England and Ireland under the name of Hassard."

PREFACE
TO THE HAZARDS OF THE MIDDLE STATES.

Since my manuscript for the Hazard family was completed I have received for publication from Mr. Willis P. Hazard, of Westchester, Pennsylvania, the following particulars of the Pennsylvania branch of the family. This branch, as held by Rhode Island tradition, descended together with the South Carolina and Georgia Hazards from a nephew—not son as Riker in his History of Newtown, Long Island, claims—of Thomas Hazard, the first settler, whom Thomas brought with him from Wales.

THOMAS R. HAZARD.

THE HAZARD FAMILY
OF THE MIDDLE STATES.

By WILLIS P. HAZARD, of Westchester, Pa.

The Hazard family take their name, we think, from the two words *has*, high, and *ard*, nature, meaning "of high disposition, proud, independent." These two words are of the ancient British or Welsh language, spoken and written by the people of that name, and more nearly allied to the Gallic than the Teutonic. As the name is written Hasard, Hassard, and Hazard, and apparently, by the old records, indiscriminately, it would lend more probability to, what has been declared by good authority to be the origin of the name. The pronunciation, too, especially by the Hazards themselves, which is long on the first syllable, would lead almost any one, a stranger to its mode of spelling, to spell it with a *z* instead of an *s*. Therefore, if it was originally spelled Hasard, according to its derivation, the pronunciation has corrupted its original spelling. And yet we have other authorities who say the two words are *haz* and *ard*, while some branches of the family, still spell their name Hassard, and they claim their mode is the correct one. For ourselves we prefer to spell the name Hazard. We have seen it spelled Hazzard, though not by any recognized branches of the family, they being mostly colored people. It would be curious, if possible, to trace where *they* get the name from, most likely from some who were formerly slaves, and adopted the name of their owners, the Hazards of Carolina, Georgia, and other Southern States—a branch of the family that settled there. There is one curious fact which I have often noticed, that is, if the address is given to strangers, they will in most cases write the name Hazzard, spelling it with two *z*'s ; most probably because we do not pronounce it in the French style, with the accent on the last syllable, Hăz-ārd. It is amusing also to notice some who wish to be extremely polite, or who desire to display their knowledge of French and the proper accent, by pronouncing it in thorough French fashion.

The Hazards are a strongly marked race, handing down and retaining certain peculiarities, from generation to generation. One is, a peculiar decision of character, a certain amount of pride, and a pronounced independence, coupled with a slight amount of reserve. Physically they are strongly marked. Generally speaking, they are of good stature, and vigorous frame, with rather a square head, high forehead, brown hair, blue eyes, straight or aquiline nose, and with their will shown by a firmly set jaw. Their complexion is fair, a little inclined to florid.

The coat of arms handed down through generations has three escalops and three bars, with an escalop rampant for a crest. These are a little varied by some, in the coloring or position ; and one that we have seen has a dove holding a branch, for a crest. The mottoes vary, as any one is at liberty to choose what he likes; we have seen "*Vive en Expoir*," "*Fortuna viam ducit*," "*Sinceritas*," and "Be just and fear not." As the last has come regularly down to us, we use that.

An anecdote I have heard of one of our kinsmen, as showing the strongly marked peculiarities of the race, I give. An American Hazard, when in Ireland, was pacing up and down the platform of a railway station, waiting the arrival of a train. Shortly a gentleman drove up, and, while he too was waiting, soon was busy watching the turns of the restless American. The American having spoken or asked some question of the railway porter, was shortly after addressed by the Irish gentleman with, "Pray excuse me, but is not your name Hazard?" The American justly astonished at being addressed in a foreign land by a stranger, at a bye-way station, replied, "It is." "Ah! I thought so," exclaimed the Irish gentleman, "for I watched you as you walked up and down, and thought how much you moved and looked like a Hazard; but when I heard you speak, I felt so sure of it, I made bold to address you. That also is my name; I live a few miles from here, and would be glad to have you go and spend some time with me." His importunities were such that the American went, and was delightfully entertained at an Irish gentleman's castle.

The leading proclivities of many of the Hazards are for literary pursuits, for mechanical operations and devices, for the pursuit of agriculture, with strong religious tendencies, which in some have made them famous and active in the church, and in others have led into spiritualism or materialism. They have usually a fair amount of ambition, preferring always to lead, rather than be led. This fact explains why so many of them are prominent in doing their duty to society as good citizens.

The descendants of the Long Island branch are connected by marriage with the Banckers, Bleeckers, Clarksons, Depeysters, Morses, Vermilyes, of New York; the Breezes,

Clarkes, Halls, Hetfields, Halsteads, of New Jersey; the Arthurs, Saulsburys, Rockwoods, of New England; the Finleys, Coxes, Ralstons, Blights, Markoes, Gilpins, Tennents, Chevaliers, Fullertons, Wistars, Snowdens, of Philadelphia.

The Hazard family is believed, according to the traditions in our branch, to have first made its appearance in this country in the person of THOMAS HAZARD[1], who came over from Wales in 1630 or 1632. Like many of the immigrants of that particular period, he is said to have first visited Jersey, then to have gone to Boston, where he was made a freeman in 1636, then to have gone to Long Island, where he founded Newtown. From there it was easy to cross to Rhode Island, where he finally settled, lived, and died, as my kinsman has already told in a previous part of this volume. He was admitted a freeman of Newport, 2nd mo. 7th, 1639, and of Aquidneck, Rhode Island, 24th 11th mo., 1639, and of Portsmouth in 1655. See Dr. Stiles' extracts from Rhode Island Records; and Bartlett's Records of Rhode Island. It is traditionary that a brother, nephew, or son of Thomas, came over with him, and was ancestor of the New York and South Carolina Hazards.*

Thomas certainly brought over with him his son Robert[2], then four years old. He finally settled in Portsmouth, R. I., and eventually in Kingstown.

ROBERT[2] (*Thomas*[1]) had five children: Thomas[3], George[3], Stephen[3], Robert[3], Jeremiah[3].

Riker in his Annals of Newtown—1852—says: "The Hazards were, prior to the Revolution, one of the most prominent families in Newtown, [Long Island]. Their ancestor THOMAS HAZARD[1] came from Wales, and was admitted to freemanship in Boston in 1636; in 1652 he became one of the founders and first magistrates of Newtown. He had several sons, one of whom Robert[2] settled in Rhode Isl-

---

*R. I. Hist. Soc: V. 3, p. 314.

and and originated the Hazards so highly distinguished in the annals of that State.

"JONATHAN[2], another son, remained at Newtown; married Hannah, daughter of James Laurenson; acquired a large property and filled various offices. He died in 1711, having had issue, Thomas[3], James[3], Nathaniel[3], Elizabeth[3] (who married Edward Hunt), and Sarah[3] (who married James Renne). Thomas[3], styled Captain, was supervisor of Newtown from 1720 till his death, which occurred August 31, 1733, at the age of 51, occasioned by a fall from his horse. By his wife Mercy, daughter of Thomas Betts, he had Thomas[4], Daniel[4], Samuel[4], John[4], and Jonathan[4], the last of whom settled in Orange County, New York. Daniel[4], a sea captain, died in New York in 1747, and his only son Thomas Hazard[5], Esq., died in New York in 1787, aged 43. His children as their births are recorded were: William Howard[6], born 1770; Charles Smith[6], born 1772; Frances S.[9], born 1773, and Benjamin[6], born 1774.

"JAMES[3], for fifteen years was a judge of Common Pleas, occupied the farm (now of John Duryea) in Newtown. The family vault on this estate fell into decay and was filled up a few years since. Judge Hazard died April 26, 1765. His children were: Rebecca[4] (married Robert Morrell), William[4], Jonathan[4]. The last married Abigail Pumroy and left a son James[5], born in 1752. William[4] was a prominent citizen in Newtown; married Miss Elizabeth Moore; born January 10, 1725, and died August 25, 1773, aged 48. He left several daughters and a son Morris[5], who was the grandfather of Wm. H. Hazard[7], of New York, shipping merchant.

"NATHANIEL[3], a merchant, finally removed to Philadelphia, and died in 1749. [Error, probably 1765.] He had issue: Nathaniel[4], Samuel[4], Hannah[4] (married Rev. Samuel Sackett), and Sarah[4], who married Captain Daniel Hazard.

"NATHANIEL[4] was a successful merchant in New York; died in or about 1764, and left sons: Nathaniel[5], Samuel[5], Joseph[5], besides nine daughters, one of whom Elizabeth[5], married Joseph Hallet, father-in-law of the late Major John Delafield. Nathaniel[5], last named, married Mary, daughter of Col. Joseph Robinson, and died in 1798; issue, Maria[6] and Nathaniel[6].

"Samuel[4], son of Nathaniel[3], was the father of the late Ebenezer Hazard[5], Esq., of Philadelphia, a former Postmaster General of the United States, and editor of valuable contributions to American history."

NATHANIEL HAZARD[3] (*Jonathan*[2], *Thomas*[1]), third son of Jonathan, was born in Newtown, Long Island. (See Riker's History of Newtown, 1852.) He was a merchant in New York, and afterwards in Philadelphia, to which city he moved in 1749. His place of business in New York was at the store of Thomas Noble, at the "old slip." He advertises "likely negroes, and a prime lot of old Cheshire cheese." "He was an elder of the Presbyterian church in New York from 1728 to 1745." "Rev. Mr. Pemberton attended synod with his elder, Nathaniel Hazard, May, 1741, and both signed the protest against the exclusion of the New Brunswick party." The time of his death is uncertain, probably after 1760. He married Deborah ———, and had four children: 1. Nathaniel[4]. 2. Samuel[4]. 3. Hannah[4]. 4. Sarah[4].

NATHANIEL HAZARD[4] (*Nathaniel*[3], *Jonathan*[2], *Thomas*[1]), married Elizabeth Drummey, who died May 27, 1811. He was first settled in business in New Windsor, on the Hudson, and afterwards for twenty years in New York. Nathaniel was active in the Presbyterian church in New York. There was but one Presbyterian church at the time, started in 1719, completed in 1730. It is not stated that he was an elder, though one of the most prominent in the church and one of two sent with a call to Rev. Dr. Bellamy, of Bethlehem, Conn., January, 1754. They met the council at Bethlehem, January 24. He was one of the commissioners to the association on the same subject May 24. His church, for years, importuned Mr. Bellamy to settle with them as their pastor. The same year he made another visit to Bethlehem. Mr. Bellamy withstood all the pleadings of Nathaniel and others. Bellamy wrote to him January 22, 1755. He was the friend and constant correspondent of Dr. Bellamy, through the years up to 1765. He most probably lived all his life in New York. Nathaniel died in 1765. He had a number of children: 1. Eliza[5]. 2. Mary. 3. Ann. 4. Catharine. 5. Catharine. 6. Nathaniel. 7. Samuel. 8. Samuel. 9. Mary. 10. Joseph. 11. Sarah. 12. Margaret. Nathaniel[5], the eldest son, was graduated at Princeton in 1764, two years later than his cousin Ebenezer[5], son of Samuel[4], was graduated. Nathaniel[4] was appointed administrator on his brother Samuel's estate, and at his own death, some property not having been yet settled, Ebenezer[5] was appointed administrator, July 21, 1766.

SAMUEL HAZARD[4] (*Nathaniel*[3], *Jonathan*[2], *Thomas*[1]), the second son of Nathaniel[3] and Deborah Hazard, was born in Philadelphia, March 20, 1713-14. He was married in New York by Rev. Ebenezer Pemberton, October, 1739, to Catharine Clarkson, daughter of Matthew Clarkson and Cornelia Depeyster, of New York, by whom he had seven children. Before he moved to Philadelphia, he was an active and consistent member and elder of the First Presbyterian church in Wall Street, New York. In Philadelphia he lived in Front street, east side, below Arch street, in a tall manor-house next above Wetherill's drug store, where most probably Ebenezer and other children were born. He was a bookseller in Philadelphia, in 1749, or at least sold books, perhaps with other merchandise, as he is designated merchant. "He was a merchant in Philadelphia, a steadfast and invaluable member and an elder in the Second church; and an original and active Trustee of the College of New Jersey. He was the father of Ebenezer Hazard, to whom we are so largely indebted for the preservation of the materials of our church history." See Webster's History of Presbyterian Church, p. 225.

He was the medium of communication between the Synods of New York and Philadelphia. See Webster's History, pp. 191, 204, 212, 225, 247, 332, 400, 503, 504, 628 to 650, 672.

Samuel[4] died at Philadelphia Friday evening at nine o'clock, July 14, 1758, aged 44 years, 3 months and 24 days, after a short but severe illness of three days. His disorder was *opistotnos*, or convulsion of the nerves, which began in his jaws and spread to his neck, breast and most of the other parts of his body, and he was thus unable to swallow either food or medicine. He died intestate, and Nathaniel H., his brother, was administrator.

Catharine Hazard, wife of Samuel, daughter of Matthew Clarkson 3d, and Cornelia Depeyster, was born in New York, January, 1720; died in New York at the residence of her son Ebenezer, Friday, 11 P. M., August 15, 1788, aged 67 years, 6 months and a half. Her disorder was complicated. She was buried on Sunday, the 17th, in the church vault No. 2, in the Old Presbyterian churchyard, Wall street, New York, and was the first person buried there. Ebenezer was one of the trustees of the church and the most active in having the vault constructed. She was the sister of Matthew Clarkson 4th, Mayor of Philadelphia, whose daughter married Robert Ralston, a very prominent merchant of Philadelphia. Catharine's sister Anna married Rev. Samuel Finley, President of Princeton College, and formerly head of a famous school at Nottingham, Maryland, at which Ebenezer H. and so many eminent pupils were educated. Among them were Rev. Dr. Rush, Dr. Benjamin Rush, Rev. Dr. McWhorter, and Rev. William Tennent. She died January 14, 1808, aged 80 years.

Samuel had seven children : 1. The first a daughter, was born dead, October 28, 1740. 2. Matthew[5], born July 3, 1742; died July 15, 1742; was baptized by Rev. Samuel Blair, July 7, 1742; and was buried in the "New Building" yard, July 16. 3. Ebenezer [5], born in Philadelphia, January 15, 1744, at five on Tuesday morning ; died June 13, 1817, aged 73 years; was baptized in the New Building, by Rev. Gilbert Tennent, on the Lord's day, January 27, 1744, being a sacramental Sabbath. 4. Anna[5], born September 20, 1746, Saturday morning, in Philadelphia; was baptized Sunday afternoon, September 28, 1746, by Rev. Gilbert Tennent in the New Building; died, unmarried, of the yellow fever in her brother Ebenezer's house, 145 Arch street, Philadelphia, October 18, 1793, aged 47 years, and was buried the same day in the Arch Street burying ground, above Fifth street, now removed. 5. Mary[5], born in Philadelphia, January 16, 1750; baptized February 17, 1750, by Rev. Gilbert Tennent; was married to Cornelius Turk, of New York, by Rev. Dr. Laidlie, July 29, 1770; died in child-bed June 21, 1772, and was buried in the Old Dutch churchyard, New York. 6. Elizabeth[5], born in Philadelphia, November 2, 1755; was baptized, November 23, 1755, by Rev. Gilbert Tennent; married Joseph West, of New York, and lived to an advanced age, dying in New York. She had six children: (a) Webley, died unmarried. (b) John. (c) Catharine, married Uriah Ryder, and had children, Uriah, Elizabeth West, Abigail, Mary Ann, Rebecca, Joseph, Catharine Phœbe. (d) Samuel, married Catharine Bantz. (e) Abigail, married Joseph Giraud, and had children, Eliza Ann, Frederick, Jacob Post, Clarissa (dead). (f) Ann, married Hugh Aikman, of New York. 7. Catharine[5], born December 13, 1758; baptized January 7, 1759, by Rev. Gilbert Tennent.

Samuel[4] was one of the founders of the Pennsylvania Hospital, and for years a manager, until his death. See printed history of the hospital. He was a trustee of Princeton College from 1748 to 1757. In 1744, it appears by records—in Rec. O. Phila. H. p. 1—that Jonathan Price and wife conveyed to Samuel Hazard (for Tennent's church?) land where the old academy was in Fourth street, west side, between High and Mulberry. In 1750, Samuel Hazard conveyed to James Logan and others, trustees of the academy (part of?) above lot on which S. Hazard afterwards erected one tenement or dwelling and stable for £289. (H. 5,p. 3.)

With the early history of Philadelphia, and the times of the great revival, under the preaching of Whitefield and the Tennents, the history of the Second Presbyterian church is closely associated ; and with that church, the Hazard family has been intimately connected for more than one hundred and twenty-five years either as elder, treasurer, or trustee. This congregation was organized through the instrumentality of the Rev. George Whitefield, in 1743, under the pastoral care of Rev. Gilbert Tennent. Many persons were induced to turn their attention to religion, under the stirring preaching of these famous men. Many also left the First church in Market street above Second. Samuel Hazard was one of the first congregation of one hundred and forty members, and was one of Mr. Tennent's first elders. In January, 1749, the church was sold to the city for an academy, and Samuel was one of the trustees to make title and select a new site at Third and Arch streets. In February, 1749, he was treasurer of the building committee and superintended the erection of the new building, which was opened June 7, 1752. In 1751, he was appointed on the Burial, and Pew Committees. Five of his children were baptized by Rev. Gilbert Tennent, in the "New Building" in Fourth street below Arch; latterly it has been known as the "old academy," belonging to the University of Pennsylvania, and kept as the Academical Department, and where the writer went to school to Rev. Samuel Wylie Crawford in 1835-9. It is now pulled down—1879—and a large Methodist church built on the academy site, and fine stores on the old play ground in front.

Samuel Hazard, Rev. Mr. Tennent and others had much trouble with the religious views of the Moravians. A letter to Count Zinzendorf, a Moravian, which Mr. Hazard wrote in Philadelphia, August 28, 1742, runs as follows:

"Yours of the 28th ult. I received and must think it but a poor proof of that Humility, Meekness and Religion you pretend to. If this be the genuine spirit of the Moravians, I must still say, 'O my soul, come not thou into their secret, unto their assembly mine honor be thou not united.' Did I think it agreeable to Christianity to answer you in your own way, you have given a great deal of room for me to be very severe upon you, but I shall endeavor to avoid rendering Railing for Railing, and just observe in answer to yours that I have already complied with all the orders I received from Mr. Stonehouse to follow your directions in relation to the disposal of the Money arising from the sale of the Snow*, so I have nothing further to say to you upon that head. I don't well understand what you mean by my returning my Directions to Mr. Stonehouse. I suppose you can hardly imagine I am so weak as to send his orders back to him again, because you tell me to do so.

Sir, Your humble servant,
SAMUEL HAZARD."

Samuel was a man of great enterprise and given to much speculation, particularly in mines and mining lands. There exist a number of deeds of such properties in all parts of the country, as follows :

May 1, 1744—Sam. Sackett, Bedford, Westchester Co., New York.

Aug. 8, 1748—Jas. Lynd, for 1-8 of 24.96 acres in Somerset Co., New Jersey.

Nov. 10, 1747—Several shares of 7 acres at Great Pond, Morris Co., New Jersey.

July 18, 1750—Part owner of Company of Adventurers in copper mine "Venus," of 200 acres, in Frederick Co., Maryland, on the Monocasie.

Sept. 1, 1750—Jacob Downer, half of all mines in three tracts of land in Lancaster Co.

Feb. 17, 1755—One-fifth share in all mines in 250 acres, Walpeck, Essex Co., New Jersey; 2 miles on Delaware river, called Minisink.

Dec. 10, 1755—200 acres of land, lead mine, at New River, Augusta Co., Virginia.

Dec. 6, 1757—1-2 of all lead mines of John Francis, Whiteland, Chester Co., Penna.

Also he entered 2400 acres of land in Augusta Co., Virginia.

He had also some interest in the Hopewell mine of 600 acres; and owned a house in Shippensburg, Pa.

But his most ambitious operation was a vast scheme for settling a portion of the great West, as granted to him for the purpose by the State of Connecticut, which he originated and, as he had between five and six thousand persons engaged to go out and settle there, would undoubtedly have carried out, if he had not suddenly died after a few days' sickness. Mr. Hazard said he could easily have induced ten thousand settlers to go. It was to be entitled " The

*The *Snow* was a name for boats, at that time.

Colony of Bereans in the Valley of Illumination." He was to have been Governor, his father and James Hazard and others, members of council. John Hazard, of Connecticut, and William Hazard, of New York, are also in the list. The object of the settlement was "for the safety of this, and all his Majesty's Colonys in North America, and would be of very great advantage to the trade and commerce of Great Britain." It was to begin at the distance of one hundred miles westward of the western boundaries of Pennsylvania, and thence to extend one hundred miles to the westward of the Mississippi, and to be divided from Virginia and Carolina by the great chain of mountains that run along the continent from the north-east to the south-west parts of America. He got the grant May 8, 1755, from the State of Connecticut, for what was known also as the Ohio settlement, "provided the petitioner obtain his majesty's (George Second) Royal grant and order for settling the said colony."

But delays occurred in obtaining the royal grant. Lord Halifax apprehended "Two Invincible Difficulties at present Lye in the way, the confusion arising from the Enemy's Being in Possession of that country, and a settlement on that Land would Disgust the Indians, who at this Juncture should by no means be offended." March 2, 1756. Whether this was overcome is not clear. "I have writ so particularly to you already about the new mission and the new colony I have nothing to add but my Impatience for Mr. Hazard's and your reply, and I told you have Lord Halifax's Honour engaged to forward the Charter and Supplies if the settlement can be Brought to Bear." London, June 9, 1757. Whatever was the result Samuel Hazard died the following year, and we have no further mention of the scheme, which probably died from want of a leader. In 1755, he requested aid from the Governor and Assembly of Pennsylvania for his project of a new settlement or colony in the West. See Watson's Annals, I, 100; see also original minutes of Assembly, in colonial records. It would have been of vast use to this country as he had over three thousand men enrolled, including a number of clergymen, and all picked men, many of them with means.

The character of Samuel Hazard both in New York and Philadelphia was that of an enterprising merchant, a man of great probity and benevolence, and one who led an upright and pious life, devoting much of his energies to advancing the cause of the Presbyterian church, even into the Indian wilds.

EBENEZER HAZARD[5] (*Samuel*[4], *Nathaniel*[3] *Jonathan*[2], *Thomas*[1]), the son of Samuel and Catharine, was born in Philadelphia, January 15, 1744-5, on Tuesday morning; was baptized in the "New Building" in Fourth street by the Rev. Gilbert Tennent on the afternoon of January 27, 1744-5—a sacramental Sabbath. In early life Ebenezer went to the famous school of Rev. Dr. Samuel Finley, his uncle, in Nottingham, Maryland, on the borders of Pennsylvania. He was graduated at Princeton college in 1762, as A. M. November, 1762, he sailed in the privateer Snow, Monckton, and was overset in her December 14, fifty leagues from Martinique and taken up by the brig Unity about six hours after. From Martinique he shipped on board his majesty's ship Scarborough, cruising in the West Indies until June 10, 1764. He then sailed for Plymouth, England, and was discharged October 23. He went to London, and taking passage on board ship Ellis, December 7, arrived at Philadelphia March 2, 1765.

He removed to New York about 1767, when he was twenty-two years of age, and that year boarded with and was employed by Garret Noel, in whose book-store he worked on a salary of two and a half per cent. on the whole sales and his board and lodging. In 1770, he became Mr. Noel's partner under the firm name of Noel & Hazard. The store was next door to the coffee-house in New York. He made a tour through Maryland from New York in 1768. As showing his strong religious sentiment thus early in life, we find in his diary of 1767, nine years after he had lost his father, that on every Sunday is recorded his attendance at church three times, the name of the preacher, and the text, as well as giving the same unvarying attendance on every Wednesday evening.

His brother Nathaniel was administrator on their father's estate and Ebenezer after the death of Nathaniel in 1765, was appointed July 21, 1766, administrator of all the property of Samuel " unadministered by Nathaniel ;" and in the same diary, he says, "January 20, applied to Aunt Hazard for my father's papers and was refused them ;" " 21st. This day the time allowed me to make an inventory expired" ; " 24th. About this time rec'd Part of my Father's papers from Aunt H. and the rest were refused and I suppose will never be got." January 26, 1767, he records he is " this day twenty-two years old" ; he was born the 15th old style, and adding the eleven days to it would make the date 26th new style.

He remained in business with Garret Noel as partner probably from October, 1772, to April, 1774. There was then some trouble, as years after Ebenezer complains of being unjustly saddled with his partner's debts, which he had not contracted. Though there is a firm name of Benedict & Hazard, and one of Thomas Benedict, April 1, 1774, it was most probably a relative.

In 1770-71, he took a voyage to England. He went in the brig Friendship, August 24, 1770, direct to Bristol. He called to see Mr. Noel's sister at Haymarket. On his return he landed at New York September 26, 1771, after a voyage of fifty days.

May 3, 1775, he was appointed by the Committee of Safety of New York as superintendent of the eastern post, with his headquarters at New York, when the post-office under the King was suppressed. He was therefore the first postmaster of New York. His first account of the New York post-office with the general post-office was January 5, 1776. His appointment was afterwards confirmed by the Continental

Congress. When that city was evacuated by the Americans, the post-office was transferred with the army in its movements. In 1777, he was appointed surveyor of the post-roads and offices throughout the United States, and traveled, while performing his duty, on horseback, between New Hampshire and Georgia, until his appointment January 28, 1782, as Postmaster General of the United States. He served as such until October, 1789. For notice of his appointment and that of James Bryson as deputy postmaster, see Pennsylvania Gazette of February 6, 1782 ; also notice of post-office being removed to Mrs. Budden's in Front street, a few doors south of the coffee-house.

As early as 1779 he began to collect materials for his Historical Collections, no doubt filling in his spare moments, while traveling in the different States, by copying documents. He also at this time was collecting information for an American Geography, but hearing afterwards that Dr. Morse was preparing a similar work he turned over all his material to him. In 1780 he wrote a life of Rev. Dr. Samuel Finley, President of Princeton College.

At this time, though 36 years of age, he writes he is " hurried through life on horseback," and later, that he was " too much hurried to think of either love or matrimony." In November, 1781, he speaks of Philadelphia as likely to be his future residence, as he is about being appointed Postmaster General, and would have to reside where Congress is. Yet the next year when he was appointed to that office, we have the first admission of the probability of his being a married man, his new "settled way of life makes me think of being more so ; and would time permit, that business should be seriously thought of." And in May, 1783, he writes "I have fixed upon a partner and *preliminaries* are settled ; but no time is yet fixed for signing the *definitive* treaty." He also had commenced building a house, a moderate-sized one, in Arch near Fifth street.

Ebenezer married Abigail Anthony, daughter of Joseph

Anthony and Jane Chevalier, of Nantucket, and was born August 5, 1759. They were married September 11, 1783, by Rev. Dr. Woodhull, at the house of Samuel Breese, in Shrewsbury, N. J. They lived long and very happily together, she surviving him three years.

They had four children : 1. Samuel[6], born May 26, 1784; married Abby Clark Hetfield, March 18, 1819; died May 26, 1870, aged 86 years. 2. Elizabeth Breese[6], born in New York March 26, 1786; married Ebenezer Rockwood, of Boston, and removed to that city. After his early death in 1815, she resided in Philadelphia, and in 1820 in New Haven, to educate her four children. Here she married Rev. Thomas E. Vermilye, D. D., of New York. She died in New York January 12, 1861, aged 75 years. 3. Erskine[6], born in New York November 30, 1789, married Mary, daughter of Alexander Fullerton; and is now dead. He was named for Rev. Dr. Erskine, of Edinburgh, a friend and correspondent of Ebenezer Hazard. 4. Ebenezer Gordon[6], born in Philadelphia September 29, 1792; died November 5, 1792, aged 5 weeks.

Ebenezer Hazard[5] died June 13, 1817, at his residence, a large house with side yard that he built in 1792, No. 145 Arch street above Fourth, where Wormath's fur store stood or stands, at the age of 73, and was buried in the Arch Street burying ground, belonging to the Second Presbyterian church, in Arch street above Fifth. This ground has since been sold, and his remains as well as those of other members of the family who were buried there, were removed to Laurel Hill. Rev. Dr. Janeway spoke at the grave. Mrs. Hazard died in New Haven July 6, 1820.

When Ebenezer Hazard and Abigail Arthur were married in 1783, they went to live at a house on the north side of Arch street below Fifth, directly opposite Christ churchyard gate, where their son Samuel was born May 26, 1784. As Postmaster General he was obliged to have his office in the city where Congress sat. Accordingly they removed to 55 Queen street, New York, in April, 1785, when Congress held its sessions in that city. May 1, 1786, he removed to the house, No. 58 Broadway ; "very near the Oswego market." Here on the 26th, his daughter Elizabeth was born. May 1, 1787, he moved again "opposite to where he lived last year," No. 29 Broadway. The following is copied from Mrs. Josiah Quincy's letters of the date of " New York, 1789" : " Mrs. Hazard, who resided in the house opposite ours, was also a valuable friend. She was distinguished for the exquisite neatness of her establishment, and for capability in every branch of domestic economy. She had many and excellent servants; but in those days it was usual for ladies to attend to housewifery, and she kindly gave me much useful instruction." The following is extracted from Pontson's paper July, 1820; " Died in this city [New Haven] on the 6th inst., Mrs. Abigail Hazard, widow of Ebenezer Hazard, Esq., of Philadelphia, and formerly Postmaster General. In this excellent woman, sound understanding and amiable dispositions were adorned by polished and dignified manners, and ennobled by their union with genuine Christian virtue. The law of kindness dwelt in her heart, governed her conduct, and guided her conversation ; producing the delightful expressions and habits of sincere, uniform, and lasting friendship. While affected by anxiety, age and ill-health, to a degree which might seem almost to excuse discontent and moroseness, she still expressed her humble reliance on the direction of Infinite wisdom, and showed the same cheerful, good will to men, which had distinguished her brighter days. Her religion was not of the tongue and the countenance, but of the life. * * * By humility, pureness, gentleness, forbearance, forgiveness of injuries, kindness, patience, fortitude, faith in God, and benevolence towards man, and especially by the control and suppression of selfish feelings, she showed that she had imbibed some measure of the spirit of Him. * * * The knowledge of Mrs. Hazard's excellence was of course most diffused among those who had longest known her; but report had brought it into a land of strangers. The residence of a few weeks confirmed the impressions which had preceded her arrival; and some even here can tell of the mild and unobtrusive form which her goodness wore. In the calm confidence of faith, she prepared for death, before its approach was visible, and that Savior in whom she trusted, was pleased to preserve her, so far as human sense could discern, from all the terrors of dissolution. * * * Her spirit rests in peace; and well may those who knew her character, and witnessed her departure, say, 'let us die the death of the righteous, and let our last end be like hers.' "

* Only a short time before her death, Mrs. Hazard had moved to New Haven to be with her daughter, Elizabeth Rockwood, who had taken up her residence there, in order that her children should be educated in New England as directed in Mr. Rockwood's will. In 1783, a committee of Congress appointed to examine the affairs of the post-office report, that " the duties of that office are discharged with the utmost industry, and economy, and with great attention at the same time to the public convenience." Upon the giving up of his position as Postmaster General, feeling it was necessary for him to make exertions, Mr. Hazard spent some time in settling up the post-office business, and looking for an occupation. In 1790, he was appointed by General H. Knox, Secretary of War, one of three to appraise West Point, about to be purchased by the United States from Stephen Moore.

He returned to Philadelphia December, 1790. He was living in 1791 at a house at No. 189 Second street above Race, west side, next door south of the sign of the Buck, between Race and Vine. While there he buried his infant child Ebenezer Gordon, named after his friend, Rev. William Gordon, the author of a history of the American Revolution, and with whom he lived while stopping in Boston, and who afterwards returned to St. Neatts', England, and corresponded with him until his death. From January, 1791, to July, 1792, he was in partnership with Jonas Addoms, as brokers and commission merchants, under the name of Hazard & Addoms, in No. 173 Market street, below Third, on the south side. They dissolved partnership in 1792. They bought and sold stocks, real estate, and sold goods on commission. See American Daily Advertiser, January 1792. His office in 1793 was at 119 South Front street. He was one of the founders of the present North American Insurance Company, 1794, which began as the Universal Tontine Association. He was secretary of the Tontine and Insurance Company for many years. In 1793, the whole family of nine were attacked by yellow fever, of whom his sister Anna died and was buried the same day, October 18. Of the servants, a Mrs. Flint, nurse, died. He was secretary and agent of the Washington Tontine, established in 1794, for buying lots, and building houses and wharfs in " the new Federal City of Washington," or " to form an extensive union of public and private benefits in its improvement."

Ebenezer Hazard was a man of fine and strong intellect, of highly cultivated mind, with a clear, cool head, and strong tendency to a sensible piety. He was one of the trustees of the Old Presbyterian Church in Wall street, New York, and the most active, during his residence there. It was the church of his ancestors, who helped to found it. He was trustee and elder in the Second Presbyterian church, Third and Arch streets, until his death, from his nomination in 1784. He was trustee of the General Assembly. He was a most excellent and deeply read Bible student, and a fine Greek scholar. When Charles Thomson, the Secretary of Congress, was making his original translation of the Bible, published in four volumes, 800 pages, he sent his MSS. in regularly to Ebenezer for his revision. We have the correspondence between the two, and while Mr. Thomson would frequently rebel against the corrections, he generally yielded to the reasons advanced. Mr. Hazard finally purchased Mr.

Thomson's share in the transaction; and afterwards disposed of them to Mr. Earle, bookseller. The printing of it was begun in 1808 by Miss Aitkin, daughter of Mr. Aitkin the printer. Mr. Hazard corrected the proof-sheets. He wrote "Remarks on a Report concerning Western Indians" in 2 Hist. Col. IV.

He published in 1792 the first volume, which was followed by the second in 1794, of "Historical Collections, consisting of State Papers and other authentic Documents," printed to preserve them and form the basis of the History of the United States; 2 vols., large quarto. With unwearied industry he traveled over the country from State to State, armed by the authority of Congress with the right to examine and copy whatever he saw fit, and thus he made copies of state papers and documents, which he said were then fast going into decay or being lost. He was materially assisted by Thomas Jefferson, John Adams, Charles Thomson, and other statesmen. This work is now extremely rare and copies of it have brought as high as $65. When he had partly prepared material for two volumes his labors were arrested by his appointment to the office of Postmaster General of the United States. He was the third to hold the office, succeeding Benj. Franklin and Richard Bache. He served from 1782 till the adoption of the Constitution in 1789. His previous labors as postmaster having eminently fitted him for the office, he applied himself thoroughly to his new position, and brought order out of chaos, conducting the department with such business tact and unswerving honesty as to make it a paying part of the government for the first time. He proposed and carried out many improvements.

It was while he was Postmaster General that the first news of the Battle of Lexington, the first Battle of the Revolution, was promulgated by him. The battle occurred April 19, 1775, and news was instantly started by post-riders to the seat of government. As the document passed through the many towns on the route, it was endorsed by members of the

Committee of Safety in each place, or by the postmaster, until it reached Ebenezer's hands and received his final endorsement. This deeply interesting paper and the first official one of our Revolution can be seen in the Historical Society's rooms.

During his useful and busy life, Ebenezer Hazard was a member of many societies, in which, notwithstanding his professional duties as bookseller, postmaster, broker, and secretary of an insurance company, he was always one of the most active. He was elected member, May 10, 1800, of the "Humane Society for Recovering Persons from Suspended Animation, or Drowning." Joseph Cruikshank was president, and Isaac Snowden, secretary. In 1805, he was chosen a member of the "Massachusetts Society for Promoting Christian Knowledge." He was for many years manager of the Schuylkill and Pennsylvania Bridge Company; also of the Delaware and Schuylkill Canal Company; of the Philadelphia Dispensary; of the Guardians of the Poor; and of the Board of Missions. Of this last organization he was a most effective member, keeping all their papers, and writing most of the annual reports for the General Assembly, as well as instructions to the missionaries. He was also Curator of the American Philosophical Society, to which he often contributed, having a turn for philosophical science. He was the first corresponding member of the Massachusetts Historical Society; and also member of the New York Historical Society, and fellow of the American Academy of Natural Sciences.

His correspondence with Rev. Jeremy Belknap, the founder of the Massachusetts Historical Society, author of the History of New Hampshire and other works, was long and very interesting, mainly on literary, historical, and scientific topics. This correspondence was published by the Massachusetts Historical Society, in 1878, in two handsome volumes.

Of himself, he wrote in a family letter in 1806, that he

"had to begin the world at the age of nineteen, without a profession, without a trade, without a shilling in his pocket, without anything but a good education, a good character, and confidence in God; he was obliged to be both industrious and economical; accommodated his wishes to his circumstances; rendered his situation as comfortable as he could by cultivating contentment with the allotments of Providence, and at length attained a sufficiency to soften the pillow of age, and smooth the rugged declivity of life."

He was a man of sound judgment, and of such liberal and enterprising turn of mind, that he was always willing to take a share of the risk which any venture that was sanctioned by his judgment demanded. He was therefore a useful promoter, with his influence and capital, of many improvements which have been of great use to the citizens of Philadelphia. Among these may be named the Schuylkill Navigation Company, for which he drew up the proposals, and the outline of the act to be passed by the Legislature, in 1813, only four years before his death. Many of his friends and relatives not only consulted him about their investments, but placed their means in his hands to be cared for, and relied on his great probity and scrupulous honesty.

SAMUEL HAZARD[6] (*Ebenezer*[5], *Samuel*[4], *Nathaniel*[3], *Jonathan*[2], *Thomas*[1]), the son of Ebenezer and Abigail; was born in Arch street, below Fifth, old No. 161, north side, May 26, 1784. He was baptized by Rev. James Sproat in the Second Presbyterian Church, Third and Arch streets, July 23, 1789.

In his childhood, in 1791, he went to Rev. Dr. Ely's school adjoining the church, Third and Arch streets; afterwards in 1793 to Rev. Dr. Andrew Hunter's school in Woodbury, N. J., for three years; then to the old academy in Fourth street. He then entered the Freshman class of Princeton College in 1797, aged about fourteen years, and left there when a Sophomore in 1799, owing to sickness which prevented his return to college.

After leaving college he entered in 1800 the counting-house of Robert Ralston, an eminent merchant and great philanthropist, whose wife was Sarah Clarkson, first cousin to his father, Ebenezer Hazard. After serving a few years' apprenticeship, it became his turn to go as supercargo. This was considered a reward to those who served their apprenticeship well. His first voyage was to the West Indies in March, 1806, returning in June. His father wrote at this time of him, "you can not exceed the truth in speaking of his diligence, punctuality and integrity."

In November, 1806, he engaged from Captain Paul Cox the front room of his house, No. 83 South Front Street, as a counting-house at the rate of $80 per annum. In December, 1806, he formed a partnership with Samuel Cabot, a young man from Boston, under the name of Hazard & Cabot, commission and shipping merchants at South Wharf, first below Chestnut street. This enterprise lasted until July 1, 1811. The business was successful until the passage of the embargo and non-intercourse act.

His next voyage, in 1812, was in charge of one of Mr. Ralston's vessels as supercargo, on a trading voyage to the Mediterranean. Here he was captured by the Turks and kept as a prisoner for four months and then ransomed. Afterwards his vessel was captured by a French privateer in the War of 1812. His vessel was finally restored to him, after lying idle during the war at Smyrna. His narrative of his experiences on these voyages was always very entertaining. In March, 1812, he applied for a passport, in which he is described as twenty-eight years old, of fair complexion, with light hair, aquiline nose, long chin, oval face, blue eyes, and of five feet seven inches in height. He was at Malta, August 9, 1812. In June, 1813, he was at Constantinople. He returned to America in 1815. While abroad he came across a marble foot, beautifully sculptured, part of a colossal statue of Minerva. This he brought home, and presented it to the Academy of Fine Arts. He carried it a long distance on horseback to Smyrna with great difficulty.

In 1817, at the request of Charles N. Bancker he went to Lexington, Kentucky, to settle some affairs. He then journeyed to Huntsville, Alabama Territory, and took an account of stock of a store which fell to Mr. Bancker in the above settlement. On his return to Philadelphia he was persuaded to take an interest in the store. Accordingly in 1818 he settled in Huntsville, as resident partner of Hazard & Co., selling goods and purchasing cotton for the northern market. While there he met Abigail Clark Hetfield, daughter of Morris Hetfield of Elizabeth, N. J., who was staying with her sister Sarah, wife of Willis Pope. He was married to her March 18, 1819, by Rev. Mr. Davis, at the residence of Col. Leroy Pope. He made a bridal tour among Colonel Percy's, Colonel Walker's, and other families, and then eastward to make acquaintances with their mutual relations. In Huntsville four children were born to them. He built a house, and was a prominent citizen and an alderman, active in establishing a church, and in bringing a missionary out.

Owing to the burning of two cargoes of cotton, the business was unprofitable, and the firms of Hazard & Co., and Hazard, Pope & Co., failed in 1826. Samuel Hazard gave up every cent's worth of property to his creditors, even to the household goods to which he was entitled. His creditors seeing the misfortune was beyond his control, as a mark of respect and confidence raised a handsome sum, nearly $3000, and presented it to him. With this, his wife, and three children, he came north to Philadelphia in June, 1827.

Being of a literary turn of mind, inherited from his father, in 1820 he commenced the publication of the Register of Pennsylvania, the first of a series of works on the history of his native State which will make his name immortal. This he published in weekly numbers, or two volumes a year, for a period of eight years. The sixteen volumes contain a vast amount of historical research relating to the city and State, which is often quoted by historians and statesmen, and is received as authority in the courts of the State. It is not too much to say that this work, together with that of Watson's Annals which first appeared partly in the Register, helped mainly to form that love for antiquarian lore which has been so fruitful in collecting and preserving many things which would otherwise have been lost. But at that time it was just forming, the number of readers was too few to support a literary periodical of that character without advertisements, and its publication had to be suspended.

Having been appointed, in 1828, Secretary of the Board of Guardians of the Poor, he fulfilled that office for seven years, and on his retirement received a vote of thanks and a sum of money, November 2, 1836.

In July, 1839, he commenced the publication of the United States Commercial and Statistical Register, a work somewhat on the plan of the Pennsylvania Register, but of wider scope, and intended for the use of merchants and for the preservation of useful statistics. This he continued for three years, until July 1842, forming six royal octavo volumes.

In 1850 he published Annals of Pennsylvania from the Discovery of the Delaware, 1609-1682, a large volume, giving the early history of New York, New Jersey, Delaware, and Maryland, besides that of Pennsylvania, and including all relating to Pennsylvania from the time of the charter to the taking possession of the country; a work full of original research.

By acts of Legislature and the commission of Governor Ritner, in 1851, Samuel Hazard was authorized to prepare and superintend the publication of a vast mass of papers in the archives of the State. He therefore edited with great labor and research, the Colonial Records, sixteen volumes, and Pennsylvania Archives, twelve volumes. The publication was commenced in 1850 and finished in 1855. He afterwards prepared a most valuable index to the whole which unlocks the contents of the twenty-eight volumes; this was published in 1860. This weary labor of eight years has produced a fund of information which no historian can overlook.

He was early a member of the Pennsylvania Historical Society, and always deeply interested in it. In 1850, he was elected honorary life member, and in 1862 the librarian by an unusually large vote. and without solicitation. The society had his portrait painted and it now graces their walls. He served as librarian until his failing sight obliged him to resign; during his service he arranged and classified a vast mass of papers, pamphlets, and books, and fully catalogued them, thus making the treasures available. At his death, Edward Armstrong was appointed to deliver an eulogy upon him. He was also a corresponding member of the New York Historical Society; and long a member of the Franklin Institute. In June, 1832, he issued proposals for publishing a Historical Journal of the Presbyterian church, in the United States.

The American Literary Association was formed in 1805 for mutual improvement. It ceased five years later, when twelve of the members formed the Phœnix Social club, which was never to be increased. Each member had a water color portrait made, all of which were bound in the book of constitution and rules, and the volume was to be the property of the last surviving member. It fell to Samuel Hazard, he having been a member sixty-five years. James West was next to the last one.

Samuel Hazard was a member of many societies, as follows:

1805, Nov. 18. Elected resident member of the American Literary Association, established in October.
1809. Elected member of Philadelphia Linnæan Society; Dr. B. S. Barton, President. The society met in the old medical college, South Fifth street, now the dispensary.
1809. Elected member of Bible Society.
1809. Elected member of Orphan Society.
1811. Elected member of Chamber of Commerce.

1814. Elected member of Academy of Natural Sciences.
1816. Elected member of Soup Society.
1817. Elected member of Society for Promoting Economy.
1818. Elected Director of Public Library in Huntsville.
1819. Elected Assistant Secretary of Agricultural Society.
1828. Elected Secretary of the Guardians of the Poor.
1828. Elected Corresponding Secretary of Horticultural Society, then just established.
1835. Elected Trustee; and as the Building Committee signed the deeds of the Second Presbyterian Church.
1836. Elected Secretary of the Board of Trustees of the Second Presbyterian Church—a position he held for twenty-eight years and missed attending only two meetings owing to absence from the city.
1839. Elected Secretary of the Buck Mountain Coal Company.
1839. Elected member of the Statistical Society of Boston.
1839. Elected Member of the Corporation of the Widows' Fund.
1845. Elected member of National Academy of Design, Washington.
1851. Appointed by the Governor and Legislature to edit the Colonial Records and Archives. This he did in twenty-nine volumes, finishing the work in 1860.
1857. Elected Honorary Member of the Moravian Historical Society of Nazareth.
1857. Elected Honorary Member of the Historical Society of Tennessee.

He was one of the founders of the Philadelphia Hose Company, instituted January 2, 1804, being the first hose company in Philadelphia. He was an active member while he remained in the city, and was one of the committee to collect subscriptions.

Busy man as he was, his religious life was a very decided one from the time of his youth. He was only nineteen when he wrote out the book of Proverbs to carry around with him for private reading. It was at Germantown, where the family had been driven by the yellow fever of 1803. He says, in his later life, "My mornings were chiefly spent in retirement and devotional exercises. * * * I look back on this period of my life as the most pleasant, being closely devoted to God, and truly days of peace and pleasantness." He maintained an ardent piety all his life, and like his ancestors it was a pleasure for him to work for the church. He was elder of the Second Presbyterian church, and Secretary of the Board of Trustees for twenty-eight years, a position he only relinquished on account of his failing eyesight, in 1864, and was Honorary Secretary till his death. He published his reminiscenses of the church and in its changes entitled a "Communication to the Board of Trustees," which has been the basis of nearly all the facts since published about the church.

From such long and steady use of his eyes in reading and writing his eyesight began to fail him, and for the last six years of his life he was totally blind. His mind was active and strong to the last, and his tenacious memory was of great use to him and to the many who consulted him. His misfortune was a heavy one to him, as his vigorous constitution would have allowed him to have done much more work and which his mental activity would have led him to do. He was of a very genial disposition, fond of society, of elevated, and improving character.

Samuel Hazard died May 26, 1870, aged 86 years, leaving four children. He had nine children:

1. Abbie[7], born December 24, 1819; died in Arch street, Philadelphia, 8 years old; and was buried in the Arch street ground, September 17, 1827. 2. Elizabeth[7], born November 6, 1821; married, June, 1845, by Rev. Albert Barnes, to Walter Kerr Halsted; died in Cincinnati, Ohio, April 5, 1861, leaving four children: (a) Elizabeth Wetherill, born May 19, 1846; died July 1, 1846. (b) Kate, married to Benjamin Shepard, of Shepardsville, now residing in Orange, New Jersey, and has two children, Benjamin Halsted, and William Ellison. (c) Walter Kerr, died December 26, 1853. (d) Samuel Hazard. 3. Samuel[7], born May 29, 1823; was drowned while bathing in the Schuylkill river, May 22, 1834, aged 11 years. The body was recovered next day, and buried in the Arch street ground. 4. Willis Pope[7], born in Huntsville, Alabama, July 22, 1825; married Susan Robinson Gilpin, daughter of Vincent Gilpin and Naomi Robinson, November 14, 1850. Inheriting the taste for bookselling that his three immediate ancestors had, he entered the book business at sixteen years of age, went into that business when twenty-five, and after publishing largely sold out when thir-

ty-eight, and finally retired at forty, and gave himself up to literary and agricultural pursuits on his farm Maple Knoll, near Westchester. He has prepared for the press several books, of which the most important is "The Annals of Philadelphia in the Olden Time," being a companion to Watson's Annals, in one volume, octavo, 520 pages; also, "The Jersey, Guernsey, and Alderney Cow," one volume, octavo; "A Treatise on Butter and Butter-making;" and one on "The Guenon System of Judging of Cows," one volume, octavo. He is chief of the Bureau of Agriculture of the Permanent Exhibition; President of the Chad's Ford Farmer's Club; Vice-President of the American Dairymen's Association; Member of the Committee to revise the Constitution of the International Dairy Fair Association; Secretary of the Pennsylvania Guenon Commission; President of the American Carburetter Company, and Member of the Microscopical Society of Westchester. He was one of the originators and Vice-Presidents of the Book Trade Association.

The children of Willis P.[7] and Susan G. Hazard are: (a) Anna Shipley[8], born September 10, 1851; died March 12, 1853; buried at Laurel Hill. (b) Vincent Gilpin[8], born January 20, 1853. (c) Kate Hood[8], born August 27, 1854. (d) Florence Naomi[8], born July 24. 1856. (e) Willis Hetfield[8], born July 29, 1866. 5. Maria Percy[7], born December 25, 1828; married William Veitch, December 30, 1869; Mr. Veitch was born August 27, 1799. 6. Spencer Halsted[7], born November 25, 1830; once a dry goods commission merchant of Philadelphia; now a broker in New York. 7. Emily[7], born September 25, 1832; died. at Germantown March 6, 1867. 8. Samuel[7], the fourth bearing the name, born March 1, 1834; was a book-seller, succeeding Willis P., which business he left to go into the war of the Rebellion.

He entered the regiment entitled "Colonel Rush's Lancers", afterward the Sixth Pennsylvania Cavalry, at its organization, and was mustered First Lieutenant of Co. D., on

September 12, 1861. He served with it until April 30, 1862, when he was forced to resign on account of ill-health, after repeated and most praiseworthy endeavors to overcome the evil effects on his constitution of the exposure of camp life.

In September, 1862, supposing his health sufficiently restored, he recruited a company for the 152d Pennsylvania Volunteers, 3rd Artillery, Colonel Roberts, and was mustered in as Captain, February 11, 1863; served with his company at Fortress Munroe during 1863. In the Petersburg campaign of 1864-5, commanded a detachment of his regiment at Fort Converse in the time of the Bermuda defences, under General Charles K. Graham, where his command was remarkable for its discipline, neatness, and precision of drill. Resigned, on surgeon's certificate of disability, February 13, 1865. Breveted Major, March 13, 1865.

He went twice to Cuba for his health, and on his return, wrote in 1870 a book entitled "Cuba with Pen and Pencil," in one volume, octavo, with many illustrations, of which some were his designs; it is a most entertaining narrative, had a large sale, and is used for and said to be, the best handbook for visitors to the island. Later, he went as correspondent for the press, and on the staff of the Santo Domingo Commission, sent out by General Grant to view and report on the country with a view of its annexation. Major Hazard wrote in 1872, "Santo Domingo, past and present, with a glance at Hayti, a history of, and travels in, that country;" in one volume, octavo, profusely illustrated, published in this country by Harper Brothers, and in London by Sampson, Low & Co., in 1873. It was universally praised, and declared the most reliable and descriptive work on the island. Shortly after his return he married, June 1, 1871, Blanche Crissy Peabody, widow of William Massey, Jr., and sailed for Europe, where he remained three years, consulting the best physicians and visiting the spas, for his health. He returned in 1875, and died January 10, 1876. While abroad two children were born to him, and still survive:

(a) Spencer[8], born in London, February 28, 1872. (b) Samuel[8], born in Dresden, 1874.

Julia Hetfield[8], ninth child of Samuel[7], born June 22, 1836; died October 17, 1844, aged 8 years.

Abigail Clark Hetfield, the wife of Samuel Hazard, the second, was connected with the best families in New Jersey. Her father was Morris Hetfield, and her mother was Abigail Clark, daughter of Abraham Clark, who was born February 15, 1726; married 1749; died September 15, 1794; he was a signer of the Declaration of Independence. The old mansion and farm of the Hetfields has been in the family in a direct line for over two hundred years. Abigail married Samuel Hazard, March 18, 1819, in Huntsville, Alabama; had nine children as stated above, and died September 15, 1863, aged 73 years. She was a very pretty woman, of medium height, brown hair, and blue eyes, and possessed of great intelligence and spirit, activity to the last, and a pious nature.

Erskine Hazard[6], the second son of Ebenezer and Abigail, the sixth generation from the first in this country, was born in New York November 30, 1789; he married Mary Fullerton, daughter of Alexander Fullerton and Mary Hall; he died March, 1865; they had eight children: Alezander[7], Erskine, Erskine, Fisher, Albert Barnes, Harry Williams, Mary, and Fanny.

He went to school at an early age in Philadelphia; afterwards to the grammar school at Princeton; then to the Quaker Academy in Philadelphia, where he was told he knew all the Latin and Greek they could teach him. Accordingly he was sent to Princeton College at thirteen years of age, where he remained till the Junior year. He then went to Boston and Andover studying with tutors. But disliking study by this time, he persuaded his father to put him into mercantile life, studying as preparatory to it, for some months, French and Chemistry. He entered Mr. Stilli's counting-house, which he left for that of Hazard & Cabot, where he remained until of age.

In 1811, he made a trip to Niagara, expecting to settle down to a life in the woods. Not liking it, he returned to Philadelphia, and, in 1812, went into the business of manufacturing wire, with Josiah White, the first mill of the kind in the country. The business, owing to the war with England, proved very lucrative, until the peace, when the imported article ruined their business. They had very largely increased their mill and machinery at the Falls of the Schuylkill. Learning there was coal up in the Schuylkill regions, they thought if the navigation of the river could be so improved as to allow the passage of boats to bring it down, it might pay. They therefore invented the plan of locks and dams, applied to the Legislature for a charter, Ebenezer Hazard preparing the bill, etc. Thus was originated the Schuylkill Navigation Company. Several wagon-loads of coal were hauled in 1814, to experiment with, at a cost of one dollar per bushel. But the workmen got tired of testing it, thinking it required constant stirring up like bituminous coal, and cleared out, shutting the door and leaving the draft on. A hand returned in about half an hour afterwards for his coat, and was surprised to see the furnace red-hot. That settled all difficulties, and enabled them to make wire so easily they cleared $50,000 per annum and could sell all they could make. In the height of success the mill took fire and destroyed everything. With new capital, the mill was rebuilt, was filled with new machinery, and had fairly got under way again, when news of peace arrived.

The low price of the imported article forced them to find every means of cheapening the manufacture until the canal was made. Erskine built a bateau of sheet-iron, and went up the Schuylkill in it, being perhaps the first iron boat ever built. He built a foot-bridge across the Schuylkill which was the first wire-bridge perhaps ever built.

Owing to too high a price being charged by the Schuylkill Navigation Company for freight and coal, Mr. White started up the Lehigh, and the result was, that finally they leased a mine, and originated the Lehigh Navigation Company in 1818. By this time the reduced wire-business had also lowered their interest in it, and the activity of White and Hazard was diverted to the carrying out of the development of the coal trade and the navigation of the Lehigh. In this undertaking they made another invention, that of the gravity road, now the famous Switchback. In 1827, they laid nine miles of track upon it and made it almost the first railroad. The cars were then hauled by mule-power. His interests were now so identified with the development of the Lehigh coal trade and the Navigation Company, that he removed to Mauch Chunk and resided there in 1819 and for many years.

He afterwards moved to and settled in Philadelphia, always retaining his interest in the Lehigh Company, and was also one of the originators of the Crane Iron Works at Catasaugua, which were also very successful.

Early endowed with a taste for mechanics, his ingenuity led him to invent many novel modes of getting at useful results, and he freely gave his ideas to others, which they carried out to their own or the public's advantage. He also invented a new cannon for carrying a great distance. In latter life, he was much afflicted with gout but he employed his active mind in writing essays on the currency, banking, and other useful topics.

He was a man of great energy, clear thought, prompt action, liberal ideas, and public-spirited, all of which enabled him to carry out the great works he undertook, and which have yielded and still yield their large benefits to the public.

GENEALOGY.

THOMAS HAZARD[1], came to this country, 1632.

JONATHAN HAZARD[2] (*Thomas*[1]), at Newtown, L. I.; married Hannah Laurenson; died 1711; had children: 1. Thomas[3], born 1682; died August 31, 1733. 2. James[3], judge at Newtown, L. I.; died April 25, 1765. 3. Nathaniel[3], a merchant; died about 1765. 4. Elizabeth[3], married Edward Hunt. 5. Sarah[3], married James Renne.

THOMAS HAZARD[3] (*Jonathan*[2], *Thomas*[1]), styled Captain, was supervisor of Newtown from 1720 till his death, which occurred August 31, 1733, at the age of 51 years, and was occasioned by a fall from his horse. By his wife Mercy, daughter of Thomas Betts, he had children: 1. Thomas[4]. 2. Daniel[4], a sea-captain, died in New York in 1747. His child was: (a) Thomas[5], died in New York in 1787, aged 48 years; had four children. 3. Samuel[4]. 4. John[4]. 5. Jonathan[4], settled in Orange County, New York.

JAMES HAZARD[3] (*Jonathan*[2], *Thomas*[1]), for fifteen years was a judge of Common Pleas at Newtown, L. I.; occupied the farm now of John Duryea, in Newtown. The family vault on this estate fell into decay and was fitted up a few years since. Judge Hazard died April 26, 1765. His children were: 1. Rebecca[4], married Robert Morrell. 2. William[4], born January 19, 1725; was a prominent citizen in Newtown; married Elizabeth Moore; died August 25, 1773, aged 58 years. He had several daughters, and a son: (a) Morris[5], who was the grandfather of William H.[7], of New York, a shipping merchant.

NATHANIEL HAZARD[3] (*Jonathan*[2], *Thomas*[1]), a merchant in New York and Philadelphia. His children were: 1. Nathaniel[4], a merchant in New York; died about 1765; married Elizabeth Drummey, who lived to be nearly one hundred years old, and died May 27, 1811. 2. Samuel[4], born March 20, 1713-14; married October, 1739; died July 14, 1758. 3. Hannah[4], married Rev. Samuel Sacket, of Bedford, a native of Newtown, and had children: (a) Nathaniel Sacket. (b) Samuel Sacket. 4. Sarah[4], married Captain Daniel Hazard, and had children: (a) Sarah Hazard, who married Captain Howard. (b) Thomas, married Martha Smith, and had children, Thomas Hazard, and Margaret Hazard.

NATHANIEL HAZARD[4] (*Nathaniel*[3], *Jonathan*[2], *Thomas*[1]), married Elizabeth Drummey, and had twelve children: 1. Eliza, or Elizabeth[5], married December 11, 1761, Joseph Hallett, and had six children: (a) Elizabeth, married Robert Gault. (b) Lydia, married Frederick Heilitz. (c) Ann, married Major John Delafield. (d) Catharine, married William Payne. (e) Sarah, died unmarried. (f) Maria, married Hon. Benjamin Talmadge. 2. Mary[5]. 3. Ann Hazard[5], married Thomas Treadwell, and had six children: Mary, Nathaniel, Elizabeth, Hannah—married Henry Davis—, Nancy, and Thomas. 4. Catharine[5]. 5. Catharine, 2d[5], married Gilbert Tennent, M. D.; one son, John Tennent. 6. Nathaniel[5], married Maria Robinson, daughter of Col. John Robinson; died 1798; had Maria[6], and Nathaniel[6]. 7. Samuel[5]. 8. Samuel, 2d[5], married and had Mary[6], who married John Tennent. 9. Mary, 2d[5], married Joseph Blackwell, and had children: (a) Harriet Blackwell, married William Howell. (b) Joseph, married Justina Bayard. (c) Frances, married Grant Forbes. (d) William Drayton Blackwell. 10. Joseph[5], married Jane Moore, and had children: (a) Jane[6]. (b) Finch[6]. 11. Sarah[5], married David Judson, and had; (a) Philander[6]. (b) David[6]. 12. Margaret[5].

SAMUEL HAZARD[4] (Nathaniel[3], Jonathan[2], Thomas[1]), born March 20, 1713-14; married, October, 1739, Catharine Clarkson; died July 14, 1758; had seven children: 1. A daughter[5], born dead, October 28, 1740. 2. Matthew[5], born July 3, 1742; died July 15, 1742. 3. Ebenezer[5], born January 15, 1744-5; married Abigail Arthur, September 11, 1783; died June 13, 1817; had four children (see previous life of Ebenezer). 4. Anna[5], born September 20, 1746; died of yellow fever October 18, 1793, aged 47 years. 5. Mary[5], born January 16, 1750-1; married July 29, 1770, Cornelius Turk, of New York; died June 21, 1772. 6. Elizabeth[5], born November 2, 1755; married Joseph West, and had six children: (a) Webley, died unmarried. (b) John C., died unmarried. (c) Catharine, married Uriah Ryder. and had children, Uriah, Elizabeth, Abigail, Mary Ann, Rebecca, Joseph, Catharine, Phœbe. (d) Samuel West, married Catharine Bantz. (e) Abigail, married Joseph Giraud, and had children, Eliza Ann, Frederick, Jacob Post, Clarissa. (f) Ann, married Hugh Aikman. 7. Catharine Hazard[5], born December 13, 1758.

THOMAS HAZARD[5] (Daniel[4], Thomas[3], Jonathan[2], Thomas[1]), died in New York in 1787, aged 43 years. His four children were: 1. William Howard[6], born 1770. 2. Charles Smith[6], born 1772. 3. Frances S.[6], born 1773. 4. Benjamin[6], born 1774.

EBENEZER HAZARD[5] (Samuel[4], Nathaniel[3], Jonathan[2], Thomas[1]), had four children; 1. Samuel[6], born May 26, 1784; married March 18; 1819; died May 26, 1870; had nine children. 2. Elizabeth Breese[6], born May 26, 1796; married Ebenezer Rockwood; had four children; married, second, Rev. Thomas E. Vermilye, D.D., and had five children. 3. Erskine[6], born November 30, 1789; married Mary Fullerton, February 28, 1822; died, February, 1865; had eight children. 4. Ebenezer Gordon[6], born September 29, 1792; died November 5, 1792.

SAMUEL HAZARD[6] (*Ebenezer*[5], *Samuel*[4], *Nathaniel*[3], *Jonathan*[2], *Thomas*[1]), the historian; married Abbie Clark Hetfield, March 18, 1819; and had nine children: 2. Abby[7], born December 24, 1819; died September 27, 1827, aged 8 years. 3. Elizabeth[7], born November 6, 1821; married Walter Kerr Halsted; died April 5, 1861; had four children: (a) Elizabeth Wetherill, born May 19, 1846; died July 1, 1846. (b) Kate, married Benjamin Shepard, and has two children, Benjamin Halsted, and William Ellison. (c) Walter Kerr, died December 26, 1853. (d) Samuel Hazard. 4. Samuel[7], born May 29, 1823; drowned May 22, 1834, aged 11 years. 5. Willis Pope[7], born July 22, 1825; married November 14, 1850; had five children: (a) Anna Shipley[8], born September 10, 1851; died March 12, 1853. (b) Vincent Gilpin[8], born January 20, 1853. (c) Kate Hood[8], born August 27, 1854. (d) Florence Naomi[8], born July 24, 1856. (e) Willis Hetfield[8], born July 29, 1866. 6. Maria Percy[7], born December 25, 1828; married William Veitch, December 30, 1869. 7. Spencer Halsted[7], born November 25, 1830. 8. Emily[8], born September 25, 1832; died March 6, 1867. 9. Samuel[7], born March 1, 1834; married June 1, 1871; died January 10, 1876; had two children: (a) Spencer[8], born February 23, 1372. (b) Samuel[8], born 1874.

ELIZABETH BREESE HAZARD[6] (*Ebenezer*[5], *Samuel*[4], *Nathaniel*[3], *Jonathan*[2], *Thomas*[1]), born in New York, May 26, 1786; married, first, September 9, 1807, by Dr. Ashbel Green, to Ebenezer Rockwood, of Boston, who was born June 2, 1781. He was graduated A. M. at Harvard, 1802, read law and settled in Boston, and died May 8, 1815, aged 34 years. In his short career, he proved his possession of great talents, and address, and his high moral worth, even among his intimate associates in the highest circle of talent and refinement. He had dignity and intelligence, his intuitions were quick and clear, his knowledge was abundant, and he was noble, generous, and affectionate. At his early death he left four children: 1. Abigail Arthur, born

September 16, 1808; resides in New York. 2. Ebenezer Hazard, born August 6, 1810; was graduated M. D. at Yale, 1832; settled at Enfield, Mass.; married, first, on November 7, 1832. Juliet Bliss, of West Springfield, who was born August 16, 1811, and died June 11, 1854. Their children were : (a) Ellen Louisa, born January 31, 1834, at Long Meadow. (b) Ebenezer Arthur, born January 6, 1839, at Enfield. (c) Charlotte Elizabeth, born February 3, 1842, at Enfield. (d) Charles Erskine, born June 20, 1847. Ebenezer married, second, Adelia O. Wilson, daughter of Ezekiel Smith, from Rehoboth. 3. William Erskine, born June, 1811; died unmarried in Havana, Cuba, 1835. 4. Charles Greene, born July 19, 1814; formerly a banker in Mauch Chunk, Pa., and now cashier of the National Newark Banking Company; married June 23, 1840, Sarah Smith, daughter of George B. Smith, of New York, and Joanna Vermilye, and had children : (a) William Erskine, born May 21, 1841; died July, 1842. (b) Charles Greene, born January 11, 1843. (c) Joanna Smith, born June 13, 1845. (d) Elizabeth Vermilye, born May 30, 1848; died May 6, 1853.

Elizabeth Breese Rockwood[6] married, second, Rev. Thomas E. Vermilye, D.D., of New York ; died January 12, 1861; and had five children : 1. Rev. Ashbel Green Vermilye. 2. Mary Montgomery Vermilye. 3. Elizabeth Breese Vermilye. 4. Thomas Edward. 5. William W.

ERSKINE HAZARD[6] (*Ebenezer*[5], *Samuel*[4], *Nathaniel*[3], *Jonathan*[2], *Thomas*[1]), son of Ebenezer and Abigail; born November 30, 1789; married Mary Fullerton, daughter of Alexander Fullerton and Mary Hall, February 28, 1822 ; died February, 1865; and had eight children: 1. Alexander Fullerton[7], born August 13, 1824. 2. Erskine[7]. 3. Erskine[7], born October 11, 1828; at early manhood entered the army, served bravely in the Rebellion, and died, January 28, 1863, of wounds received at Fredericksburg. 4. Fisher[7], born October 14, 1830; married February 7, 1854, Elizabeth, daughter of Rev. J. B. Clemson; resides at Mauch Chunk; and had six children: Mary Fullerton[8], John Clemson, Bessie Fisher, Erskine Hazard—dec'd—, Erskine Hazard, Ethel. 5. Albert Barnes[7], born December 3, 1832; married Mary Ann West, and had: (a) Harry Williams[8], born December 12, 1856. 6. Harry Williams[7], born October 20, 1834; died in Rio Janeiro, Brazil, 1851. 7. Mary[7], born January 15, 1836; married James S. Cox, June 25, 1857, and now resides in Orange, New Jersey. They have had nine children: Mary Hazard—born August 18, 1858; died April 26, 1864, Martha Lyman, Fanny Hazard, Julia Biddle, John Lyman, Edith, Erskine Hazard, Alice, and Edward Vermilye—born December 28, 1873. 8. Fanny[7], born September 28, 1838; married Samuel N. Dickson June 5, 1867; and had two children: (a) Erskine Hazard, born February 26, 1872. (b) Arthur Gillespie, born November, 1873.

Genealogy and Memoir of the Sweet Famliy.

CHAPTER XXII.

JAMES SWEET[1], son of Isaac and Mary, came to America from Wales in 1630; settled at the foot of Ridge Hill in North Kingstown, Rhode Island, where the family burial ground is yet to be seen; was made a freeeman in 1655; married Mary Green, daughter of the first John Green. Their children were: 1. Philip[2], born July 15, 1655. 2. James[2] born May 8, 1657. 3. Mary[2], born February 2, 1660. 4. Benoni[2], born November 28, 1663. 5. Valentine[2], born February 14, 1665. 6. Samuel[2], born November 1, 1667. 7. Jeremiah[2], born January 6, 1669. 8. Renewed[2], born July 18, 1671. 9. Sylvester[2], born March 1, 1674. All the children of James and Mary Sweet were born in North Kingstown, Washington county, Rhode Island.

BENONI SWEET[2] (*James*[1]), fourth child of James, married Elizabeth ——, and had children: 1. James[3], born June 28, 1688. 2. Margaret[3], born September 22, 1690. 3. Benoni, Jr.[3], born March 23, 1692. 4. Mary[3], born December 8, 1696. 5. Elizabeth[3], born February 12, 1700. 6. Thomas[3], born August 12, 1703. All of the children of Benoni and Elizabeth Sweet were born in North Kingstown.

JAMES SWEET[3] (*Benoni*[2], *James*[1]), married Mary——, and had children: 1. Benoni[4], born April 2, 1715. 2.

Eben[4], born June 5, 1716. 3. Mary[4], born November 4, 1717. 4. James[4], born December 4, 1719. 5. Elisha[4], born October 18, 1721. 6. Freelove[4], born April 12, 1723. 7. Job[4], born December 1, 1724. 8. Elizabeth[4], born May 13, 1727. 9. Margaret[4], born April 4, 1729.

JOB SWEET[4] (*James*[3], *Benoni*[2], *James*[1]), seventh child of James, married Jemima Sherman July 5, 1750, in South Kingstown, and had children: 1. Rufus[5], born September 3, 1753. 2. Jeremiah[5], born November 7, 1754. 3. Gideon[5], born April 11, 1758. 4. James[5], born October 17, 1760. 5. Benoni[5], born October 16, 1762. He was father of Stephen[6], who was father of the present Charles Sweet[7], bone-setter in Hartford, Conn. 6. Jonathan[5], born September 6, 1765. 7. Margaret[5], born December 4, 1767. 8. Lydia[5], twin to Margaret. 9. Hannah[5], born April 3, 1770. 10. Sarah[5], born April 4, 1774.

JONATHAN SWEET[5] (*Job*[4], *James*[3], *Benoni*[2], *James*[1]), bone-setter at Sugar Loaf Hill, South Kingstown; married Sally, daughter of Thomas Sweet, and had children: 1. Job[6], born 1792. 2. Fanny[6], born 1795. 3. Mary Ann[6], born March 28, 1798. 4. William[6], born October 25, 1802. 5. Sarah[6], born July 3, 1807. 6. Jonathan[6], born 1810.

JOB SWEET[6] (*Jonathan*[5], *Job*[4], *James*[3], *Benoni*[2], *James*)[1], first son of Jonathan; married Deborah Greenman, and had children: 1. James[7]. 2. Betsy[7]. 3. Jonathan[7]. 4. Hannah[7]. 5. Susan[7].

WILLIAM SWEET[6] (*Jonathan*[5], *Job*[4], *James*[3], *Benoni*[2], *James*[1]), second son of Jonathan; now bone-setter at Sugar Loaf Hill, South Kingstown; married Martha Tourgee, February 23, 1825, and had children: 1. Sarah[7], born November 8, 1826. 2. Job[7], born October 13, 1828. 3. William[7], born November 8, 1830. 4. Thomas[7], born March 10, 1832. 5. Frances[7], born October 1, 1834. 6. Jonathan[7], born April 16, 1838. 7. Benoni[7], born September 23, 1840. 8. Mary[7], born May 13, 1844. 9. George[7], twin to Mary. 10. Edward[7], born October 3, 1846.

The above genealogical table was furnished me by the present Dr. Job Sweet, of New Bedford, Mass.

There is a tradition in the Narragansett family of Sweets that their ancestors, including James the first immigrant to Rhode Island, had been long gifted by nature with the faculty of setting dislocated and broken bones. James reared a large family of children, among whom was Benoni, who died at the age of ninety, June 19, 1751. To him a son James was born, June 18, 1688. This James and his father Benoni both possessed the "natural" gift of setting dislocated bones, but to what extent it was exercised is not definitely known.

Job, the son of the second James, the first great "bone-setter," was born December 1, 1724, and died on the farm now owned by Peleg Anthony and situated about a mile south of Narragansett Pier in Point Judith, Rhode Island.

Updike, in his History of the Narragansett Church, page 94, says: "James Sweet, the father of Benoni, emigrated from Wales to this country and purchased an estate at the foot of Ridge Hill—so called—, in North Kingstown, the same on which the late William Congdon lived and died. Benoni had been a captain in the British service, was well informed and of polished manners. He was a natural bone-setter and the progenitor of the race in Rhode Island. He was styled Doctor Sweet, but he practiced in restoring dislocations only. He was a regular communicant of the church, and officiated as a vestryman until his death, July 19, 1751. Says the record, 'Died, Captain Benoni Sweet, of North Kingstown, in the 90th year of his age. Dr. MacSparran preached his funeral sermon, and buried him in the cemetery of his ancestors.'

"Job, one of the family, obtained an eminent and widespread reputation as a bone-setter. During the Revolution he was called to Newport to set the dislocated bones of the French officers, an operation which their army surgeons were unable to perform. After the Revolutionary war, Colonel Burr, afterwards Vice President, invited him to New York, to restore the dislocated hipbone of his daughter, Theodosia, afterwards Mrs. Allston. In this operation, which had previously baffled the skill of the city surgeons, Dr. Sweet was successful. The fear of taking the small-pox deterred him from accepting Colonel Burr's invitation when first applied to; but this difficulty having been obviated, he embarked in a Newport packet.

"Dr. Sweet used to relate the adventure in this wise. That when he arrived in New York, Colonel Burr's coach was waiting at the wharf for his reception. Having never ridden in a coach he objected to being transported in a vehicle that was shut up. He was fearful of some trick, and farther, he did not like to ride in a thing over which he had no control, but fearing the small-pox he was induced to enter it. He said, he never was whirled about so in his life; at last he was ushered into the most splendid mansion that he ever saw. The girl was alarmed at his appearance when he was invited into her chamber. The family surgeon was soon introduced, and he proposed that the operation should be performed the succeeding day, and ten o'clock was agreed upon, when other surgeons would attend. But Dr. Sweet meant to avoid their presence, if he could; he did not fancy learned men. In the evening he solicited an interview with his patient; talked with her familiarly, dissipated her fears, asked permission, in the presence of her father, just to let the old man put his hand upon her hip; she consenting, he in a few minutes set the bone. He then said, ' Now walk about the room,' which to her own and her father's surprise, she found herself readily able to do. Dr. Sweet would detail the operation with great *naiveté*.

"He early in life moved to South Kingstown and settled near Sugar Loaf Hill, where some of his descendants in the fifth generation are in popular practice as natural bone-setters now [1847]. Benoni, one of the sons of Doctor Job, emigrated to Lebanon, in Connecticut, where he continued to practice, as some of his sons have since his decease. Numbers yearly visit South Kingstown to have their dislocations replaced by the lineal descendants of the first Benoni, at their residence opposite Sugar Loaf Hill, near Wakefield."

Spiritualists and clairvoyants of the present day understand something of the philosophy in accordance with the laws of which Dr. Job Sweet avoided the presence of the learned surgeons whilst he was performing his seemingly miraculous cure. We read that Jesus was compelled to "put them all out" who "laughed him to scorn," before the conditions could be sufficiently harmonized to enable him to restore the suspended vitality of the daughter of Jairus.

Though totally unlearned in surgery, Dr. Job Sweet seldom, if ever, failed in his bone-restoring operations. Many characteristic anecdotes of him have been retained in the neighborhood. Among others, it is told that a skeptical young *sprig of science*—" falsely so called"—once sent for the doctor to set his dislocated elbow. The old man went and found his patient apparently in great pain, with his bandaged arm in a sling. He scarcely touched the limb, before he discovered the trick and left. Dr. Job was, however, overtaken on his way home by a messenger, who implored him to return and restore the young man's elbow joint, which had been really dislocated by the touch of the doctor's hand as a punishment for deceit. On another occasion, it is said, he was shown through an anatomical hall in Boston, by a city doctor. In glancing at a human specimen as they passed along the old man remarked that he had never seen a "*tominy*" before, but that there was a little bone put in wrong side up in the foot of the one before him. This was for a time controverted by his learned friend, but he was ultimately forced to admit the correctness of the natural bone-setter's assertion after permitting him to change the position of the bone in question.

Benoni, a son of Job, born October 17, 1762, removed to Lebanon, in Connecticut, where until his death he was very celebrated as a natural bone-setter.

Jonathan, another son of Job, born September 6, 1765, settled at Sugar Loaf Hill, near Wakefield, in Rhode Island, where he continued to reside until his death, about the year 1820. I knew Jonathan well, and have been present when he restored dislocated and broken bones in members or employés of my father's family. Once, when he was setting in my presence the thigh bone of a colored boy, I asked him to tell me how he did it. He answered that he did not know himself, but that he was just as certain of the position of all the bones he operated upon as if he saw them with his naked eye. Spiritualists will readily recognize this as clairvoyance, a gift that doubtless the Sweet family have been endowed with for many generations without being aware of it. Gideon, an elder brother, used occasionally to set bones when Jonathan was out of the way, but on no other occasions.

Job, son of Jonathan, commenced setting bones on the death of his father, and acquired great renown. Both were blacksmiths, and it used to be said that when called from their work, as they often were, to restore shattered and dislocated limbs—the healing of some of which would have conferred a world-wide fame on any regularly bred surgeon— all either of them asked for the *hindrance* was just change enough to pay them for the time lost in shoeing a horse or other work in the shop.

I remember well when a young Boston lawyer by the name of Warner, a friend of Daniel Webster, who had suffered much at the hands of the first surgeons in America without relief, was brought to South Kingstown, to try, as a forlorn hope, the unlearned and unpretentious Job Sweet. I do not know but this gentleman may be now living in Boston. I think his ailment was of a complicated nature, located in the leg, which had been aggravated by maltreatment, and had become so chronic that it could be overcome only by a very slow and gradual process of treatment. For this reason he boarded in or near Sweet's family, and occasionally visited my father's house, who lived at that time within a mile. On these occasions he always dwelt with great enthusiasm upon the remarkable powers possessed by Sweet, as not only evinced in the gradual but sure process of restoring his own limb to soundness, but also as exemplified in his successful treatment of other patients who were brought to him. Among others he used to speak of the case of a boy, I think by the name of Day, who came from some point on the North River. As he described it, this boy's leg was void of flesh, and as straight and hard as "his walking stick," the joints being stiffened and immovable through the presence of ossified matter. Sweet examined the boy's leg in the presence of Warner, and the latter remarked: "You certainly can do nothing with that leg, for there are no joints in it." "Then," replied the doctor, "I must make some." And sure enough, by the application of certain vegetable emollients and liniments—in the compounding of which all of the Sweets seem to be intuitively directed—and frequent manipulations of the leg, the ossification was gradually loosened and expelled, so that the joints assumed their natural play, and the leg became again clothed in flesh.

Mr. Warner evinced much gratitude for the restoration of his own limb, and persuaded the doctor to remove to Boston, where there was an unlimited field for the exercise of his wonderful gift. But, owing probably to his different mode of living, Job did not long survive the change, and died in that city about the year 1827.

On the removal of Job to Boston, William, his brother, born October 28, 1802, who has always resided where he now does, at the homestead at Sugar Loaf Hill, commenced in the bone-setting line, but in accordance with the usages of the family, whereby only one of its members habitually practices in a neighborhood at the same time, he gave way to his brother John, son of Gideon, who had relinquished farming that he might devote his whole time to the business of bone-setting. After a time John removed to New Bedford, and

William resumed bone-setting in South Kingstown, and has probably been as successful in his calling as any one of the name.

Like all of his ancestors, he has reared a large family of children. Job, his eldest son, is now a skillful bone-setter, practicing in New Bedford and its vicinity. George, a younger son, lives with Job, and sets bones when his brother is away. William N. Sweet, another son of William, lives with Job, but practices principally in Boston, Fall River, and their vicinities. He, too, is said to be very successful in his calling. Jonathan, another son, lives in Providence. where he practices bone-setting with great success. Thomas, another son, also practiced in Providence for ten years, until his death in 1867. Edward, youngest son of William, lives in the homestead at Sugar Loaf, and occasionally sets bones when his father is absent.

Jonathan Sweet, son of the last named Job and grandson of William, practices bone-setting successfully in Newark, N. J. James, also a son of Job, and Samuel, son of Gideon, now both living in South Kingstown, inherit the gift, and occasionally, in cases of necessity, replace dislocated and broken bones.

I have heard of instances wherein persons of the same name, who are not allied to the family of bone-setters, have professed to practice the Sweets' profession. Of course, the genuine bone-setters are not responsible for the failures of their imitators.

I have known Doctor William Sweet from boyhood, and have been present several times when he has restored broken and dislocated bones for employés or members of my own family, and although some of these were very complicated and bad, he always treated them successfully, and in no instance ever had to repeat an operation. He has been called during his practice to hundreds, and no doubt thousands, of injured persons, and yet he assured me a few days since that he had never had a patient die on his hands. On my asking what cases he had treated lately, he replied, "None of account." This expression he applied to simple fractures, dislocations and broken bones, which he restored without trouble, and for which he received but little pay. I asked him to narrate to me some of the cases he had treated that he thought were of "account." He mentioned several, and among them these which I now relate, as he told them to me.

"Several years ago John Moon was caught by a belt in Reynolds' factory in West Greenwich, and thrown over a drum through a space eight inches deep. His hips and whole frame were all mashed up in a heap; his knees were both out of joint, and stretched so that his legs hung like threshing flails; one arm broken, the other badly damaged. Put him together so that he got about, and after awhile went to work again. Saw him some years after. He was then pretty well, but not exactly straight, as I could not get everything just as it was before he was broken to pieces so.

"Whitman Phillips went over a drum in Dutee Hall's factory in Exeter; had one arm broken and both badly damaged; had both thighs broken, and both legs below the knee broken short off. Two doctors got there before me, and had just finished sawing off one arm. I fixed up what was left of him in about six hours, and could just as well have saved his arm. The young man got well, but has now to peddle for a living, owing to the loss of his arm. Dutee Hall sat by and cried while I was fixing Phillips up, and said I was doing God's work.

"George Church got caught in the running gear of the Locustville factory, now called Hopedale, in Richmond. Both legs were broken, both above and below the knee, and fractured and lacerated badly besides. He was also badly injured inside. I put him all right, however, and healed him up; and he is now well, and carting wood and doing other work for a living.

"Michael Flaherty caught by a belt in the factory at Wakefield, his leg was turned clean round and spaltered from the knee, and the bone left naked down to the ankle. The bone was split, and lay like splinters on the flesh. I put the pieces all in their places and worked on him with my liniments and washes off and on about nine or ten months, when he went to work, and is now well; but I got nothing for it.

"A man by the name of Mirick, a cooper from Nantucket, smashed his wrist all to pieces. Doctor Warren and other doctors worked on him till his wrist got stiff and cold through ossification. When he came to me he said I might put a live coal on his arm and he would not feel it. I went to work, and after a while broke it all up, and got the blood to circulate, and then put all the bones in their places again, and nature soon did the rest, so that his wrist was about as good as ever."

The doctor told me that in making his liniments, decoctions, etc., for washes, he uses, with the exception of alcohol, but little besides barks, herbs and vegetables, such, in fact, as an apothecary would say could be found almost anywhere, and therefore could be of no value to medical science. The simple but yet all but perfect art the Sweets possess, to stay and reduce inflammation, relax the sinews and muscles and prevent mortification, is quite as remarkable as their extraordinary intuitive gift of setting bones.

In instances where these "natural bone setters" have been called to patients who have suffered intense agony through fruitless attempts to replace a joint by means of ropes and pulleys, and other violent malpractices, they have, by the skillful application of their simple emollients and laxatives and soothing manipulation of the hand, removed the inflammation and tension of the parts and replaced the bone with little comparative effort on the part of the operator, or pain on that of the patient.

I am aware that many readers will think the facts I have given are exaggerated. If such will take a trip by rail to the town of South Kingstown, where such things have been doing for a century and more past, and inquire among the old settlers of that town of the cures that have been made by the Sweet family, I think they will learn that but a very small part of these most wonderful performances have been narrated.

In further illustration of the remarkable healing powers possessed by the Sweet family of Narragansett, I append the following extracts in addition to those from the New Bedford Star, taken from a pamphlet of 124 pages which the writer compiled in 1876, entitled " Civil and Religious Persecution in the State of New York," published by Colby & Rich, Boston. In that State, as in many others, the organized medical societies have recently succeeded in obtaining the enactment of laws making it a misdemeanor for natural bone-setters and clairvoyant healers to practice their professions, punishable with fine and imprisonment. This includes those who heal by the laying on of hands—a mode of cure not only prescribed but enjoined upon his disciples by Jesus of Nazareth.

In consequence of the existence and enforcement of these laws the Sweets, and other natural healers of human infirmities, can no longer practice their benign gifts in New York with safety to themselves, and many have in consequence been compelled to forego their calling or abandon their homes and flee the State—in some instances that have come to the writer's knowledge—greatly to their pecuniary detriment. A further movement is now pending in the New York legislature to intensify the requirements of the law to meet the inroads that the natural healers are still making upon the practice and profits of the regular diplomated physicians.

I well knew the blacksmith, Jonathan Sweet, of Sugar Loaf Hill—a son of Job—, who seldom left home but on extraordinary occasions, and who, when patients were brought to him whose cases had perhaps in some instances baffled the skill of the most renowned doctors, was wont to ask the customer whose horse was left only partly shod, to excuse him a few minutes whilst he put the stranger *to rights*. Having done this he would charge his patient a pistareen or quarter for the loss of time incurred by the interruption, and return to finish his more important job of shoeing the horse.

Jonathan's son, William, is quite as skillful as his father. On one occasion I remember sending for William to an adjacent hay field, where he was at work for a neighbor, to set the wrist of a boy who had been thrown from his horse. This he did in an instant, after the bandages had been prepared. I supposed the work was completed; "not quite," said the doctor, as he pressed his thumb on the back of the boy's hand, and replaced with a snap a little bone that had been also disarranged in the fall. This he no doubt detected through his clairvoyant gift.

Again, I sent for him to restore the displaced collar bone of a daughter. I then lived many miles away, and as the doctor did not arrive until over twenty-four hours after the accident happened, my daughter's sufferings had become exceedingly acute. When Sweet arrived he evidently comprehended the exact difficulty at a glance, doubtless not by his external, but by his internal, vision, and replaced the bone at one touch of his hands, so that after being bandaged and carried in a sling for a few weeks the shoulder was made apparently as sound as ever.

On another occasion a boy of seven or eight years of age, who lived with his mother in my family, by falling from the back of a donkey had his arm broken above the elbow. I sent at once for William Sweet. It was a very bad break, and the wound was much lacerated. The end of the fractured bone was easily felt, and I think, was to be seen. The weather being hot the arm had swelled to fully twice its usual dimensions before Sweet arrived, one or two days after the accident. I was absent for a few hours at that time, and on my return home learned that the boy's arm had been set, splintered and bandaged, and that the bone-setter was assisting my workmen in the hayfield. I found by inquiry that after Sweet's arrival he glanced at the arm, and then went out in the grounds in search of wild cherry and some other barks or roots. With these he made a compound wash, that quickly reduced the inflammation and swelling so that he could set the bone. The boy was wilful, and to restrain him within proper bounds, we shut him in a long entry. But the next day he got out of this through an open window, and thenceforward continued to run at large with his arm in a sling. In a few weeks, however, the bones knit, and he was as well as ever, without the slightest disfigurement.

At this time the doctor went with me to see Thomas Durfee, an old man who occupied one of my tenements and one of whose hands was disabled. He had shown the injured member to many physicians, but none of them could detect anything out of place. Sweet fixed his eyes momentarily on the back of the old man's hand, then putting his fingers on the palm, he gently pressed his thumb on the back, above where the forefinger joined, and told the old man to open and shut his hand. This he at once did, and continued to use it ever after as well as the other. In explanation Sweet said that there was a little bone somewhere in the hand so slightly raised and set out of its proper place on edge, that it was very difficult to perceive it through the sense of either sight or touch.

Besides the bone-setting gifts the Sweet family possess in a remarkable degree another faculty scarcely less wonderful— that of compounding liniments or washes from the roots and barks that are to be found in almost every neighborhood, and which are highly efficacious in reducing inflammation and swellings and in preventing mortification.

Some forty or more years ago, as Mr. Samuel Curtis, of Peace Dale, was proceeding to a manufactory of mine with a heavily laden ox-team, he was thrown from the tongue of the cart upon a rough, stony place in the road, so that a wheel passed over and crushed his thigh bone, besides dreadfully bruising and lacerating the flesh. He was brought home, a distance of some five or more miles, and it was thought that no treatment could save his limb, if peradventure it might his life. Dr. "Bill Sweet," however, was sent for, and after washing and *mopping* the wound in his accustomed fashion with vegetable decoctions, he put all the bones in place, and splintered them with sole leather. Under his care, notwithstanding the summer heat that prevailed, inflammation was kept down and mortification entirely prevented. After lying on his back in bed a few weeks the sufferer was again walking about, and it was not long before he was seen on the road with his team, as well as ever, with the exception of a trifling limp, occasioned by the slight shortening of the limb—the result of the tension of the tendons and muscles while the broken and shattered bones were in the process of knitting together. Curtis died not long since, aged about eighty years, as liberal in mind and as highly respected as any man in the neighborhood.

A striking peculiarity of the older branches of the Sweet family is their utter unconsciousness of the magnitude of the cures they perform. Exploits of healing that if done by regular practitioners would place them in the foremost rank of the profession, and give them a world-wide reputation, are accomplished by the Sweets without its apparently entering their minds that they have done anything worthy of especial note. I have been amused to hear the old man William Sweet's narrations of some of the most remarkable cures that were perhaps ever performed by man, for which he claimed no more credit than he might have done for merely setting a broken bone of the finger.

Since writing the above, I have received a letter, dated February 7, 1876, from a lady who resides near Pittsfield, Mass., in which she incidentally mentions this circumstance. "Mr. Olmstead, who lives not far from us, had not long since his shoulder all crushed to pieces by the fall of a cask of molasses which he was steadying down a gangway. He went to a doctor in Pittsfield, and when he left his care at the end of some weeks, the arm had grown to his side, so that the flesh was continuous, and the arm, of course, utterly useless. Olmstead then went down to Dr. Sweet at Hartford, who cut the flesh, re-broke the bones and re-set them, so that the arm, though somewhat disabled, does not prevent his leading a very active life, besides following his trade as a butcher." Dr. Sweet, of Hartford, is a descendant of old Job Sweet of Narragansett. It is well for him that he is not located in New York instead of Connecticut, as in that case the M. D. of Pittsfield might be after him with a sheriff's *posse*, and have him before a New York court of justice, to be fined and imprisoned for interfering with the privileges of the profession, nor could Sweet avoid conviction, as the law stands on the statute book.

It is not long ago that while passing with a stone-drag through a gateway, a very near neighbor of mine caught his foot between it and the post, and dislocated the great toe. As small an affair as it might be deemed, the M. D. that was called to his aid managed to inflict in one or more bungling operations an untold amount of anguish on his patient, without succeeding in moving the member from the upright position it had been thrown into by the accident. Finding that he could get no relief at the hands of the regular M. D., the sufferer finally applied to Dr. Sweet, of Fall River, a lineal descendant of old Job Sweet, who put the bones of the toe in their proper places in a very short time, and with but little pain.

David J. Gould, of Newport, R. I., furnishes the following facts relating to the Sweet family.

"Thomas N. Dale, of New York City, in passing from one car to another in Pennsylvania, just on the turn of a curve, was thrown off the cars and fell clear off the track, having his wrist and ankle broken and his shoulder started in the socket so as to break the cell containing the lubricating matter. Of course, he had no use whatever of his arm, and was not able even to lift it from his side. Mr. Dale was taken to the first station, where a surgeon set his ankle and wrist, but could do nothing for his shoulder. When he recovered sufficiently to be moved, Mr. Dale was brought to Newport and placed under the care of Dr. William Sweet, of Sugar Loaf Hill, Narragansett, who after several operations removed the ossification that had formed in the cup of the joint, and in a few weeks the patient was completely restored to his usual health and bodily powers.

"Amos R. Little, of Philadelphia, was accidentally thrown, and fell with his whole weight on his right shoulder. He was immediately placed under Dr. Pancoast's care, who treated him for several weeks without any visible benefit. The arm gradually wasted and became much smaller than the other it was entirely helpless and carried constantly in a sling. Dr. Pancoast said that he had done all he could, but proposed as a forlorn hope to cauterize it. A day was set on which the operation should be performed. In the meantime Mr. Gould had written his friend Little, recommending him to come to Newport and put himself under the care of Dr. Sweet, of Fall River—a son of William. Mr. Little received the letter on the day that Dr. Pancoast had concluded to make the cauterizing operation, and immediately left Philadelphia for Newport. On his arrival, accompanied by Mr. Gould he proceeded to Fall River, and placed himself under the care of Dr. Sweet, who, no sooner examined the shoulder than he told what the trouble was—that the cell containing the lubricating matter was broken and the joint was filling with a fungus-like substance that oozed therefrom. Dr. Sweet went to work on his patient's arm and shoulder, and followed it up for about seven days, one hour each day. At the end of that time Mr. Little could use his arm and throw it around his head. He then returned to Philadelphia to keep his appointment with Dr. Pancoast. He went at the hour appointed to the doctor's office, and greeted him by putting out his right arm and shaking hands, at which Dr. Pancoast started and exclaimed, ' What in God's name have you been doing to your arm!' Mr. Little told him that Dr. Sweet, of Fall River, had been operating on it for the week past with the result he now witnessed. Dr. Pancoast said he would like to see Dr. Sweet, for he had made a marvelous cure and one that he could not have accomplished under any circumstances."

Mr. Gould further said that whilst Sweet was attending on his brother-in-law Little a patient applied for aid who said he had spent nearly all he had on doctors, trying to help his arm without their doing any good. The doctor examined it about fifteen minutes, and then said the injury must have been caused by his frequent pushing of some weight above his head, suiting the action at the time to the word. The man then said that he was a peddler, and had been accustomed for a long time to take a heavy box from overhead in the back of his wagon, and replace it again, after his cus tomers had been served. Mr. Gould said that after a few weeks' treatment by Dr. Sweet this man's arm was entirely restored.

Since the preceding account of the Sweet family appeared in the Newport Mercury and the Narragansett Times, I have received from my brother, Joseph P. Hazard, a letter dated Paris, October 12, 1878, and containing the following additional particulars in relation to the family.

"In the autumn of 1828 or 1829, in jumping, I so severely

injured the joint of my right knee that I was unable to bring my heel down and could walk at all only by touching my toes lightly to the ground. The least pressure produced pain in the injured part. After some days of suffering finding that I got no better, I went to Newport and consulted that most kind and excellent physician and surgeon, the late Dr. Enoch Hazard. Upon examination of the part he told me there was a displacement of the semi-lunar cartilage, and that but one case of the kind, as far as he knew, had ever occurred in the United States. The doctor then brought a book from his library in which he showed me the printed account of the case he referred to, and said it was at the time decided by a college of physicians—though, I think, perhaps a council—that the semi-lunar cartilage had got doubled under itself, so as to act as a wedge in the joint and thereby prevent the straightening of the limb, and that it was *beyond the power of surgery to replace it, though peradventure an accident to the part might do so!*

"I then proceeded to Dr. William Turner, a noted physician and surgeon of Newport, who took the same view of the case as Dr. Hazard. I then went to Providence, where I consulted Dr. Parsons. He coincided in opinion with Doctors Hazard and Turner. I will here remark that I was then about twenty-one years of age, that every one of the physicians named gave his opinion without any knowledge of the case until I presented it myself, and no one of them made any charge.

"I returned to Narragansett much disheartened. From the first my father had counseled and urged me to send for John Sweet, a natural bone-setter who lived within half a mile of us. This I finally consented to do. About dark the same evening John Sweet was ushered from the kitchen into our sitting-room, where father and I were seated by the fire. As Sweet entered I perceived he was somewhat under the influence of liquor, though he was not an intemperate man, but an honest, hard-working tenant farmer. As the door closed after him Sweet said, ' Mr. Hazard, I heard this morning that you wanted to see me, but I have been very busy all day, and so have come over now. If you want me to do any thing I would like you to be ready soon, as I have not yet finished my chores and am somewhat in a hurry to get back.'

"I was greatly alarmed lest Sweet's condition, if nothing else, might be a dangerous factor in the case, and made no reply. My father strove to reassure me and said ' Joseph, let John set it.' I pretty promptly yielded to father's request. Sweet then knelt down before me and, taking my foot with the hollow of his hand beneath it, twisted it so as to turn the toes outward somewhat. He then pressed the part just above the injured knee with his other hand and with a sudden, quick movement of my foot in a proper direction brought the heel of the foot in contact with the lower portion of my body, which motion he repeated three times in quick succession. Sweet then rose from the floor and told me to walk. I replied that I could not without its hurting me. He answered that he was sure my heel would now reach the ground as usual, and that I could walk as well as ever except that the knee would be very weak, which he would at once bandage and send me an ointment to heal it. To my great surprise I accordingly got up and walked about the room as well as ever, save that a feeling of great weakness prevailed in the joint. Sweet applied the bandage and sent me the ointment, which I used as directed, and in a few days I was about as usual except that the joint did not recover its usual strength for some weeks, if it ever has entirely to the present day. Some weeks after this I met Sweet in the road and asked him what I should pay him for his services. ' Mr. Hazard, 'said he 'I must charge you a pretty big price, for most of the bones I set are for poor people for which I charge nothing. So I must ask two dollars for your job.'

"I asked Sweet why it was that he always took a drink of liquor before he set a bone. He replied that it was 'to harden my heart, as I cannot bear to hurt people.' I suppose, however, that a more potent reason may have been that the spiritual influence is facilitated by a little stupefying of the physical senses, although he may not have been aware of it.

"In the year 1831 or 1832, our father, then living at Washington Hollow, Dutchess county, New York, was thrown violently from a 'Dearborn,' and falling forward dislocated or broke nearly all the bones in the back of one hand. He was then nearly seventy years of age. He was attended by a local physician, and the hand soon healed apparently, but was of little service to him. Some months after the accident he came to Narragansett and stayed at brother Isaac's house in Peace Dale, where I was also dwelling. Our cousin, William R. Peace, of Philadelphia, was then spending some time with us. Father had determined to call on Job Sweet, then the senior bone-setter in Narragansett, and proposed that my cousin William and myself should go with him. I shrank from the trial that would have followed my acceptance of father's invitation, but Mr. Peace, who had heard a great deal of the 'natural bone-setters of Narragansett,' gladly accepted the proffered opportunity to witness their mode of operation.

"In the course of a very few hours father and William Peace both returned, and a more amazed man than the latter I never saw. It seems that on their arrival at Sweet's house—rather more than a mile from Peace Dale—they learned from Job's son, a lad of about seventeen years of age, that his father had been called to a distant case of broken or dislocated bones, and would not be home for some days to come. 'but,' said the boy, "I can fix that hand as well as my father can.'! Strange to say our father consented that the lad should try. The boy then examined the hand, and said that the bones had all knit together but had not been set right.

'But,' said he, 'I can soon fix *that*.' He then re-broke the bones, that had proved nearly useless though healed, and reset them all in their proper places. Father made daily visits to Sweet, and erelong the fractures and dislocations were all restored and the hand healed, so as to become almost as supple and useful as it was before the accident, and it so continued during the remainder of his life.

"Many years ago I was spending a few weeks at Townsend's Hotel in Newport, R. I. Lieutenant William Griffin, U. S. Navy, was stopping there at the time, also Captain Gedney, of the U. S. Navy, a good specimen of a good South Carolinian. We three were much together, and one day I took a walk with Captain Gedney down to Rocky farm. In getting over a wall Gedney sprained his ankle so badly that even with my assistance it was with great difficulty he got back to the hotel. I suggested that he send to Narragansett for one of the Sweets, but he decided to employ a regular surgeon of high reputation, who decided that his ankle was only sprained and treated it accordingly. Captain Gedney was thereafter confined to his chamber, where I saw him daily. Two weeks had passed but he got no relief under the surgeon's treatment, but he still declined to send for John Sweet, when I occasionally suggested it to him. One day as I left the dinner table, I observed John Sweet at the bar of the hotel taking a glass of liquor. I asked him to go with me up-stairs, and he followed me to Captain Gedney's room. Thus confronted, Captain Gedney without hesitation consented that Sweet should look at his sprained ankle. Said Sweet, "It is out of joint, but I can set it in a minute." Sweet then asked me to stand behind the captain, who as usual was sitting in his arm-chair, and hold him forward as hard as I could. I accordingly put my arms around the captain and braced myself. Sweet got down on his knees, and, placing the sole of Captain Gedney's foot against his own shoulder, he gave a tremendous heave forward, that nearly sent Captain Gedney and myself over backward. Sweet without further ado told Captain Gedney to get up and walk The latter hesitated to try an experiment in which he had no faith, but finally did as he was bid and got up and walked across the room without aid. That same evening Captain Gedney walked half a mile to visit his friend, Miss Lawrence, daughter of Commodore Lawrence; and he afterwards told me more than once that if he ever met with a like accident though he was as far off as the South Seas, no one should treat him until he got back to John Sweet.

"Of the William Sweet who is now living in Wakefield—an old man—I have to say, that happening to see him some twenty years ago at Peace Dale with a bandana bundle under his arm, I supposed he might have been called to a distance, and I asked him where he had been. He replied that he was on his way back from the island of Rhode Island where he had been to set a man's arm which had been broken by a fall from a hay-mow. I asked him what he charged for such a visit. 'Why,' said he, 'I have been very unlucky' In going I was detained all night and most of the next day on Conanicut by bad weather, and I got over so late I was obliged to stop all night at a tavern in Newport. Then I had to walk six miles out of town to fix the man's arm, and to stay another night on the island. And now,' says he 'it is nearly sundown again and I have not got home yet. So I had to charge him pretty bad—eight dollars!' Out of eight dollars were to be deducted four ferry fares from forty to sixty cents, and two tavern bills for supper, lodging and breakfast, to say nothing of four days lost time and twenty-one miles traveled on foot!"

"Many years ago I was talking with this same William Sweet about the mysteries of his bone-setting faculty, and I asked him how he explained it. This he said he could not do, but said he, 'Why, Mr. Hazard, I see the bone I am going to set just as plainly as if it had no flesh on it. I say I see it, but, of course, I do not *see* it.' Now here is clairvoyance, plainly enough, before it had ever been heard of as such. Sweet had no language to explain his mysterious gift except such as he used; and having no conception of the possibilities of clairvoyant seeing, he had no words at his command to give expression to what he saw with his internal or spiritual vision, but was not reflected on his external sense or instrument of sight.

"The Sweets have been numerous in Narragansett for several generations, and are a remarkably innocent people. I never heard of any one of them committing any violence in any way, nor anything against any of them which I can recollect; certainly, not against any of the numerous 'bone-setters.' With two exceptions only, as far as I have ever known or heard they have always been, and still are, void of avarice, or any inordinate desire to be known, much less distinguished. They are for the most part industrious farmers, mechanics, laborers, and fishermen, all of them in humble circumstances but none in poverty. Without ambition, they are respected by all; without wealth, they are comfortably situated, almost to a man. Their gentleness and quiet demeanor seem to be universal characteristics of the family. They are temperate except those who make bone-setting their most prominent occupation, and those resort to liquor—probably as a stimulant to the interior senses—only when immediately engaged in the line of their profession. They seem to be as distinct from the communities about them in their general character as they are in their peculiar gift of bone-setting. They are children, as it were, and as guileless."

Those versed in the principles that govern in spiritualism both ancient and modern may best understand that it is the harmonious conditions induced by the simplicity and unambitious character of the Sweet family and their freedom from the lust of avarice and the desire to be distinguished, that for so many successive generations have made them the father's recipients and instruments for beneficent ministering spirits to use in signally ameliorating so large a class of the most serious accidents that are liable to befall suffering humanity.

FINIS.

List of Subscribers

TO

⁂RECOLLECTIONS OF OLDEN TIMES.⁂

Isaac P. Hazard............... } Eliza G. " .... } Newport, R. I............Fifty copies. Anna " .... }		
Thomas R. Hazard..............Vaucluse, R. I..............Fifty copies.		
Rowland G. Hazard.......... } Peace Dale, R. I............Fifty copies. John N. Hazard............. }		
Rowland Hazard..............Peace Dale, R. I..............Fifty copies.		
Joseph P. Hazard..............South Kingstown, R. I.......Ten "		
Willis P. Hazard..............Westchester, Pa.............. " "		
Stephen Hazard...............Ferrisburgh, Vt.............Seven "		
Samuel L. Hazard.............West Castleton, Vt..........Five "		
George H. Wilson..............Newport, R. I................ " "		
George P. Hazard..............Providence, R. I..............Four "		
Mrs. Anna H. B. Ward..........New York.................. " "		
Jacob Dunnell.................Pawtucket, R. I................Three "		
Mrs. Lloyd Minturn............Ferrisburgh, Vt.............. " "		
Edwin Noyes..................Waterville, Me.............. " "		
George C. Robinson, Jr........Brooklyn, N. Y.............. " "		
Jeremiah P. Robinson.......... " " .... " "		
Andrew P. Bashford............Newport, R. I................Two "		
William W. Battey.............Providence, R. I.............. " "		
James C. Dillon................Narragansett Pier, R. I...... " "		
J. R. G. Hassard.... ....New York.................... " "		
Mrs. L. L. Hazard..............Newport, R. I................ " "		
Dr. David King................ " " .... " "		
Attmore Robinson..............Wakefield, " .... " "		
J. Peace Vernon...............San Francisco, Cal.......... " "		
Benjamin S. Babcock...........Wakefield, R. I..............One "		
George A. Armstrong..........Newport, R. I................ " "		
George H. Babcock............Pennsylvania................ " "		
Mary E. Babcock..............Liberty Hill, Conn.......... " "		
Mrs. James Birckhead..........Newport, R. I................ " "		
J. M. Bokee...................Brooklyn, N. Y.............. " "		
G. A. Boyce...................Rensselaer, N. Y............ " "		
Rev. Charles T. Brooks........Newport, R. I................ " "		
Arnold L. Burdick............. " " .... " "		
Col. Thomas L. Casey..........U. S. A., Washington....... " "		
Mrs. Wm. G. Caswell..........Narragansett Pier, R. I...... " "		
Raymond Chappell.............Wakefield, R. I.............. " "		

LIST OF SUBSCRIBERS.

Wendall Chappell	Wakefield, R. I.	One copy.
Joseph J. Cooke	Providence, R. I.	" "
John B. Cozzens	Newport, R. I.	" "
Benjamin R. Curtis	Peace Dale, R. I.	" "
Mrs. George L. DeBlois	San Francisco, Cal.	" "
Alice Dixon	Peace Dale, R. I.	" "
William D. Frost	Hammonton, N. J.	" "
John E. Groff	Boston, Mass.	" "
Miss Abby Hazard	Peace Dale, R. I.	" "
Anthony Hazard	Providence, "	" "
Benjamin Hazard	Newport, "	" "
Charles L. Hazard	Watchemoket, "	" "
Charles T. Hazard	Newport, "	" "
Daniel Hazard	Wakefield, "	" "
Daniel L. Hazard	Newport, "	" "
Edward W. Hazard	Chicago, Ill.	" "
Emily L. Hazard	Newport, R. I.	" "
Frank S. Hazard	" "	" "
George A. Hazard	" "	" "
George B. Hazard	" "	" "
George J. Hazard	" "	" "
George M. Hazard	" "	" "
Henry B. Hazard	" "	" "
H. S. Hazard	" "	" "
James Hazard	Providence,"	" "
James L. Hazard	Newport, "	" "
Jeffrey Hazard	Providence,"	" "
Mary W. Hazard	Newport, "	" "
Rufus Hazard	No. Ferrisburgh, Vt.	" "
R. N. Hazard	New York.	" "
Simeon Hazard	Newport, R. I.	" "
T. D. Hazard	Brooklyn, N. Y.	" "
Thomas G. Hazard	Narragansett Pier, R. I.	" "
William C. Hazard	Cranston, R. I.	" "
Dr. William H. Hazard	Wakefield, "	" "
Thomas R. Hubbard	Brooklyn, N. Y.	" "
Mary Roach Hunter Kane	Newport, R. I.	" "
Horace Knowles,	Marcellus, N. Y.	" "
Mrs. Minkler	Newport, R. I.	" "
J. F. Noyes, M. D.	Detroit, Mich.	" "
Jeremiah Quinlan	Peace Dale, R. I.	" "
E. A. Robinson	Chicago, Ill.	" "
George C. Robinson	Brooklyn, N. Y.	" "
George T. Robinson	Milwaukee, Wis.	" "
J. P. Robinson	New York.	" "
Robert A. Robinson	Providence, R. I.	" "

LIST OF SUBSCRIBERS.

Rowland T. Robinson	Ferrisburgh, Vt.	One copy.
Thomas Robinson	Pawtucket, R. I.	" "
Thurston R. Robinson	Providence, "	" "
William H. Robinson	South Kingstown, R. I.	" "
William H. Robinson	Wakefield, R. I.	" "
Robert Rodman	Lafayette, "	" "
Mrs. George W. Sanford	Newport, "	" "
Hon. William P. Sheffield	" "	" "
Mary A. Sherman	Providence, "	" "
Benj. R. Smith	Germantown, Pa.	" "
Hazard Stevens	Boston, Mass.	" "
Benjamin C. Sweet	Hamilton, R. I.	" "
Gilbert Sweet	New York	" "
James D. Sweet	Jewett City, Conn.	" "
Smith S. Sweet	Providence, R. I.	" "
H. B. Tompkins	Newport, "	" "
Dr. Henry E. Turner	" "	" "
Gov. C. C. Van Zandt	" "	" "
Rev. E. F. Watson	Wakefield, "	" "
Mrs. Dr. Watson	Newport, "	" "
John Hazard Watson	" "	" "
Walter Watson	Wakefield, "	" "
Mrs. William A. Whaley	Newport, R. I.	" "
Mrs. Elizabeth W. Wilbour	Newport, R. I.	" "

www.ingramcontent.com/pod-product-compliance
Lightning Source LLC
Chambersburg PA
CBHW022110230426
43672CB00008B/1335